Creating and Managing
International Joint Ventures

Creating and Managing International Joint Ventures

Edited by **Arch G. Woodside**
and Robert E. Pitts

Q

QUORUM BOOKS
Westport, Connecticut • London

Library of Congress Cataloging-in-Publication Data

Creating and managing international joint ventures / edited by Arch G.
   Woodside and Robert E. Pitts.
      p.   cm.
      Includes bibliographical references and index.
      ISBN 0–89930–970–4 (alk. paper)
      1. Joint ventures—Management.   2. International business
   enterprises—Management.   3. Joint ventures—Europe—Management.
   I. Woodside, Arch G.   II. Pitts, Robert E.
   HD62.47.C74   1996
   658'.044—dc20   95–3781

British Library Cataloguing in Publication Data is available.

Library of Congress Catalog Card Number: 95–3781
ISBN: 0–89930–970–4

First published in 1996

Quorum Books, 88 Post Road West, Westport, CT 06881
An imprint of Greenwood Publishing Group, Inc.

Printed in the United States of America

The paper used in this book complies with the
Permanent Paper Standard issued by the National
Information Standards Organization (Z39.48–1984).

10 9 8 7 6 5 4 3 2 1

Contents

Preface   ix

I. THEORY AND RESEARCH ON INTERNATIONAL JOINT VENTURE STRATEGIES

1. Toward a Behavioral Theory of   3
    International Joint Venture
    Strategies
    Arch G. Woodside
    Robert E. Pitts

2. Reciprocal Agency: Toward a Theory   21
    of International Joint Ventures
    Frank L. Winfrey
    Anne L. Austin

3. Strategic Auditing of International   33
    Joint Ventures Using a Triangulation
    Research Approach
    Arch G. Woodside
    Matthew D. Heaps

II. RESEARCH ON KEY SUCCESS FACTORS FOR INTERNATIONAL JOINT VENTURE STRATEGIES

4. Key Issues in the Creation of   63
    International Joint Ventures
    with China
    Guo-Liang Xuan
    Gunnar Gräf

5. Joint Ventures in Hungary: Criteria   77
    for Success
    Jim Hamill
    Graham Hunt

6. Parent Company Characteristics and   107
    International Joint Ventures' Success
    in England and the U.S.A.
    Barbara Parker
    Yoram Zeira

III. ASSESSING SUCCESS AND FAILURE
      OF CROSS-HEMISPHERE INTERNATIONAL
      JOINT VENTURES

7. Where Have the U.S.-Dutch Joint   127
    Ventures Gone? In Search of
    Dimensions That May Bring Down
    Untimely Dissolutions
    Theo Roebers

8. European Ventures in China: 141
    Characteristics and Entry
    Strategies
    David K. Tse
    Kevin Y. Au
    Ilan Vertinsky

IV. RESEARCH ON INTERNATIONAL
     JOINT VENTURE STRATEGIES
     IN WESTERN AND CENTRAL EUROPE
     AND RUSSIA

9. Development of International   159
    Joint Ventures in Russia: Risks
    and Opportunities
    Vladimir L. Kvint

10. Foreign Investment and Joint   175
    Ventures in the Former
    Yugoslavia, 1967-1990: A Success
    Story in Southeastern Europe
    Mile B. Jovic

11. The Strategic Behavior of Dutch   189
     Multinational Enterprises Toward
     International Joint Ventures: A
     Multidimensional Analysis
     John Bell
     Pieter K. Jagersma

12. The Evolution of Polish Joint   203
     Ventures
     Stanley J. Paliwoda
     Zbigniew Dobosiewicz

Index   221

About the Contributors   231

Preface

Research on international joint ventures (IJVs) is a hot topic for strategists and scholars. Answers to three principal questions are sought by both groups: (1) in real-life, why are IJVs created; (2) what are the key success factors in creating and managing successful IJVs, and why do so many have such short lives (< 5 years); (3) how can the decision-action processes in creating and managing IJVs through time be described accurately, and what important insights can we learn from studying these processes?

A fourth question concerns deductive and inductive development of IJV theories: scholars are interested in developing useful theories to describe-explain-predict the creation and management of IJVs. Much of this book's focus is on describing and evaluating the nitty-gritty thinking-and-doing that occurs in real-life decision-processes in creating and managing IJVs. The findings reported in the following chapters support the major propositions in Cyert and March's *A Behavioral Theory of the Firm* (1963); see also Tallman and Shenkar (1994), and Chapter 1 of this book. Here are some central propositions (P_i) in a behavioral theory of the firm applied to creating and managing IJVs:

P_1: IJVs are created and managed in a series of small steps that link (1) finding-searching-thinking-deciding with (2) doing and evaluating opportunities and actions; consequently, to describe and understand IJV decision processes requires the examination of the streams of thinking and behaviors (through time) of participating firms and persons in IJV finding-searching-thinking-deciding-doing-evaluating.

P_2: In most cases, search for partners in creating IJVs is limited, biased, and messy; firms search and evaluate potential partners sequentially—evaluating and deciding are not delayed until a consideration set of several (say 3 to 10) potential partners is found—potential partners are usually accepted or rejected without thorough and comparative evaluations. Firms that are more thorough and comparative in selecting IJV partners are likely to be successful in moving from creation the on-going operation of an IJV.

P_3: The principals involved in creating and managing IJVs initially overestimate the level of agreement of shared vision among their partners in the specific objectives and day-to-day management of the IJV. Continual and deep communications, daily face-to-face discussions, are necessary to achieve consensus on implementing actions for achieving the shared vision. Otherwise, trust is reduced, communication breakdowns occur, and the IJV is judged to be a failure.

P_4: Multi-national enterprises (MNEs) are more likely to use IJVs in centrally planned or hybrid economies when the local government prefers such cooperation, even if wholly-owned subsidiaries (WOS) are permitted (see Tallman and Shenkar 1994). National governments often create incentives for MNEs to create IJVs with domestic partners; centrally-planned government interference is believed to be greater for WOS than IJVs (in reality, such interference appears to be similar in kind and degree for both).

P_5: Most created and operating IJVs that include an MNE and a small domestic partner have life spans of less than five years. The success and failure of such IJVs should not be judged by the length of their lives; the ability of the IJV in achieving multiple performance objectives should be the focus in valuing an ongoing IJV (see Gomes-Casseres 1987).

P_6: Most IJVs created by two small-size enterprises never become operational. Delays become permanent because of shallow product-market knowledge, inability to operationalize a shared vision, and limited financial resources (see Woodside and Kandiko 1991).

ORGANIZATION OF THE BOOK

The book includes 12 original chapters written to provide theory/research reports and strategy briefings on IJV decision processes. Each chapter is written by experts on their respective topics.

The book is organized in four parts. Part I, Theory and Research on IJV Strategies, is the foundation of the next four parts.

Part I: Theory and Research on IJV Strategies

In Chapter 1, Woodside and Pitts use case study research findings to explore applications of a behavioral theory of the firm to IJV creation and management. In Chapter 2, Winfrey and Austin offer theoretical insights into why IJVs often break down, even before they become really operational. In Chapter 3, a detailed example of how to do a strategy audit of an IJV is described by Woodside and Heaps.

Part II: Research on Key Success Factors for IJV Strategies

Note that key success factors for creating-operating IJVs in three different industrial national environments are included in Part II.

In Chapter 4, Xuan and Gräf offer a detailed chronology of IJV creation in the People's Republic of China; they focus on why some of these IJVs succeed and why some fail. In Chapter 5, the ability to cultivate good working relationships among three parties is the IJV Key Success Factor (KSF) in Hungary identified by Hamill and Hunt. In Chapter 6, Parker and Zeira answer the following question: what are six preincorporation KSFs for building trust among partners?

Part III: Assessing Success and Failure of Cross-Hemisphere IJVs

In the chapters in Part III, findings and insights on creating and operating IJVs across long distances are described.   In Chapter 7, Roebers traces the development of 27 U.S. and Dutch joint ventures in the Netherlands; Roebers emphasizes that multiple reasons are always present as causes of IJV creation. In Chapter 8, Tse, Au, and Vertinsky describe the unique strategies implemented by European firms in forming IJVs with domestic firms in China.

Part IV: Research on IJV Strategies in Western and Central Europe and Russia

What do we really know about IJVs in Russia? Many details about such IJVs are reported by Kvint in Chapter 9. IJVs have a history longer in Yugoslavia than other former Communist European countries; detailed descriptions of operating IJVs in Yugoslavia are provided by Jovic in Chapter 10. The Dutch, more than strategists from any other countries, have deep experience at creating-managing successful IJVs; details on how they do it are provided by Bell and Jagersma in Chapter 11. Finally, in Chapter 12, Paliwoda and Dobosiewicz provide a detailed assessment on the state-of-development and quality of operations of IJVs in Poland.

CENTRAL VALUE OF READING THIS BOOK

Creating and managing IJVs include making lots of messy decisions reached initially by partners who really do not know each other very well. Lots of instances for breakdowns in communications and trust can be expected to occur among IJV partners between the time of initial contact and ongoing operation of the new venture. To gain knowledge and insight into how IJVs are created and managed, both strategists and scholars need to focus on building useful descriptive models of the actual streams of decisions and behaviors of real-life IJVs. Reading this book is a useful step toward achieving this goal.

REFERENCES

Cyert, Richard M., and John G. March (1963), *A Behavioral Theory of the Firm*, Englewood Cliffs, NJ: Prentice-Hall.

Gomes-Casseres, Benjamin (1987), "Joint Venture Instability: Is It a Problem?" *Columbia Journal of World Business,* 22 (2), 97-102.

Tallman, Stephen B., and Oded Shenkar (1994), "A Managerial Decision Model of International Cooperative Venture Formation," *Journal of International Business Studies,* 25 (1), 91-113.

Woodside, Arch G., and Jozef Kandiko (1991), "Decision-Processes in Strategic Alliances: Designing and Implementing International Joint Ventures in Eastern Europe," *Journal of Euromarketing, 1* (1/2), 151-187.

Creating and Managing
International Joint Ventures

Part I

THEORY AND RESEARCH ON INTERNATIONAL JOINT VENTURE STRATEGIES

Toward a Behavioral Theory of International Joint Venture Strategies

Arch G. Woodside
Robert E. Pitts

An international joint venture is a distinct enterprise, or multi-organizational agreement, created as an alliance between two or more parent organizations working across country borders in designing-managing the venture. The central reason for this book is to provide managers and executives with knowledge and insight useful for creating and implementing better international joint venture (IJV) strategies. With this focus on creating-implementing better IJV strategies, the central proposition of this chapter is that the study of real-life, planned, and implemented IJV strategies is necessary. The point made by Fleck (1973) and Peter (1981) should be heeded: in order for participants in a decision to make better decisions, they need to know how current decisions are made. How do managers involved in creating IJVs actually think about the problem? What information do they actually use? What rules do they use in making choices? To gain knowledge and provide insights about IJVs, we need to examine the thinking and doing processes through time of decisionmakers involved in working together in creating and running IJVs.

In real-life, designing and implementing an IJV usually takes six months to three years. In some countries, the legal creation of an IJV generally does not result in implementation—no products-services are created, no customers are served, and no sales are made. The IJV never gets off the ground; for several reasons, the creation-implementation process breaks down. Often the prime reason for such breakdowns is the poor fit in working out the operating details when attempting to convert the early shared vision between the two principal parties.

Why do only some designed IJVs ever get implemented? Are most implemented IJVs successful? What decisions and actions are associated with successful versus unsuccessful IJVs? What are the key success factors (KSFs) associated with IJVs? The answers to these questions are the focus of this book.

Tallman and Shenkar (1994) emphasize the point that most scholarly researchers have used (i.e., theoretically grounded their research) industrial organization models and transaction cost economics to explain different forms of foreign direct investments, including the creation of IJVs. "However, such models do not provide a sufficient explanation of the original decision by multinational enterprise (MNE) managers to establish an international cooperative venture (ICV), nor do they adequately address the contractual joint ventures that comprise a majority of ICVs" (Tallman and Shenkar 1994, 92; see also Contractor and Lorange 1988). Thus, executives involved in creating-implementing IJVs are unlikely to gain much knowledge into making better IJV decisions from the industrial organization and transaction cost economics literatures. These literatures do not get into the nitty-gritty thoughts-decisions-actions and interactions of people involved in IJV decisions.

In making decisions, all managers carry simplified models in their heads of how they perceive bits of reality, and how they should utilize such bits in making decisions. These perceptions of bits include planning and observing sequences of steps of: (1) what-why-how to make-implement decisions, and (2) summary explanations of decisions processes that have been completed recently and the results of these processes.

NOTEWORTHY CHARACTERISTICS ABOUT THE DECISIONS INVOLVED IN CREATING AND IMPLEMENTING IJVs

Several noteworthy observations should be emphasized about the creation and implementation of IJVs. Here is a summary of these observations to be kept in mind while reading this book.

(1) IJVs are one form of international cooperative alliances between two or more organizations. Other forms include licensing deals, research consortia, supply agreements, minority investments, and agent contracting. About 90% of all alliances in recent years have been between firms from industrial countries, "and most of them involve activities in the rich world itself" (Emmott 1993, p. 18). Approximately 25 percent of IJVs involve combinations of firms from industrial and developing and/or former Communist European countries. However, "there are no reliable data on the rise of the alliance. No government collects the figures rigorously, for there is generally no need to register such alliances, especially in the industrial countries, and no value need be put on them" (Emmott 1993, 18).

(2) The real-life, decision process in creating an IJV is messy, time-consuming, and (in most cases) alternative partners and design configurations are not carefully researched by either of the two principals. Breakdowns and delays occur in valuing the opportunities and costs associated with creating and running the IJV; additional breakdowns and delays occur in assessing the operating doability of the IJV. Specific discussions about such breakdowns and delays are described by Woodside and Kandiko (1991) and Parkhe (1993).

(3) Important third-party stakeholders are always involved in the design and implementation of IJVs. For example, banks, government agencies, union officials, suppliers, distributors, and legal officials often make critical contributions in designing-implementing parts of an IJV. Enterprises with little prior experience in setting-up IJVs almost always underestimate the impact of third party involvement (see Biemans 1989).

(4) For the two principal parties considering the design and start-up of an IJV, the decision-process to form the alliance can be classified usefully into one of four 2 X 2 categories: a product-market opportunity for both firms A and B; a product-market opportunity for firm A (usually from an industrial country) and a business-competitive crisis for firm B (usually from a developing or former Communist country); a business-competitive crisis for firm A and an opportunity for firm B; and a business-competitive crisis for both principals to the new enterprise. Only the first IJV category, opportunity, has a reasonable chance for success. Attempting to manage the crisis engulfing one, or both, principals in the other three categories (coupled with the concurrent needs to build the trust and working relationships required in creating-managing the IJV) can be expected to present insurmountable hurdles.

(5) Most IJVs are inherently unstable organizational arrangements. One or both principals involved in the design and operation of the IJV can be expected to seek other organizational arrangements within the first five years of operating the IJV. For example, a multi-national enterprise may use joint ventures to penetrate foreign markets quickly, and within a few years, replace their established IJV with wholly owned subsidiaries (WOS) by buying-out other principals. Joint ventures allow firms to use the resources of other firms, and, in the process, to increase their own capabilities. As a firm's capabilities grow, such cooperation of its joint venture partner can be expected to diminish.

Consequently, years of operating should not be the sole, or even a major, criterion in evaluating the success or failure of an IJV. Multiple goals and multiple performance criteria should be used in valuing the investments in designing and operating an IJV.

(6) In examining IJV operations involving principals from industrial countries and developing or former Communist countries, one of the following five major causes of failure is usually present in early operating failures of IJVs: (1) government agencies that interfere in industrial management of the venture; (2) lack of quality and a dependable supplier and distributor infrastructure; (3) perception of unequal benefits and costs among the principals, including conflicts over the repatriation of profits; (4) a decline in resource contribution by the MNE participating in the IJV; and (5) substantial differences in the strategic goals of the IJV (e.g., profit versus employment goals). See Hisrich (1992) and many of the chapters in the present book for deep discussions on key success factors and reasons for failures of IJVs.

FOCUS ON RESEARCH ON IJV CREATION AND
MANAGING DECISION PROCESSES

In the remainder of this chapter we present the findings from a programmatic case research study on creating-managing two IJVs that include the following combination of principals: an MNE from an industrial country and a large enterprise from a former Communist country. Information on the details of the decisions, activities, and interactions through time of persons among the two principal enterprises is provided.

Answers to the following questions are provided. What are the key yes/no turning points in the design and implementation of successful international joint marketing ventures that are starting-up in East Europe? What are the streams of decisions, interactions of people, and events that actually occur in designing and implementing new marketing enterprises located in countries moving from centrally planned to market economies? From the study, what strategic insights—things to do and things not to do—should be considered in deciding on starting-up new marketing enterprises to be located in transition market economies?

Thus, the primary concern of the study is describing the phenomena of how decisions are actually made in designing and implementing joint retailing ventures in Eastern Europe. The secondary purpose of the study is to compare the degree of similarity of actual decisionmaking with the decisionmaking predicted by behavioral theories of the firm.

METHOD

The case study research method recommended by Yin (1989) was employed to gain useful information for answering the key questions. The major goal of this research method is analytical generalization based on the degree of fit (i.e., "pattern matching," see Campbell 1975) between observed decision processes and a series of propositions of how the decisions are supposed to occur. The propositions developed for study are based on the Bounded Rationality Model (March and Simon 1958; Cyert and March 1963) and the Garbage Can Model (Cohen, March, and Olsen 1972) of decisionmaking. The basic proposition of the Bounded Rationality Model is that decisionmakers intend to be rational but are constrained by cognitive limitations, habits, and biases. The Garbage Can model posits that organization decisions are analogous to garbage cans into which problems, solutions, choice opportunities, search for alternatives, and people are dumped.

The key theoretical question is: how well do the decision processes that emerge in the design and implementation of international joint ventures reflect the propositions generated from the Bounded Rationality versus the Garbage Can Models? The results from the present study indicate partial fits of reality to both models.

The following additional propositions follow from the Bounded Rationality Model. Problem definitions are simplified; search is sequential and limited to familiar areas, and information exchange is biased by individual preference. Preferences originate from either the personal or departmental sub-goals related to persons in the firm. Evaluation of alternatives follow conjunctive decision rules where go/no go criteria are expressed in terms of cutoff levels. Choice depends on which alternative first exceeds the minimum cutoff levels of evaluative criteria.

The following predictions follow from the Garbage Can Model of decision-making. Problem solving definitions are variable, changing as new problems or people are attached to choice opportunities. Data are often collected and not used. Preferences are unclear and may have little impact on choice. Evaluation criteria are discovered during and after the decision process, and choices are mostly made when problems are either not noticed or are attached to other choices.

The findings from intensive case research studies on complex decisionmaking by organizations among Finnish firms (see Bjorkman 1989), German firms (see Witte 1972), and Canadian firms (see Mintzberg, Raisinghani, and Theoret 1976) support several of the propositions from these two theoretical models. The main conclusion of these studies is that the "phase theorem" from the Rational Model of organizational decisionmaking (that problems are defined before search for solutions occurs and that search is completed before evaluation of alternatives takes place, and choice occurs only after evaluation) is a poor match of the reality of decisionmaking.

Having a theoretical basis for case research is important to overcome the common complaint about case studies: that it is difficult to generalize from one case to another. "The problem lies in the very notion of generalizing to other case studies. Instead, an analyst should try to generalize findings to `theory', analogous to the way a scientist generalizes from experimental results to theory. (Note that the scientist does not attempt to select `representative' experiments.)" (Yin 1989, 44).

Decision systems analysis (DSA) was used to collect the data on decision-making for the study. DSA involves a series of personal interviews with several managers participating in one or more phases of the decision process, as well as an analysis of available documents related directly to the decision process. The aim of DSA is to describe the structure and flow of how and why a decision process actually occurs (see Howard, Hulbert, and Farley 1975).

In the process of using DSA, series of flow-diagrams, or maps, of the decision phases, specific decisions, behavior and interactions of managers are prepared. In follow-up interviews, these flow-diagrams are shown to the managers initially interviewed to learn additional details of the decision processes and to make corrections. In the present study the flow-diagrams are summaries of the decision processes used by the organizations participating in designing and implementing the joint retailing ventures. The flow-diagrams and accompanying descriptions of the decision processes are based on the first round of interviews of managers in the two joint ventures in this case research study.

RESULTS

While recycling of activities and decisions occurred in both decision processes, the identification of four phases in the decision processes is useful for describing and understanding the flow of decisions, interactions of people, and the behaviors that occurred: (1) solution-opportunity assessment; (2) evaluation of the basic proposal to form a joint venture; (3) design; and (4) implementation and operation of the joint venture. Figure 1.1 is a summary of these four phases and some of the issues related to each phase that were examined in the study.

While not all the central issues in designing and implementing international joint ventures are summarized in Figure 1.1, several very useful insights may be suggested from the figure. First, a substantial length of time is implied from scanning Figure 1.1, for example, the reality of each of the four decision phases depicted may involve one or more years. Second, the decision phases depicted do not suggest that the participants will be engaged in the four decision phases with more than one potential joint venture at any one time: the reality of international joint venture search and evaluation is that the search is limited and very focused; simultaneous extensive search and evaluation of several options is unlikely to occur. Third, philosophical fit, the compatibility of visions, is a factor crucial for reaching the design stage in joint venture formation; the reality observed in joint venture evaluation is that the potential partners do worry about the fit among the strategic goals of the potential participants in the new enterprise.

The McDonald's-Babolna Fast-Food Joint Venture

The decision process resulting in the first McDonald's fast food retail store in Hungary occurred over a five-year period starting in 1984. Details of the decisions, interactions of people, and behaviors in this decision process are summarized in Figures 1.2, 1.3, and 1.4.

For the two principal enterprises in this joint venture (McDonald's USA and Babolna Agricultural Cooperative), this joint venture problem definition is best described as two firms attempting to exploit an opportunity for sales and profit growth. Unlike other cases research reports on joint ventures in Hungary (see Woodside and Kandiko 1990), a crisis situation of plant shut-down and the layoff of all employees was not facing the Hungarian enterprise, Babolna.

Solution-Opportunity Identification Phase

The strategic orientation of McDonald's was the impetus and driving force in developing the opportunity and in designing the joint venture in Budapest. The company recognized in the 1970s that it would finally run out of room to grow in the United States without cannibalizing its own stores. The chain also was aware that the U.S. consumer base outgrows its menu as customers become older and recognized that massive marketing spending isn't enough to boost sales in

Figure 1.1. Design Phases and Key Issues in Designing and Implementing International Joint Ventures (IJVs)

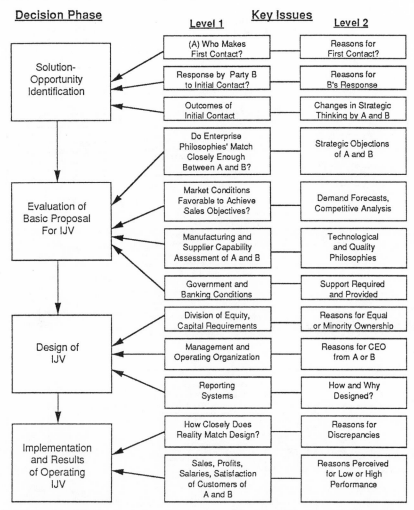

the face of industry saturation, lower demand, and tougher competition (Hume 1990).

Given the huge potential markets, McDonald's retailing expertise, and comparatively weak fast food competition, focusing on international markets became a major part of the philosophy of senior management. The firm made the commitment early to overcome a major obstacle (the poor infrastructure) in successful marketing in Eastern Europe; for example, the firm spent 14 years and $50 million setting up its first Moscow hamburger restaurant. To insure a regular supply of quality meat and potatoes, McDonald's runs its own Soviet farms,

Figure 1.2. Solution-Opportunity Identification in Hungarian-U.S. Fast-Food Retailing Joint Venture

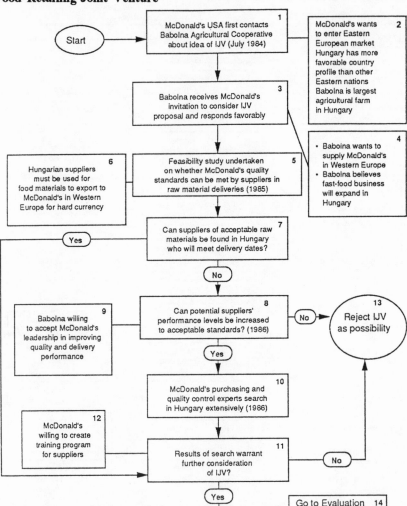

processing plants, and delivery lorries (*The Economist,* 7 April 1990, p. 82).

McDonald's decision to achieve aggressive growth in international markets included Eastern European markets because of the size of these markets and the advantages of being first: followers rarely overcome the market share of the market innovator unless the innovator commits a major blunder.

Before McDonald's restaurant was to open in Moscow in 1990, the joint venture in Budapest was planned and implemented. During the 1980s the Hungarian agricultural industry was noted by McDonald's to be effectively

**Figure 1.3. Evaluation of Proposed Hungarian-U.S. Fast-Food Retailing
Joint Venture**

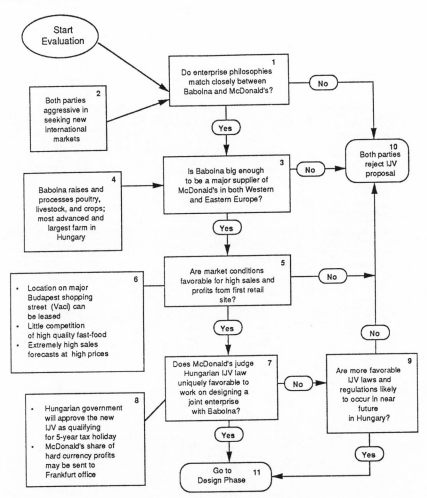

run in comparison to those in other Eastern European nations. Enterprises in the
Hungarian agricultural industry have many customers in Western Europe and the
United States, and their managements were more experienced in meeting Western
standards of supply. Also, early on in McDonald's search for potential joint
venture partners in Eastern Europe, a large agricultural, Hungarian enterprise
(Babolna) that was experienced in working with Western customers was
identified, had political clout in the Hungarian national government, and whose
leadership was committed to aggressive sales growth was identified. Thus, for
both the Hungarian and U.S. joint venture partners, the reasons for exploring the
possibility of the joint venture were similar: both sought aggressive sales and

Figure 1.4. Design/Implementation of Hungarian-U.S. Fast-Food Retailing Joint Venture

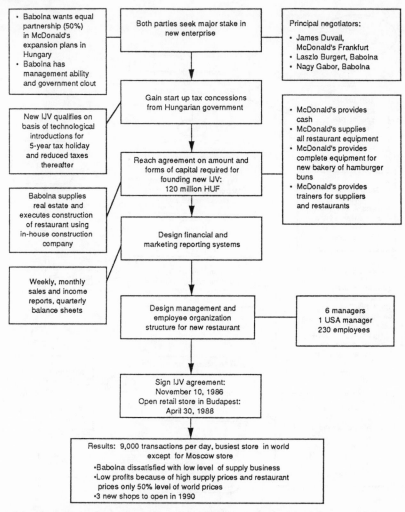

market share growth, and neither was facing a crisis situation caused by poor product quality or customer dissatisfaction.

Note in Figure 1.2 that solution-opportunity identification involved extensive search done in Hungary by McDonald's supply experts to learn whether or not the quality required of raw materials could be delivered to the potential joint venture (it could not) and whether or not McDonald's could train potential suppliers to meet McDonald's quality requirements. Conclusion reached: the potential suppliers could be trained and wanted such training.

Evaluation of the Proposed Hungarian-U.S. Fast-Food Joint Venture

Note in Figure 1.3 that McDonald's sought and gained the possibility of a highly visible joint venture with Babolna in two ways. First, Babolna is a largest and most well-known agricultural enterprise in Hungary; unlike most industrial enterprises, Babolna has had successful performance records both within Hungarian markets and international markets.

Second, the principal shopping street in Budapest and the most well-known shopping district in Hungary is the Vaci, the principal street reserved for pedestrian shopping traffic in Budapest; McDonald's viewed the question of retail site location as a strategic issue for the first McDonald's store in Hungary. The question of achieving an outstanding retail site location was resolved early in the negotiation process for the joint venture.

Design and Implementation of the Fast-Food Joint Venture

The strong desire to enter into the joint venture by senior managers in both of the two principal firms is the foundation for the activities summarized in Figure 1.4. Note in this figure that McDonald's agreed to provide the necessary operating capital, supplier training, and retail management skills to insure for the success of the new enterprise. Babolna agreed to provide the retail site and build the retail store. Part of the proposed agreement was the requirement that Babolna would provide a majority of the raw food materials in several food categories and that the new restaurant had to make use of Hungarian raw materials. In return to these conditions, the new joint venture did receive government approval to qualify to receive a 5-year tax exemption and reduced taxes thereafter.

After the initial year of operation, the principal Hungarian joint venture partner judged the operating results of the new enterprise to be 40 percent of expectations. Babolna's senior management had hoped for sales to be substantially higher (by a factor of 1.5) with higher profits than realized by the new enterprise. McDonald's senior management judged the new enterprise to reach 70 percent of their expectations; they viewed the restaurant's performance to be successful, but they perceived the new investment to be too expensive and the price of the planned, new retail, locations to be increasing too rapidly to permit future success.

The IKEA-Butarker Retail Furniture Joint Venture

IKEA has long had furniture made in Eastern Europe for sale in the West. The plan for the 1990s is for its Eastern European stores to generate soft-currency earnings to pay suppliers or to invest in new production facilities in Eastern Europe.

In 1968 IKEA had completed negotiations for a joint retail venture in Czechoslovakia and the contract for the joint venture was scheduled to be signed one week after the country was invaded. The Swedish-Hungarian joint retail venture summarized in Figures 1.5, 1.6, and 1.7 represents IKEA's first retail store in a Eastern European country during the country's transition to a market economy.

Solution-Opportunity Identification

Both of the two principal firms participating in the identification, design, and implementation of the Hungarian-Swedish furniture joint venture perceived the new enterprise as a strategic opportunity, not as a problem or crisis situation. In Figure 1.5, the need to be the dominant partner in the new enterprise held by both the Hungarian and Swedish firms is apparent. Initially, both firms agreed (without much discussion) to ignore the potential conflict of control of the joint venture until the strengths and weaknesses of the proposal could be examined.

Figure 1.5. Solution-Opportunity Identification of Hungarian-Swedish Retail Furniture Joint Venture

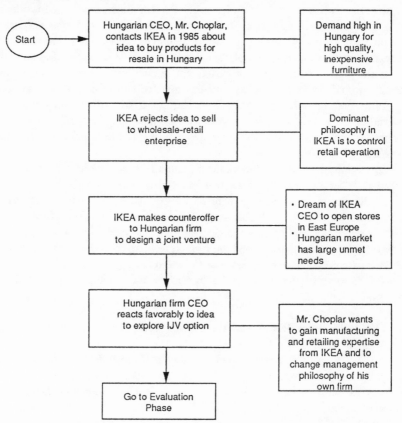

Figure 1.6. Evaluation of Proposed Hungarian-Swedish Retail Furniture Joint Venture

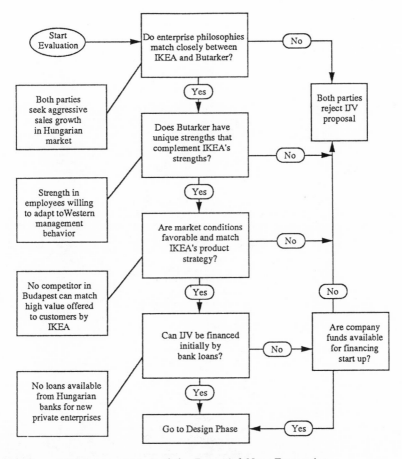

Evaluation and Implementation of the Potential New Enterprise

The basic steps in the evaluation phase of the joint venture shown in Figure 1.6 occurred in a relatively short period of time (less than one year) but concurrently with the initial steps shown in the implementation phase (summarized in Figure 1.7).

Central to the evaluation phase in the decision process was the recognition by both of the principal participants that the strategic orientation of IKEA uniquely matched the furniture needs for the majority of Hungarian households: moderate quality, low-priced furniture that is well-designed for small apartments.

The postponement of the issue of the relative amount of control of the new joint venture until after the evaluation of the proposal helped result in a favorable outcome in the design and implementation of the joint venture.   The potential

Figure 1.7. Implementation of Hungarian-Swedish Retail Furniture Joint Venture

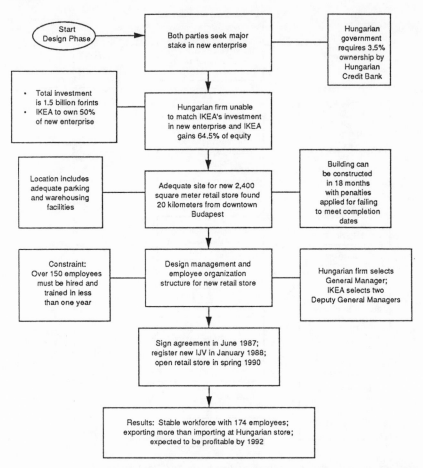

problem of management control was resolved by the fact that the Hungarian enterprise was unable to match IKEA's investment in the new enterprise (as agreed initially); see Figure 1.7. Consequently, Butarker agreed to a minority ownership position in the new enterprise.

Both the Hungarian and IKEA senior managers judged the new joint venture to be operating between 80 to 90 percent of their expectations after the first three months of operation. The implementation of new accounting systems and financial reporting systems was of immediate concern for senior managers when the interviews were completed.

CONCLUSIONS

The central theoretical conclusion from this case research approach to examining the identification and design of joint venture opportunities in Europe is that several of the propositions of the bounded rationality model do appear to apply to the two decision processes.

In both of the cases, the participants viewed the possible new joint ventures similarly: as strategic opportunities, not as problems or crises for their respective firms. Search for possible alternative solutions was indeed limited. Potential solutions were not considered simultaneously and were not compared to one another; the observations reported by Bjorkman (1989) about search processes among Finnish firms for foreign direct investments also held for the two cases reported here.

The data collected to evaluate the two proposed joint ventures were not to discover an optimal decision but to judge the feasibility of success of the new enterprises. The information collected did appear to be biased in favor of designing and implementing the new enterprise in both cases. What is of value about the search for evaluating future joint ventures is the depth of search carried out by McDonald's as part of the evaluation stage and before the design of the joint venture. Surprisingly, such depth of search of potential supplier operations and quality of materials supplied may be the exception rather than the operating rule-of-thumb in evaluating proposed joint ventures (cf. Woodside and Kandiko 1990).

A finding from an in-depth case research study of the foreign direct investments (FDIs) of seven Finnish firms reported by Bjorkman (1989) also fits the decision-making patterns observed in the two cases described in the present study. Bjorkman (1989) reported that FDI decisionmaking almost entirely consisted of development of one and only one FDI alternative at a time, "This concerned the country to be investigated, the location within the country, the choice of whether to acquire a firm or to make a greenfield investment, the choice of JV partner, and the choice of which firm to acquire. Although earlier studies have shown that the development of alternative solutions is relatively uncommon, the consistent absence of such activities was striking in our data" (Bjorkman 1989, 163).

In the two cases reported here, none of the four major participants reported making any attempts of searching for alternative joint venture partners from other countries or from the same countries of their future partners. The fact that the four joint venture participants across the two cases were the most well known and successful enterprises in their respective industries within their respective domestic markets may have served as the principal reason for eliminating search for alternative joint venture partners. The result was that the final choice of joint venture partners was the first enterprise that exceeded a set of minimum cutoff criteria (a conjunctive decision-making rule). The application of such a decision making rule for final choice fits within the predictions expected from the bounded rationality model of decisionmaking (cf. Cyert and March 1963; Wilson and Wilson 1988).

What are the strategic management lessons to be learned from a case research approach to international joint venture planning? The answer is, in part, the actions and decisions by the parties in the identifying and planning of joint venture opportunities indicate that no one sequence of decisions is likely best for designing successful international joint ventures. Specific decisions can be postponed and the order of the phase in process can be rearranged in such ways that may solve potential stalemates and circumvent roadblocks.

The case research findings indicate the necessity of achieving a good fit in strategic thinking among senior managers of the major participating enterprises. With both cases reported here, the senior Hungarian and foreign managers all recognized aggressive growth to be their respective firms' valued strategic orientations. This match of strategic orientations appeared to have served well in overcoming obstacles in both designing and implementing the new enterprises.

REFERENCES

Biemans, Wim G. (1989), *Developing Innovations Within Networks*, Groningen: University of Groningen.

Bjorkman, Ingmar (1989), *Foreign Direct Investments: An Empirical Analysis of Decision Making in Seven Finnish Firms*, Helsinki: The Swedish School of Economics and Business Administration.

Campbell, Donald T. (1975), "Degrees of Freedom and the Case Study," *Comparative Political Studies, 8* (July), 178-193.

Cohen, M., John March, and J. Olsen (1972), "A Garbage Can Model of Organizational Choice," *Administrative Science Quarterly, 17,* 1-24.

Contractor, Farok J., and Peter Lorange (1988), "Why Should Firms Cooperate: The Strategy and Economics Basis for Cooperative Ventures," in *Cooperative Strategies in International Business*, Farok Contractor and Peter Lorange, eds., Lexington, MA: Lexington Books, pp. 3-30.

Cyert, Richard, and John March (1963), *A Behavioral Theory of the Firm*, Englewood Cliffs, NJ: Prentice-Hall.

Economist (April 7, 1990), "Retailing in Eastern Europe: A Shortage of Shopkeepers," p. 82.

Emmott, Bill (1993), "A Survey of Multinationals," *The Economist, 326* (March 27-April 2), 26 pages.

Fleck, Robert A. (1973), "How Media Planners Process Information," *Journal of Advertising Research*, 13 (May), 14-18.

Hisrich, Robert D. (1992), "Joint Ventures: Research Base and Use in International Markets," in *The State of the Art of Entrepreneurship*, Donald L. Sexton and John D. Kasarda, eds. Boston: PWS-Kent.

Howard, John A., James Hulbert, and John U. Farley (1975), "Organizational Analysis and Information Design: A Decision-Process Perspective," *Journal of Business Research, 3* (April), 133-148.

Hume, Scott (1990), "McD's Faces U.S. Slowdown," *Advertising Age, 61* (May 14), 1 ff.

March, John, and Herbert Simon (1958), *Organizations*, New York: Wiley.

Mintzberg, Henry, Duru Raisinghani, and Andre Theoret (1976), "The Structure of `Unstructured' Decision Processes," *Administrative Science Quarterly, 21* (June), 246-275.

Parkhe, Arvind (1993), "`Messy' Research, Methodological Predispositions, and Theory Development in International Joint Ventures," *Academy of Management Review, 18* (2), 227-268.

Peter, J. Paul (1981), "Construct Validity: A Review of Basic Issues and Marketing Practices," *Journal of Marketing Research, 18* (May), 133-145.

Tallman, Stephen B., and Oded Shenkar (1994), "A Managerial Decision Model of International Cooperative Venture Formation," *Journal of International Business Studies, 25* (1), 91-113.

Wilson, Elizabeth J., and David T. Wilson (1988), "Degrees of Freedom in Case Research of Behavioral Theories of Group Buying," *Advances in Consumer Research, 15*, 587-594.

Witte, Erhard (1972), "Field Research on Complex Decision Making Processes—The Phase Theorem," *International Studies of Management and Organizations, 2*, 123-132.

Woodside, Arch G., and Jozsef Kandiko (1990), "Decision-Processes in Strategic Alliances: Designing and Implementing International Joint Ventures in Eastern Europe," 90-INTB-01, New Orleans, Freeman School of Business, Tulane University.

—— (1991), "Decision-Processes in Strategic Alliances: Designing and Implementing International Joint Ventures in Easter Europe," *Journal of Euromarketing, 1 (1/2)*, 151-187.

Yin, Robert K. (1989), *Case Study Research*, Newbury Park, CA: Sage Publications.

2

Reciprocal Agency: Toward a Theory of International Joint Ventures

Frank L. Winfrey
Anne L. Austin

Globalization of the economy and the unification of Europe have stimulated the formation of international joint ventures (IJVs). Numerous examples have been reported in the business press (Barnard 1992). East and West German shipyards have discussed cooperating to meet competition from the Pacific Rim. A West German bank, seeking market expansion in Asia, discussed cooperation with a Japanese bank that wants access to the asset management skills of the German bank. Three European national airlines considered a joint venture for global operations (Lafayette Publications 1990a). Despite the continuing interest, most discussed joint ventures remain on the drawing board; of those formed, fewer still survive and profit.

This paper develops an agency-theoretic basis for the study of IJVs. Although IJVs have been studied from numerous perspectives (Blodgett 1986; Geringer and Hebert 1989; Beamish and Banks 1987), agency theory provides a unique and under-utilized perspective (Austin and Winfrey 1989; Bergen, Dutta, and Walker 1992). The objective of this chapter is to focus on the control of the venture members and the coordination of their actions for the mutual benefit of all members. By identifying the IJV partner performing the role of the agent in an agency relationship, reciprocal agency provides a theoretical framework to anticipate where problems arise and suggests the appropriate actions for resolving those problems (Austin and Winfrey 1989).

AGENCY RELATIONSHIPS

Agency theory suggests that the principal contracts with an agent to conduct the necessary transactions of the business in an integrated fashion. The transactions are the foundation for the profitable conduct of the firm and must be based upon decisions that are rationally taken to advance the objectives of the principal (Levinthal 1988). Jensen and Meckling (1976) define an agency relationship as a contract under which one or more individuals (the principal) engage another individual (the agent) to perform some service on their behalf that involves delegating some decisionmaking authority to the agent. Agency problems arise when a principal has employed an agent to perform a service that necessitates the delegation of choice authority to the agent under circumstances in which there is a conflict of interest between the agent and the principal (Pratt and Zeckhauser 1985). Agency costs, in turn, arise in circumstances where conflicts of interest coupled with the exercise of self-interested behavior under conditions of rational expectations result in suboptimal business decisions (Jensen and Meckling 1976).

Contracts and Enforcement

Agency theory focuses on the utilization of rules with which the principal seeks to motivate the agent to direct business activities in ways that are advantageous to the principal (MacDonald 1984; Starks 1987). Therefore, a fundamental understanding of agency costs and contracts is an essential element in understanding the nature of agency agreements. Because contractual relations are the very essence of the firm (Coase 1937; Alchian and Demsetz 1972; Jensen and Meckling 1976), agency relationships are ubiquitous in business structure. The business firm may be defined as a set of contracts among factors of production (Fama 1980; Cheung 1983). The set of contracts describes a multitude of complex relationships (i.e., contracts) between the legal fiction (i.e., the firm) and the suppliers or owners of labor, material and capital inputs, and the consumers of the output (Jensen and Meckling 1976).

A contract may be defined as "a promise or set of promises for which the breach of which the law gives a remedy, or the performance of which the law in some way recognizes as a duty" (Goldberg 1976). The crucial aspects of this definition are the notions of "promise" and the consequences of "breach." A key dimension of contracts is that they "are designed to direct individual interests toward some joint interest" (Heckathorn and Maser 1987). However, a contract providing compatible incentives to both principal and agent is unlikely to achieve optimal risk-sharing and allocative efficiency. The contracting problem may be described as one of nonrepeated asymmetric information. If the state of nature is only revealed ex post, the optimal contract may involve the risk preferences of the participants (Easley and O'Hara 1988). The structure of the firm may be a response to these risk preferences.

The notion of promise requires the definition of a performance standard as "a signal which enters the compensation function as a parameter" which is not observable at the time the contract is agreed upon by both parties (Christensen 1982). Christensen noted that, "the determination of standards is an element of choice at the time of contracting."

To analyze the conditions of the exchange process in the real world, the basic single-period agency model must be extended to a multiple-period model. In such instances, reputation is the integral, albeit implicit, monitoring mechanism or contract enforcement device. Reputation may be defined as a perception of effectiveness by an individual or group (Tsui 1984). Reputation has both a temporal and dynamic focus, grounded in role theory and social structure perspectives. The chief benefit to reputation in the agency perspective is that reputation provides an incentive to assure contract performance and reduce opportunism (Buckley and Casson 1987; Klein and Leffler 1981; Milgrom and Roberts 1988; Noorderhaven 1992).

Moral Hazard

The situation in which information is asymmetric or the agent's actions are unobservable produces a problem of moral hazard. The problem of moral hazard exists when the agent acts opportunistically or breaches the contract. The outcome of the agent's action is sub-optimal to the principal's performance standard.

Arrow (1985) has identified two such types of moral hazard. In the Hidden Action Model, the actions of the agent are not observable to the principal, but the outcome of those actions is observable. For example, it may be difficult to tell whether a worker is shirking when the group's output is examined. The agency problem has to do with the enforceability of the contract and the related costs of monitoring the agent's actions.

The second type of moral hazard is the Hidden Information Model. In this case, the actions of the agent are observable, but the contingencies on which the actions are decided are not. For example, a manager's investment decisions may be observable, but it is difficult to know why the decision was made. The outcome of the decision may be sub-optimal to the principal, but not to the agent, who is maximizing his own utility (Hart and Holmstrom 1987).

INTERNATIONAL JOINT VENTURES

A great deal has been written about international joint ventures, from why they are formed (Contractor and Lorange 1988), to how they can best be managed (Sullivan and Peterson 1982; Newman 1992), to why they succeed or fail (Killing 1983). Much of the literature draws on an economic cost-benefit analysis (Contractor and Lorange 1988) or on a dependency-cooperation notion (Buckley and Casson 1987). Koot (1987) has identified five recurrent themes in the joint venture literature: rationales for joint ventures; ownership and control; venture autonomy; choice of partner; and legal agreement and protection. Much of the research pertaining to these themes focuses on the formation and start-up phases of the venture. For example, using a transaction cost paradigm to explain a preference for joint ventures over wholly owned subsidiaries, internalization theory is extended to include equity joint ventures (Beamish and Banks 1987). Contractor and Lorange (1988) develop a cost-benefit framework to analyze whether a direct investment or a cooperative venture is a better strategic alternative. Other authors have examined the criteria for partner selection or the structure of the joint venture arrangement. Through its emphasis on a carefully planned and negotiated venture, this literature implicitly recognizes the difficulty of managing the venture. However, relatively few papers focus on strategies, such as control and coordination, for managing the inevitable conflict.

Geringer and Hebert (1989) integrate two conceptual frameworks, transactions costs and strategy-structure, to study control in IJVs. Control is considered on three dimensions. The focus of control refers to the scope of activities over which a partner exercises control. The extent of control is the degree of control achieved by the partners. The mechanisms describe the ways the partners have of exercising control. The performance of the IJV is a function of the fit between partners' and IJV strategy and the parameters of control.

In a theoretical perspective on conflict and cooperation, Buckley and Casson (1987) utilize the fifty:fifty equity joint venture as an exemplar that symbolizes the cooperative ethos. Cooperation is defined as coordination through mutual forbearance. Mutual forbearance builds trust and, through trust, commitment to the venture. Forbearance occurs where an agent chooses to honor his full contractual obligation. Alternatively, the agent may fail to honor minimal obligations (strong cheating) or may choose to honor only minimal obligations (weak cheating). Mutual forbearance occurs when parties forbear on a reciprocal basis and punish cheating. Activities that enhance each party's reputation for forbearance serve to build trust. As trust builds, agents' preferences change so that through commitment to the venture, cooperation becomes an end in itself.

Buckley and Casson's (1987) conceptualization is analogous to Thompson's reciprocal interdependence (1967). Reciprocal interdependence refers to the situation in which outputs of each system element become the inputs for other system elements. This is precisely what occurs in a joint venture relationship. The distinguishing aspect of reciprocal interdependence is that each entity poses a contingency for the other (Thompson 1967). With reciprocal interdependence, concerted actions are achieved through coordination.

Koot (1987) takes a more practical approach to the conflict-cooperation problem in joint ventures by identifying four dilemmas that reoccur in joint venture management. Partners must make choices between: exploiting or investing in finance and know-how; molding or letting the operation grow; fighting or producing a team-like cooperative effort; and selecting its own joint venture manager or allowing the manager to develop his own staff. Koot points out that while some of these issues can be resolved early, the same issues are likely to reoccur at later stages in response to changes in the joint venture and its environment.

It is clear that the problem of the control of venture activities is of central importance because the parties are mutually dependent on each other to accomplish activities and achieve goals. The agency nature of the relationship has been implicitly recognized by several scholars. Geringer and Hebert (1989) note that partners are "often unable to rely solely on their ownership position" to determine behavior and must relinquish control to the IJV. Blodgett (1986) recognizes that while partners form a joint venture hoping for mutually beneficial outcomes, control is relinquished grudgingly. Greater specification of the cause and solution to conflict in the joint venture is necessary. A useful framework may be developed by explicitly considering the joint venture as a reciprocal agency relationship.

RECIPROCAL AGENCY IN THE CONTEXT OF JOINT VENTURES

A joint venture could be defined as simply the set of agency contracts covering the way inputs are joined to create outputs and the way receipts from outputs are shared among inputs (Fama 1980). In agency theory, the contract structures of most organizational forms limit the risks undertaken by most agents through the specification of either fixed promised payoffs or incentive payoffs tied to specific measures of performance (Itoh 1992). This is congruent with the joint venture literature, where emphasis is placed on negotiating an agreement that details the obligations of both partners (Collins and Doorley 1991; Nichols 1950). It has long been recognized that partners in a joint venture share mutual dependencies, the extent of which depends on the share of the venture (Pfeffer and Nowak 1976). Also recognized is that the legal agreement is insufficient to keep the venture going, or to resolve problems when it runs into trouble.

As examined above, the standard agency model involves a principal and agent in clearly superior-subordinate roles. An interesting conceptual problem arises when the identity of the principal and agent is not readily apparent because the roles played by each party are not explicit, and furthermore, may shift over time or in response to contingencies. A joint venture embodies just such a situation.

The principal-agent relationship as it pertains to joint ventures is a reciprocal one. The partners enter the relationship seeking mutually beneficial outcomes. Each partner owns some asset, tangible or intangible, that the other partner seeks access to. In order for the joint venture to succeed, each partner must relinquish some autonomy to the other. The non-fixed identity of the agent in a reciprocal agency relationship means that identifying the agent in the context of an agency problem is critical to determining the resolution of that problem.

It is possible to conceptualize the joint venture within the context of agency in one of two ways. First, and more traditionally, the joint venture may be considered as an agency relationship between two partners, one of whom plays the role of the principal and one the role of the agent. If the joint venture is not split equally, as is most often the case, it is traditional to think of the majority partner as assuming the role of the principal. A second way to conceptualize the joint venture is to consider the relationship between the partners and the joint venture they form. In actuality such a conceptualization views the relationship as a network of agency relationships. In this conceptualization it is most common to think of the partners as principals and the joint venture as the agent of the partners.

In either conceptualization, however, it is possible that the traditional roles played by the partners may be reversed. Thus, the agency relationship becomes reciprocal. The reciprocal, interdependent nature of the joint venture relationship is recognized as the source of information asymmetry and monitoring problems that lead to interorganizational coordination and conflict problems (Buckley and Casson 1987).

Even though the joint venture has a contractual structure, the problem of moral hazard still arises. The contract is insufficient for two reasons (Arrow 1985). First, it is impossible to specify a contract that covers all contingencies. Second, even if it were possible to specify all contingencies, it would be impossible to enforce such a contract. This reality implies that other means beyond the contract must be found to monitor and control the principal-agent relationship.

A framework is developed by considering the international joint venture relationship between partners as a reciprocal agency relationship with the problem of moral hazard. Two hypothetical joint ventures are explored to illustrate the reciprocal roles assumed by the partners. The framework considers the identity of the agent in each moral hazard problem in order to determine an optimal resolution.

Hidden Action Model

In the Hidden Action Model, the outcome of the agent's actions may be observed, but not the actions themselves. There are several instances when the parties are unable to observe each others' actions, but are able to observe outcome indicators such as increased revenues, decreased sales, increased friction, or decreased productivity.

The moral hazard problem is the level of effort expended by the agent. Some level of effort is needed to honor the terms specified in the contract. Such effort may represent a disutility to the agent. Utility may occur instead from other actions, likely those not specified in the contract. The level of effort expended by the partners in an IJV may be in part culturally determined. Beamish and Banks (1987) observe that "while the foreign partner may possess the requisite knowledge about the local economy, politics and culture at the outset he may not continue to put forth the effort necessary to maintain this knowledge." Variations in production, such as style of labor organization, willingness to work third shift, and traditional August vacations, are factors that can impact both the expectations and actual levels of effort. The resolution of the moral hazard problem is to induce the necessary level of effort from the agent. At issue is the ability of the principal to police and alter the agent's actions.

The Hidden Action Model may be illustrated with a hypothetical joint venture. An American multinational and a European manufacturer form a joint venture. The American firm (AM) owns a valuable proprietary technology and is the majority partner. The European firm (EM) has market power within its country, a country that the AM does not operate in, and is the minority partner.

A traditional assessment of this joint venture would conclude that the EM is the agent of the AM. The AM has contracted with the EM, in the form of a joint venture, in order to secure access to a market in which it has no presence. The AM expects the EM to expend effort so that the AM, through the joint venture, develops market presence. The EM has market expertise and a good grasp of the factors determining consumer demand. In order to expend sufficient effort to satisfy the AM's expectations, the EM must divert effort from its own operations to the joint venture. It is possible, therefore, that the EM will not devote sufficient effort to the joint venture and will opt instead to perform activities that create utility for itself. In order to achieve the requisite level of consumer demand, the IJV may need to develop a new package. The effort it takes to do this, using the EM's knowledge of European packaging preferences, is effort that the EM cannot expend on its own packages. The outcome of the EM's efforts will be observable to the AM in the form of unmet expectations of the joint venture's performance.

A reciprocal assessment of this joint venture realizes that while the EM can act as the agent of the AM, the AM may also act as the agent of the EM. From this perspective, the EM has contracted with its agent, the AM, in order to gain access to proprietary technology. In order to honor its contract, the AM must divulge this technology to the joint venture. It may be hesitant to fully disclose because such disclosure would be detrimental to the AM's other operations. The outcome of the AM's efforts will be observable to the principal, the EM, in the level of access to technology accorded to the joint venture.

The resolution of the Hidden Action problem involves several elements. Although it is expensive to construct a contract that covers all contingencies, each party can specify what actions are absolutely required of the other. Such a contract will be difficult to determine and expensive (if not impossible) to enforce. Contractor and Lorange (1988) note that increased administrative overhead to monitor and enforce contracts is a direct cost of venture activity. Contract specification is generally a solution where the Hidden Action problem arises under circumstances when the minority partner, here the EM, is acting as the agent. The majority partner is more able to bear the costs associated with contract specification. It is possible that the unification of Europe may make contract specification a less costly alternative as business activities and operations become more standardized.

An alternative resolution to the Hidden Action is to focus on the creation of a climate that encourages voluntary cooperation. This solution is more likely where the joint majority partner is acting as the agent because due to the unbalanced power relationship created by the joint venture share, cooperation is the minority partner's tool to co-opt the majority partner's economic power. If the goals of both partners are compatible and fully understood, each partner is more likely to be committed to the relationship, and less likely to pursue sub-optimal actions. A similar outcome is likely to the extent both partners are satisfied with the relationship created by the joint venture.

Both solutions are most effective if used proactively, even to the extent of creating the solution before the problem arises. The extensive literature on joint venture creation, including the work on partner selection, speaks to the realization that the Hidden Action problem can be addressed at an early stage of the relationship and a structure created that will address the problem as it occurs.

Hidden Information Model

In the Hidden Information Model, the principal can observe the agent's actions, but cannot observe the agent's contingencies. Such a scenario is common in joint ventures, and in the international context, may be more common because of culturally-influenced managerial strategies and geographic distances. The moral hazard problem arises because the agent has information the principal does not. The agent uses this information to make decisions, but the principal is unable to verify if the use of the information best serves the principal. The solution to this moral hazard problem is unlikely to occur by contract specification. The issue for the parties is to convince the other party to select mutually beneficial contingencies. It is in instances such as these that reputation provides the incentive to assure contract performance and reduce opportunism (Buckley and Casson 1987; Klein and Leffler 1981; Milgrom and Roberts 1988).

The Hidden Information Model may be illustrated with a hypothetical joint venture. Two European companies with compatible technologies form a joint venture. The majority partner (MJ) is the larger company, operating exclusively in the European market. The minority partner (MN) is a smaller company, but operates in the American market as well as the European market.

The traditional agency perspective assumes the MN is acting as the agent of the MJ in the formation of the joint venture. The MJ has entered the joint venture in order to gain access to the agent's knowledge of the American market. The MJ expects that because of the MN's knowledge, the joint venture will be able to successfully compete outside of Europe. However, since the MJ does not know the contingencies that are known to the MN, the MJ is unable to verify that the decisions the MN makes about the joint venture's activities best serve the MJ's interests. It is likely that the MN makes decisions that are more optimal for it than for the joint venture. For example, the MN has developed a supplier network in the United States. It knows of the inadequacies of the supplier selected by the IJV. However, because the MN is anxious to develop the IJV, it does not reveal these inadequacies to the MJ. The MN has made a decision that is sub-optimal for the IJV, but that preserves its ties to its own supplier network.

A reciprocal assessment of the joint venture will notice that the partner in the ostensibly stronger position, the MJ, can act as the agent of the MN. Because it is a larger company with a different sphere of expertise, the MJ has knowledge not available to the MN. It is equally likely that the MJ will make decisions that enhance its operations, but are sub-optimal to the MN. The transfer pricing decisions of the MJ are one example. The MJ knows its own cost structures, it may decide to transfer components to the IJV at a price that, while good, is not optimal for the IJV. However, the price is optimal to the MJ because such a price allows it to optimize its own tax and profit strategies.

The resolution of the Hidden Information problem is based in reputation. The reputation of the partners involved in the joint venture may reassure the other partner that whatever the contingencies, the actions of the other party will be optimal since the other partner would be unlikely to select a course of action that would damage the viability of the joint venture arrangement. This is an informal enforcement strategy based on trust (Arrow, 1985). Communication and reciprocity between the parties are required. Participation and negotiation allow both parties inputs to the process, and through the stages of bargaining, may enhance goal alignment and move the parties toward mutual commitment.

CONCLUSIONS

Additional insights into the joint venture relationship are obtained when the relationship is considered in the framework of reciprocal agency. Under certain circumstances of autonomy and choice, either partner may fulfill the role of principal or agent. By focusing on the level of effort expended and the access to information, rather than the equity shares of the partners, the partner assuming the role of the agent may be identified. Successful resolution of joint venture problems should begin with the identification of the partner acting as the agent and the characterization of the source of the agency moral hazard: hidden action or hidden information. The possible resolutions to the problem of moral hazard demonstrate that interorganizational structure and contracts are insufficient to alleviate the problem. Close attention should be paid to attaining coalignment of interests through noncontractual means, such as cooperation and coordination. Reputation is an essential element to insuring trust between partners.

The framework developed in this paper utilizes two hypothetical joint ventures to illustrate the reciprocal nature of the agency relationship in joint venture arrangements. Although the two types of moral hazard have been discussed separately, the reciprocal nature of a joint venture ensures that the two problems may occur simultaneously, or that one may serve as the impetus for the other. Although the resolution of either type of moral hazard is the same regardless of the identity of the agent, it is critical to note the source of the problem. The reciprocal nature of the joint venture agency relationship complicates the resolution because the identity of the agent may not be assumed *a priori*. By considering whether the partner is acting in the role of principal or agent, the roots of the moral hazard problem are more clear and a resolution more easily determined.

The reciprocal agency framework developed in this paper yields important considerations for future IJV research. The framework must be further developed such that a model with testable propositions may emerge. It should be noted that empirical testing of agency models is problematic (Arrow 1985), and data about internal operations of IJVs difficult to acquire. Nonetheless, a profitable approach might be the ethnographic-style case study.

From a practical perspective, the reciprocal agency framework allows a consideration of the roots of the problem and a better understanding of the partner's motivations. It is axiomatic that problem identification is the initial step to problem resolution.

REFERENCES

Alchian, Armen A., and Harold Demsetz (1972), "Production, Information Costs and Economic Organization," *American Economic Review 62* (December), 777-795.

Arrow, Kenneth J. (1985), The Economics of Agency, in *Principals and Agents: The Structure of Business*, J.W. Pratt and R.J. Zeckhauser, eds., Boston: Harvard Business School Press, pp. 37-51.

Austin, Anne L., and Frank L. Winfrey (1989), "Reciprocal Agency in Franchise Channels of Distribution." *Proceedings of the Fourth Annual Society of Franchising Conference*, Scottsdale, AZ (October 3-5). Paper 17.

Barnard, Bruce (1992), "U.S. Firms Diving into Europe," *Europe: Magazine of the European Community 319* (September), 8-11.

Beamish, Paul W., and John C. Banks (1987), "Equity Joint Ventures and the Theory of the Multinational Enterprise," *Journal of International Business Studies 18* (Summer): 1-16.

Bergen, Mark, Shantanu Dutta and Orville C. Walker Jr. (1992), "Agency Relationships in Marketing: A Review of the Implications and Applications of Agency and Related Theories. *Journal of Marketing 56* (July) 1-24.

Blodgett, Linda Longfellow (1986), "Partner Contributions as Predictors of Equity Share in International Joint Ventures," *Journal of International Business Studies 22* (First Quarter), 63-78.

Buckley, Peter J., and Mark Casson (1987), "A Theory of Cooperation in International Business," in *Cooperative Strategies in International Business*, F.J. Contractor and P. Lorange, eds., Lexington, MA: Lexington, pp. 31-53.

Cheung, Steven N.S. (1983), "The Contractual Nature of the Firm," *Journal of Law and Economics 24* (April), 1-21.

Christensen, John (1982), "The Determination of Standards and Participation," *Journal of Accounting Research 20* (Autumn Part II), 589-603.

Coase, Ronald H. (1937), "The Nature of the Firm," *Economica 4*, 386-405.

Collins, Timothy M., and Thomas L. Doorley III (1991), *Teaming Up for the 90s: A Guide to International Joint Ventures and Strategic Alliances*, Homewood, IL: Business One Irwin.

Contractor, Farok J., and Peter Lorange (1988), "Competition vs. Cooperation: A Benefit/Cost Framework for Choosing Between Fully-Owned Investments and Cooperative Relationships," *Management International Review Special Issue*, 5-18.

Cremer, Jacques, and Michael H. Riordan (1987), "On Governing Multilateral Transactions with Bilateral Contracts," *Rand Journal of Economics 18* (Autumn), 436-451.

Easley, David, and Maureen O'Hara (1988), "Contracts and Asymmetric Information in the Theory of the Firm," *Journal of Economic Behavior and Organization 9* (April), 229-246.

Fama, Eugene F. (1980), "Agency Problems and the Theory of the Firm," *Journal of Political Economy 88* (April), 288-307.

Geringer, J. Michael, and Louis Hebert (1989), "Control and Performance in International Joint Ventures," *Journal of International Business Studies 20* (Summer), 235-254.

Goldberg, Victor P. (1976), "Toward an Expanded Economic Theory of Contracts," *Journal of Economic Issues 10* (March), 45-61.

Hart, Oliver, and Bengt Holmstrom (1987), "The Theory of Contracts," in *Advances in Economic Theory Fifth World Congress,* T.F. Bewley, ed., Cambridge, U.K.: Cambridge Univ. Press, pp. 71-155.

Heckathorn, Douglas D., and Steven M. Maser (1987), "Bargaining and Sources of Transaction Costs: The Case of Government Regulation," *Journal of Law, Economics, & Organization 3,* 69-98.

Itoh, Hideshi (1992), "Cooperation in Hierarchical Organizations: An Incentive Perspective," *Journal of Law, Economics, & Organization 8* (April), 321-345.

Jensen, Michael C., and William H. Meckling (1976), "Theory of the Firm: Managerial Behavior, Agency Costs and Ownership Structure," *Journal of Financial Economics 3* (October), 305-360.

Killing, J. Peter (1983), *Strategies for Joint Venture Success,* New York: Praeger.

Klein, Benjamin, and Keith B. Leffler (1981), "The Role of Market Forces in Assuring Contractual Performance," *Journal of Political Economy 89* (August), 615-641.

Koot, William T.M. (1987), "Underlying Dilemmas in the Management of International Joint Ventures," in *Cooperative Strategies in International Business,* F.J. Contractor and P. Lorange, eds., Lexington, MA: Lexington, pp. 347-367.

Lafayette Publications, Inc. Business Briefs (1990a), *Europe 1992: The Report on the Single European Market 2* (March 21), 581-586.

Lafayette Publications, Inc. Business Reports (1990b), *Europe 1992: The Report on the Single European Market 2* (April 4), 599-604.

Levinthal, Daniel (1988), "A Survey of Agency Models of Organization," *Journal of Economic Behavior and Organization 9* (March), 153-185.

MacDonald, Glenn M. (1984), "New Directions in the Economic Theory of Agency," *Canadian Journal of Economics 17* (August), 415-440.

Milgrom, Paul, and John Roberts (1988), "Economic Theories of the Firm: Past, Present, and Future," *Canadian Journal of Economics 21* (August), 445-458.

Newman, William H. (1992), "'Focused Joint Ventures' in Transforming Economies," *Academy of Management Executive 6* (February), 67-75.

Nichols, Henry W. (1950), "Joint Ventures," *Virginia Law Review 36* (May), 425-459.

Noorderhaven, Niels G. (1992), "The Problem of Contract Enforcement in Economic Organization Theory," *Organization Studies 13* (2), 229-243.

Pfeffer, Jeffrey, and Phillip Nowak (1976), "Joint Ventures and Interorganizational Interdependence," *Administrative Science Quarterly 21* (September), 398-418.

Pratt, John W., and Richard J. Zeckhauser (1985), *Principals and Agents: The Structure of Business,* Boston, MA: Harvard Business School Press.

Starks, Laura T. (1987), "Performance Incentive Fees: An Agency Theoretic Approach," *Journal of Financial and Quantitative Analysis* 22 (March), 17-32.

Sullivan, J., and R.B. Peterson (1982), "Factors Associated with Trust in Japanese-American Joint Ventures," *Management International Review* 22 (2), 30-40.

Thompson, James D. (1967), *Organizations in Action.* New York, McGraw-Hill.

Tsui, Anne S. (1984), "A Role Set Analysis of Managerial Reputation," *Organizational Behavior and Human Performance* 34 (August), 64-96.

3

Strategic Auditing of International Joint Ventures Using a Triangulation Research Approach

Arch G. Woodside
Matthew D. Heaps

> An audit of auditors would be scathing. They have missed impending company collapses and become too close to company managers. Reforms are overdue. ("Accountancy" 1992)

The severe criticism of auditors arises from the unexpected corporate failures, such as the thrift mess in the United States and the failures of the Bank of Credit and Commerce International (BCCI). "Accountants respond defensively to these attacks. They say the public expects more from an audit than it can deliver—the so-called expectations gap. The responsibility for drawing up a company's accounts rest with its directors; it is, they claim, unrealistic to expect a one-off outside audit always to pick up a complex fraud or imminent collapse" ("Accountancy" 1992, 19).

Accounting myopia may be a substantial cause of the failure of audits to detect serious problems and impending company failures: auditors check some but not all of the accounts drawn up by their client for the previous year and then declare that these accounts represent a true and fair view of the company's position. "Yet as Roger Davis, head of audit at Coopers & Lybrand, points out, shareholders are more interested in two forward-looking questions: how good is a company's internal management, and will it remain a going concern" ("Accountancy" 1992, 20).

Answering these fundamental, forward-looking questions requires creating and implementing a strategy audit of an enterprise, that is, designing and applying a research method for assessing the strategic focus, skills, activities, distinctive competencies, and the performance of an enterprise or nonprofit organization. The theory and tools for such assessments are available now from the evaluation research, strategic management, organizational science, and administrative science literatures (e.g., Dess and Robinson 1984; Mintzberg 1988; Conant, Mokwa, and Varadarajan 1990; Patton 1990; Lee 1991; Morrison and Roth 1991; Dougherty 1992; Miller 1992; Doyle, Saunders and Wong 1992).

The present chapter is a report on a strategy audit of an ongoing, international joint venture (IJV) involving members from a developed, industrial nation (Japan) and a former COMCON nation (Hungary). Given that most IJVs created by enterprises from Western, industrial nations and former European communist nations never become up-and-running enterprises, and those IJVs that do usually fail within three years (Woodside and Kandiko 1991), detailed information on the strategies of a successful Hungarian-Japanese IJV may be useful for both IJV theory-building and strategy planning. Our purpose includes illustrating strategic auditing research in the context of the international enterprise.

The case study we describe is focused on one of the first successful (i.e., profitable and operating for more than five years) East-West IJVs in a former COMCON country. The detailed, strategic audit method and results may offer insights for designing and implementing successful IJV enterprises; such audit reports may also be useful for theory-building in the field of IJV management. Our strategy-audit report includes: (1) identifying the strategic goals of the Hungarian-Japanese enterprise, (2) identifying the strategies employed to achieve these goals, (3) learning how these realized-strategies affect the performance of the enterprise, and (4) demonstrating an application of triangulation methods in strategic auditing research.

The following propositions concerning enterprise success factors provide the theoretical framework for the study (see Clifford and Cavanaugh 1985; Buzzell and Gale 1987; Doyle, Saunders, and Wong 1992). (The strategy audit issues are whether or not the strategy implemented for the IJV studied reflects the foci and behaviors of more or less successful enterprises.) (1) The more successful firms are focused on aggressive market growth and less on defending existing market positions. (2) When describing their firms, focusing on "good short-term profits" is reported more often by executives in less successful firms. (3) Successful firms more often focus simultaneously on both market and financial objectives compared to less successful firms. (4) Product superiority is more often reported as a distinctive competency among more versus less successful firms. (5) More successful firms have a greater number of distinctive competencies compared to less successful firms. (6) More successful international enterprises have more responsibility at the local operating level compared to the less successful enterprises. (7) The management style of more versus less successful firms includes group responsibility and teamwork, less hierarchical distinctions, and variable and ad hoc job specifications.

Our study is unusual in two respects. First, the detailed results of a strategy audit of an ongoing IJV is reported. By contrast, most studies on IJV strategies and behaviors use cross-sectional databases (e.g., Kogut 1989; for a review, see Geringer and Hebert 1989; Franko 1989). While such studies are useful for testing and generalizing theory across firms, such research reports do not provide the details necessary for firm-specific evaluations; that is, details on the strategic foci, actions, and performance of specific IJVs. Here we sacrifice breadth to gain depth to learn the strategies, behaviors, and performance of an ongoing IJV.

Second, the reported study is unusual in the application of triangulation to strategic auditing. Triangulation is broadly defined by Denzin (1978, 291) as "the combination of methodologies in the study of the same phenomenon." The triangulation metaphor is from navigation and military strategy that use multiple reference points to locate an object's exact position. Multiple viewpoints allow for greater accuracy. The effectiveness of triangulation rests on the premise that the weaknesses in each single method will be compensated by the counter-balancing strengths of another.

Triangulation, however, can be something other than scaling, reliability, and convergent validation. It can also capture a more complete, *holistic*, and contextual portrayal of the unit(s) under study. That is, beyond the analysis of overlapping variance, the use of multiple measures may also uncover some unique variance which otherwise may have been neglected by single methods. (Jick 1979, 603)

Following a description of the IJV participating in the study and a background section on strategic auditing and managing IJVs, the details on the triangulation method used in the study are presented; then, the findings of the study are described; the chapter closes with a section on conclusions and suggestions for future research.

THE ENTERPRISE FOCUS OF THE STUDY:
POLIFOAM CORPORATION

The study is focused on an ongoing Hungarian-Japanese manufacturing enterprise, the Polifoam Corporation. Polifoam manufactures both industrial and consumer polyethylene foam products (e.g., insulation for buildings and pipes, sound-proofing materials, camping mats, large playhouses for children, and inserts for footwear). Polifoam was selected because this firm met several criteria: relatively small in size (less than 100 employees), and thus, possible to study using a small research team in a relatively brief period of time; an ongoing enterprise that was ongoing for more than five years; and an IJV that includes parent enterprises from a developed, market economy and a formerly, centrally planned economy.

Polifoam is located in an industrial park in Budapest. The enterprise was founded in 1984 with an initial working capital of 160 million (Hungarian Forints) by five enterprises; the two enterprises most involved in the creation process were Pannonplast, a large Hungarian chemical manufacturing firm, and Furukawa, a Japanese manufacturing conglomerate. Polifoam's manufacturing location and management offices had their start-up in 1985-86 on a greenfield site. The first production runs were made in 1986; the company was profitable in its first year of operation and in all subsequent years. For the first year of production, most sales were to industrial customers in the construction industry. Sales in the second year of production were 180 percent of first year's sales. Annual sales growth continued; it was more than 15 percent in 1991 compared to 1990 for exports; domestic sales remained level in 1991 versus 1990.

Polifoam's export sales to West European customers were forecasted to be 61 percent of total sales in 1992; total sales for 1992 were expected to be above 360 million (Hungarian Forints). A total of 80 persons were employed full-time at Polifoam in 1992: 15 managers and staff and 65 production workers. Details of the reasoning behind the principals creation of Polifoam and the design of the IJV are reported elsewhere (Woodside and Kandiko 1991; Woodside and Somogyi 1993).

BACKGROUND ON STRATEGY AUDITING AND RESEARCH ON IJVs

Progress has been made in assessing the strategic focus, the distinctive competencies, and the performance of an enterprise, as well as learning the linkages between these three concepts. Most firms can be segmented by their strategic focus. For example, using Miles and Snow's (1978) strategic typology, most enterprises can be classified as being defenders, prospectors, analyzers, or reactors (see Conant, Mokwa, and Varadarajan 1990); or, companies can be classified by their market share/sales strategies: prevent decline, defensive, maintain position, steady growth, aggressive growth, or dominant share (see Doyle, Saunders, and Wong 1992).

Second, enterprises segmented by strategic focus have specific patterns and levels of distinctive competencies that differ between such segments. For example, firms seeking aggressive growth in market share more often report entering newly emerging market segments, while firms focused on preventing decline tend to focus predominantly on cost reductions and improvements in productivity. Also, prospectors tend to have a greater number of distinctive competencies compared to analyzers or defenders, and all three have greater numbers of distinctive competencies compared to reactors (Woodside, Sullivan, and Trappey 1991).

Third, while attaining and using distinctive competencies does not guarantee high performance, the lack of such competencies are associated with low performance. Thus, attaining and using distinctive competencies appear necessary, but they are not sufficient, for high performance; environmental factors and situational factors (e.g., good/bad luck) are important noncontrollable factors affecting performance.

Fourth, performance might be best viewed as a multi-dimensional rather than a single-dimensional construct. Profitability, sales growth, market share growth, and customer satisfaction are each dimensions of performance. While these dimensions are often related positively to each other, their associations are not necessary high (the associations among these four dimensions are often small to moderate, $r^2 < .25$). Consequently, multi-dimensional measures of performance should be taken, and enterprises differing in strategic focus are likely to use different principal measures of performance.

In summary, clear links appear in the literature between strategic types and distinctive competencies. Also, attaining and using distinctive competencies are linked positively with achieving high performance.

In a recently released three-year study of the focus, operating strategies, and organization of 30 American and 30 matched Japanese subsidiaries operating in Britain (Doyle, Saunders, and Wong 1992), American subsidiaries were found to be less ambitious, more oriented toward delivering short-term profit performance and less adapted to local market conditions than their Japanese competitors. Over a five-year period, only one in three U.S. subsidiaries exhibited successful profit and market performance, against more than three of four Japanese subsidiaries. Some of the detailed findings from the Doyle, Saunders, and Wong 1992 study are compared to the findings for the Hungarian-Japanese international joint venture (IJV) later in this chapter.

An IJV is a distinct organization created by two or more legally distinct organizations (the parents) with the parents' headquarter operations being located in different nations. IJVs are perceived often to be strategic weapons for gaining entry in emerging markets (see Harrigan 1987) and for gaining knowledge and skills in using new technologies (Perlmutter and Heenan 1986; Kogut 1988; Geringer and Hebert 1989; Kogut 1989).

Research reports on IJV operations indicate that, while many are created, few actually are implemented, and almost none (less than 2% of those created) succeed. For example, in 1990 less than 50 of the 1,400 IJV agreements signed in the former Soviet Union were operating (Dean 1990). A total of only 10 of the 70 created Hungarian-U.S. IJVs were operating in 1989 (Dyson 1989).

A key finding from Kogut (1989) for IJVs located in the United States is that those ventures actually performing research and development in R&D intensive industries tend to be dissolved less often than other ventures. "A plausible interpretation of this result is that ventures motivated by the transfer or creation of knowledge reflect more potent cooperative incentives relative to other kinds of ventures. Whether this cooperation reflects the gains from enhanced efficiency or more effective means to enhance market power awaits more rigorous specifications of the downstream competitive market" (Kogut 1989, 197).

DETAILS ON TRIANGULATION RESEARCH

Triangulation demands the blending and integrating of a variety of data and methods (Jick 1979). For example, archival materials, such as written annual plans, financial reports, and internal memoranda, are examined and their contents compared to data collected from semi-structured, probing interviews. Triangulation research applications often include long periods of field observation: "the studied commitment to actively enter the worlds of interacting individuals" (Denzin 1978, 8-9). "*Going into the field* means having direct and personal contact with people under study in their own environments" (Patton 1990, 46), over long time periods (e.g., several months or years).

Although not a requirement for triangulation research applications, long periods of time on-site (in the field) are helpful in particular for crystallizing findings: "the field worker knows what he [she] knows, not only because he's [she's] been in the field and because of his [her] careful verification of hypotheses, but because 'in his [her] bones' he [she] feels the worth of his [her] final analysis" (Glaser and Strauss 1965, 8).

Many examples are available of triangulation research applications from the marketing, management, and organizational science literatures. Howard and Morgenroth (1968) used multiple data collection methods (including long periods of direct observation) to map the pricing decisions in a petroleum enterprise; Pettigrew (1983) reviews several studies in which the convergent validity of data from several sources are examined in each study; Lee (1991) calls for (and demonstrates) the value of integrating positivist and interpretative approaches within the same study in organizational research designs.

RESEARCH METHODS

Three principal research methods were used for data collection in the study. First, the 38-page, semi-structured, strategic auditing survey form used by Doyle, Saunders, and Wong (1992) was used in interviewing five senior and middle mangers of Polifoam, the Hungarian-Japanese IJV manufacturing enterprise participating in the study. The Doyle, Saunders, and Wong (1992) survey is an open-ended, strategy-audit form particularly suitable for assessing strengths and weaknesses of enterprises with operating/reporting units in different nations. Given this suitability and the cooperation and considerable depth in responding to the questions described later in the results section, we conclude that substantial face validity exists in our reported application. An industry-specific study using the nearly identical strategy audit form is reported by Doyle, Shaw, and Wong (1993).

The central rationale for incorporating multiple interviews of different executives located at different levels of management in a strategic audit is that different persons have different perspectives of reality, and to learn about such different perspectives requires multiple interviews. Direct observation of decisions, interactions of people, and activities, along with an analysis of available documents, are additional research methods used to help answer the questions of who did what, with whom, when and where and why. Such information is useful for assessing the quality of internal management and the viability of the enterprise.

Second, on-site document analyses were completed on all company records, including articles of the IJV incorporation in Hungary, sales data and history for each customer account, minutes of all quarterly meetings with parent representatives and Polifoam senior managers, and all quarterly and annual financial reports.

Third, in 1992 one of us (Matthew Heaps) was in the field, on-site at Polifoam's manufacturing location in Budapest, for a six-week period of direct observation. During this on-site period, the researcher shared office space with Polifoam's Deputy Managing Director (D-MD); the researcher attended meetings (among senior and middle managers, managers and manufacturing supervisors, managers and customers, supervisors and production workers, and managers and parent representatives); the researcher kept a daily journal of significant events (i.e., the decisions, interactions and conversations, and small and large critical incidents) occurring on-site.

The data collection for the present study concluded with a two-hour interview by one of the researchers (Arch Woodside) with both the Managing Director (MD) and the D-MD; this final interview focused on intended strategic directions of these managers and Polifoam itself.

Initial Contact with Polifoam's Senior Management

The initial contact with a Polifoam manager occurred in 1989 when the D-MD (Ms. Piroska Somogyi) became a participant in a new executive training program in Budapest, the Young Managers' Program (YMP). In 1989-90, working in the evenings and on weekends, Ms. Somogyi continued to serve as the D-MD of Polifoam.

During November 1989, it was requested of Ms. Somogyi and she agreed to a lengthy interview to learn the process of Polifoam's creation. A semi-structured personal interview form was used during an initial two-hour interview. This initial interview was followed by a four-hour, personal interview with the Managing Director, Miklos Arvai, in December 1989.

In August 1990 she received a ten-month leave-of-absence from the company; she and her husband travelled to Tulane University to attend the second-year of the Freeman School's M.B.A. program. In May 1991, she graduated first academically in the M.B.A. class and returned to her position at Polifoam.

Second Round of Interviews

In 1991, while attending Tulane University as an M.B.A. candidate, Ms. Somogyi arranged for telephone interviews with senior managers at both of the principal parent organizations, Pannonplast in Hungary and Furukawa in Japan, to collect additional details on the process of creation of IJV. These interviews and a review of company documents resulted in a revised and deeper report on the creation process for Polifoam (Woodside and Somogyi 1994).

Procedure

Early in 1992 the senior managers, Ms. Somogyi and Mr. Arvai, were contacted with a request to sponsor a Tulane M.B.A. summer international intern at Polifoam's manufacturing location in Budapest and for permission to conduct a strategic audit of Polifoam. The details of a strategic audit were described to the senior managers; the request included an on-site period-of-residence by Matthew Heaps, an M.B.A. student, for a period of six weeks.

The on-site field work for the strategic audit also included work on a new product planning report for Polifoam. Matthew Heaps worked on designing and marketing a new consumer product, "Our House," a playhouse for young children constructed of polyethylene. Thus, the student worked on two assignments jointly while at Polifoam: collecting data for the strategic audit, and collecting data and writing a product design and marketing plan for Our House.

Each in-depth strategic audit interview was completed in two to four sessions at Polifoam. The average interview time for these interviews was five hours. Four of the five interviews were completed during the last three weeks Matthew Heaps was at Polifoam.

In the late afternoons and early evenings of his field work, daily journal entries were made by Matthew Heaps on the key events, decisions, and interactions of people. Impressions of the sentiments and reported feelings among executives and production workers were also recorded. Late in the field data collection period, a personal interview was completed with both the Managing Director and Deputy Managing Director of Polifoam by Arch Woodside. The interview was focused on the relationships among the parent enterprises and on future directions of Polifoam.

FINDINGS

Organizational Design

The organizational design of Polifoam's management is summarized in Figure 3.1. The floor plan for the production facility is summarized in Figure 3.2. All mid-level executives reported to the D-MDs, Piroska Somogyi. The D-MD's responsibilities included all phases of production, new product development, and marketing operations of the enterprise. Both the Managing Director and the D-MD had university degrees in chemical engineering with extensive industrial engineering manufacturing experience; both executives were employed by Polifoam from the inception of the company.

Based on daily journal entries, the D-MD left her office and supervised manufacturing operations on the plant floor four to ten times per day. She met with visiting customers and suppliers directly, and worked to solve technical production problems on a daily basis. The D-MD personally handled most production as well as marketing problems. For example, in one instance the D-MD renegotiated (by telephone) a price with an export customer in Germany after receiving the sales order from Polifoam's sales agent for Germany; the agent had set the price lower than authorized by the export sales manager. All middle level managers met with the D-MD on a daily basis. Based on direct observation and strategic audit interviews, the mid-level executives and workers viewed the D-MD as highly competent; very focused on achieving high quality production, new customers for Polifoam, and sales growth; and sometimes as being abrasive in her relationships with mid-level managers.

Based on the organizational design and daily journal entries, the Managing Director (MD), Miklos Arvai, focused on two activities: (1) preparation of written reports for the parent organization and directing the company's

Figure 3.1. Organization of Senior and Middle Management at Polifoam Company

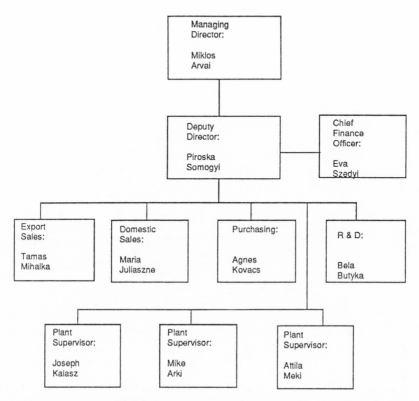

interactions with the parent enterprises, and (2) reducing and solving supervisory conflicts among executives and executives and workers.   The MD rarely went onto the production floor more than once or twice per day, and on some days he did not visit the production facility at all. The MD successfully arbitrated major conflicts about marketing, purchasing, and production operations among company executives. When such conflicts were focused on decisions made by the D-MD, the MD served well to reduce the tension between the D-MD and a mid-level executive and sometimes to modify parts of the planned actions in conflict.

With reference to the persons in Figure 3.1, the in-depth interviews for the strategic audit were completed with the MD, the D-MD, the head of export sales, the Chief Finance Officer (CFO), and the Chief Purchasing Officer (CPO).

Two Noteworthy Incidents During the Field Data Collection Period

Anecdotal evidence helps to increase understanding of the interactions among participants, why decisions are made, and how things get done in organizations. The following report of two noteworthy incidents are examples of such evidence.

Figure 3.2. Manufacturing Plant Layout of Polifoam Company

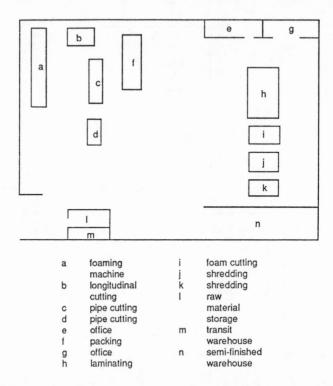

a	foaming machine	i foam cutting
b	longitudinal cutting	j shredding
c	pipe cutting	k shredding
d	pipe cutting	l raw material storage
e	office	m transit warehouse
f	packing	n semi-finished warehouse
g	office	
h	laminating	

Mr. Bela Butyka, the head of Research and Development, resigned from Polifoam during the second week of field data collection. He had founded a trading company with three friends; the trading company was founded to import polyethylene products for food packaging. Matthew Heaps met with Mr. Butyka several times during the nine days before he resigned. Mr. Butyka mentioned to Matthew Heaps that no conflict of interest would occur between his work for the new trading company and Polifoam because Polifoam products can not be used with food. The MD and D-MD disagreed; they met with Mr. Butyka and told him to choose between the two firms. Mr. Butyka explained the situation over a three day period to Matthew Heaps; after Mr. Butyka resigned and had left the company, the D-MD commented about the situation, "I like Bela but this was his second conflict of interest for him this year, and he had to go." The D-MD assumed most of the R&D responsibilities for the remaining field data collection time period.

During the third week of the field data collection period, a major Austrian customer informed the Head of Export Sales, Tamas Mihalka, that the Austrian firm had bought a small Hungarian retail chain that carries Polifoam products. The Austrian manager planned to replace some of Polifoam's products with competitors' products; at this point the D-MD telephoned the Austrian manager and told him that the retail chain would need to continue to carry Polifoam's entire retail product line or none of it. The Austrian customer agreed to continue to carry the complete Polifoam retail product line.

These two vignettes illustrate unique and overlapping theme elements in decisionmaking at Polifoam. The first illustrates the complementary and close-working relationship between the MD and D-MD in making strategic decisions: they consulted with each other several times before the D-MD informed Mr. Butyka that he would need to choose between working strictly for Polifoam or leaving Polifoam for his new venture. The second vignette is an example of the strong presence of the D-MD in decisions of sales managers with customers: the D-MD stepped in directly in an important negotiation between the Export Sales Manager and the Austrian customer.

Strategic Objectives

In the 1992 Doyle, Saunders, and Wong (DSW) study, four out of five Japanese companies operating in Britain gave aggressive growth or market domination as their objective, against only half the U.S. companies operating in Britain and only one in five of 30 British companies. In the present study, four of the five Polifoam executives interviewed for the strategic audit reported than maintaining the current market share/sales position was the major strategic objective of the firm. These results are summarized in Table 3.1.

Thus, the current strategy for Polifoam appears substantially less ambitious than found for the Japanese firms in the DSW study. This view is supported by Polifoam's belief about short-term profit objectives of the firm. Similar to the majority of the British and American firms in the DSW study, all five Polifoam executives reported that "good short-term profits are the objective" describes Polifoam well. See Table 3.2 for results.

The Japanese managers in the DSW study reported that their headquarters were not unduly unsettled by low profits provided that long-term market performance showed steady improvement. In 1992 the strategic focus for Polifoam is more focused on profits here-and-now than on future market share growth. However, additional responses indicate that the strategic focus at Polifoam is somewhat unique compared to the British, U.S., and Japanese approaches. For example, probably because of the daily focus on new product and new market R&D by the D-MD, four of the five Polifoam executives reported that the strategic focus of the firm included working hard to enter newly emerging market segments. However, only one Polifoam executive reported that the firm was focused on winning share by beating competitors, and most agreed that the strategic focus was centered on cost reduction and improved productivity. Additional details appear in Table 3.3.

Thus, Polifoam does appear to be focused on winning new customers and developing new products but not on beating competitors to win additional market share. Most Polifoam executives do not perceive their firm to be in a competitive battle for gaining market share.

Competitive Advantages

Assuming that market success and profit performance depends on an ability to match the needs of customers more effectively than competitors, then an enterprise should be found to be superior on some marketing dimensions respective to their competitors. Polifoam's executives saw this view to be the case, especially for bringing product innovations to market and providing a wide product range, high quality, and reliability. The detailed results are summarized in Table 3.4.

Table 3.1. Which Best Describes Your Market Share/Sales Strategy?

Strategy	U.S. %	Japanese %	British %	Polifoam %
Prevent decline	7	3	27	0
Defensive	3	0	17	0
Maintain position	17	0	23	80
Steady growth	23	17	13	20
Aggressive growth	33	57	13	0
Dominate market	17	23	7	0
Sample Size (n)	30	30	30	5

Source: Data in first three columns from Doyle, Saunders, and Wong (1992); data from last column collected in study reported here.

Table 3.2. How Well Does "Good Short-Term Profits Are the Object" Describe Your Company?

Firms	Response Yes in Percent	Sample Size
Japanese	27	30
U.S.	80	30
British	87	30
Polifoam	100	5

Source: Adapted from Doyle, Saunders, and Wong (1992 Table 4, 425) for Japanese, U.S. and British data; original study for Polifoam data.

Table 3.3. How Well Do These Statements Describe Your Strategic Focus?

Strategic Focus	Firms (in percent)			
	U.S.	Japanese	British	Polifoam
Expand market by converting non-users of product	n.a.	n.a.	n.a.	0%
Expand market by creating new uses for the products	n.a.	n.a.	n.a.	20%
Enter newly emerging market segments	50%	77%	40%	80%
Enter segments already established in the market but are new to our company	n.a.	n.a.	n.a.	80%
Increasing usage rate of product	n.a.	n.a.	n.a.	0%
Winning share by beating competition	73%	83%	53%	20%
Focus on cost reduction and improved productivity	70%	43%	83%	80%

Source: Adapted from Doyle, Saunders, and Wong (1992) for U.S., Japanese, and British firms (Table 5, 429), and original study for Polifoam.
n.a. − not available.

Table 3.4. In Which Dimensions Do You Have Competitive Superiority?

Dimension	Firms (in percent)			
	U.S.	Japanese	British	Polifoam
Quality and reliability	77%	93%	47%	80%
Service and support	50	70	44	60
Product range	63	60	43	80
Product innovation	63	68	33	100
Low prices	40	60	60	0
Product performance	n.a.	n.a.	n.a.	40
Product design (aesthetics, ergonomics)	n.a.	n.a.	n.a.	80
Advertising	n.a.	n.a.	n.a.	0
Personal selling	n.a.	n.a.	n.a.	20
Distribution effectiveness	n.a.	n.a.	n.a.	40

Source: Based, in part, on Doyle, Saunders, and Wong (1992 Table 7, 431), and original study for Polifoam data.
n.a. = not available.

Table 3.5.   Have You Responsibility for Marketing and Distribution Decisions Versus "Big" Decisions Made by Parent Organizations?

	Not Responsible		Sole Responsibility		
Firms	1	2	3	4	5
U.S. %	0	0	13	40	47
Japanese %	0	0	0	41	59
Polifoam %	0	0	20	0	80

Source: Adapted from Doyle, Saunders, and Wong (1992) for U.S. and Japanese data (Table 8, 433), original study for Polifoam data.

Note in Table 3.4 that the profile for the first four dimensions listed match closest to the Japanese responses in the DSW 1992 study. Also, note that four of the five Polifoam executives do not report Polifoam to be superior to competitors in offering low prices or being effective in personal selling. Having competitive prices and being effective in selling in the field at customer locations appear to be current weak points in Polifoam's marketing strategy.

Four of five of the Polifoam executives reported that important decisions were made with Polifoam management having the sole responsibility for the decisions. Details appear in Table 3.5. The observed decisionmaking and reporting process at Polifoam followed closely with the Japanese loose-tight management style of subsidiaries: the local managers have sole responsibility for decisions but reporting systems are extensive and frequent.   Continuous informal monitoring and formal performance reviews (four times annually) were the main modes of control of Polifoam by its parent enterprises. The monitoring and review activities were the major daily focus of the MD. Thus, Polifoam's executives viewed the headquarters of the parent enterprises as being very well-informed of the activities, problems, and progress of Polifoam.

Management Style

Management style at Polifoam is unique and does not match closely, any one of the three groups of firms in the DSW 1992 study. Details appear in Table 3.6.

Unfortunately, four of the five Polifoam executives do not believe that "group responsibility and teamwork" describes Polifoam. This situation is likely due, in part, to the management style in Hungary prior to the collapse of the centrally planned government, that is, managers and workers were told what to do and their views rarely sought. "Group responsibility and teamwork" appeared to be new, and somewhat dangerous, concepts at Polifoam. One executive (the D-MD) reported that "the adoption of such a management style reduces the opportunity to assign blame, mistakes, on someone else, a management trait developed and perfected under Communism."

The good news about Polifoam's management style was the view that both top-down and bottom-up communications occurred regularly. This view was held by three of the five executive interviewed. Such communications were observed to occur daily at Polifoam, mainly because the D-MD asked questions of plant supervisors and production workers on the production floor. In summary, the management style at Polifoam appears to be effective but over-reliant on the

Table 3.6. How Well Do These Statements Describe Your Company's Management Style?

Statement	Firms (in percent)			
	U.S.	Japanese	British	Polifoam
Group responsibility and teamwork	63%	73%	50%	20%
Strong hierarchical distinctions in management	57%	35%	83%	40%
Both top-down and bottom-up communications	30%	62%	27%	60%
Variable and ad hoc job specifications	30%	73%	33%	40%

Source: Adapted from Doyle, Saunders, and Wong (1992) for U.S., Japanese, and British data (Table 12, 437); original study results for Polifoam.

activities of the D-MD. The ability of the current management team to perform effectively in the absence of the current D-MD is a disturbing strategic issue.

How Does Each Polifoam Executive Evaluate the Firm's Strengths?

High levels of agreement among Polifoam's executives are found on the company's strategic strengths and weaknesses. For example, none of the executives believed Polifoam to be efficient at large-scale production runs, and four reported that Polifoam was flexible in responding to problems and opportunities. Detailed answers for the five Polifoam executives and an independent view held based on the field observations, prior research of Polifoam, and document analysis are summarized in Table 3.7.

The main conclusion from the profile of responses in Table 3.7 is that substantial agreement does exist about Polifoam's strengths among the firm's executives. However, the executives do differ in their perceptions about the firm's capability in being first to enter new markets and possessing strong product design capabilities. The CFO, CPO, and export sales head viewed the firm with more limited strengths than did the MD and D-MD. Possibly, the combination of the D-MD's strong technical ability, her relative youth (age in the mid-30s), aggressiveness in achieving production and sales results, and her more senior executive position resulted in some discounting of the firm's product strengths by the firm's mid-level executives.

Distribution Effectiveness

The results summarized in Table 3.8 confirmed that distribution strategy is very important to Polifoam, but the firm's current distribution strategy is less than highly effective. Note in Table 3.8 that the MD has a more rosy view of the performance of Polifoam's distribution strategy relative to the firm's competitors versus the view held by the three mid-level managers and the independent, observer responses. Current sales support needs to be improved at Polifoam.

One improvement was completed during the field data collection period: a high quality, three-dimensional sales brochure of the firm's major products was prepared; the brochure included small sample pieces of 30 products along with their descriptions. However, deep knowledge of customer applications of Polifoam products and relationship marketing practices by Polifoam executives is missing from the company currently.

Marketing Mix

Details on the executive's views about the superiority of the firm's marketing mix are summarized in Table 3.9. Note that product quality and product range are the major areas of marketing mix strength for Polifoam relative to competitors. Possible weaknesses include pricing, advertising, and personal selling efforts.

Contact with Customers/Dealers

Most Polifoam executives believe contact with customers and dealers to be very important for the long-term survival of the enterprise. However, the final three dimensions concerning customer/dealer contacts reported in Table 3.10 indicate that such contacts are not receiving substantial attention according to most Polifoam executives. Some marketing program to activate and maintain close customer/dealer contact is needed at Polifoam.

Planning at Polifoam

Surprisingly, high agreement among the five executives interviewed for the strategic audit is not found for the type and level of planning activities in the firm. Details are summarized in Table 3.11.

Formal long-term plans are prepared and revised annually at Polifoam. However, both the CFO and CPO were unaware of this activity or the contents of these plans. Both the CFO and CPO reported that the firm did engage in medium-range to short-range formal planning, however. All the executives recognized that formal planning did occur at Polifoam.

New Product Development

Details of Polifoam's new product development activities are summarized in Table 3.12. The company has been successful in developing two to seven new product applications in each year of its life; note, however, that this success is based on little concept testing or business analysis. Some form of new product business analysis tools are likely necessary, and such tools are missing currently at Polifoam.

The final interview of Polifoam's two senior managers included the statement by the D-MD that she was searching actively for a MD position at one of several Hungarian industrial manufacturing enterprises. She reported that she believed she was ready to assume the responsibilities of a managing director. Polifoam's current MD reported regretting, but understanding, her decision.

Conclusions about the Strategy Audit of Polifoam

Polifoam is at a major strategic crossroads. The firm is now entering a maturing phase in its company life cycle. Annual sales growth is slowing down. The company has both substantial technical and marketing strengths as well as weaknesses. Polifoam is overly dependent on the abilities and workaholic lifestyle of its current D-MD, who is currently seeking to leave the company. Specific improvements in distribution and customer relationship strategies have been noted in this report.

Table 3.7. Evaluation of Polifoam's Strengths

Company Activity	Respondent					
	MD	Deputy MD	CFO	CPO	Export Sales	Observer
First to enter new markets	Yes	Yes	No	No	No	Some-times
Strong product design capability	Yes	Some-times	Some-times	No	No	Some-times
Strong process development and cost reduction capability	No	No	No	Some-times	No	No
Flexible with medium scale production runs	Yes	No	Yes	Yes	Yes	Some-times
Efficient large-scale production runs	No	No	No	No	No	No
Financial resources: easy access to risk capital	No	No	No	No	No	No
Access to capital in moderate quantities	Yes	Yes	Yes	Yes	No Re-sponse	Yes
Flexible organization	No	Some-times	No	No	No	No

Table 3.8. Effectiveness of Polifoam's Distribution Strategy Compared to Main Competitors

Distribution Factor	Respondent					
	MD	Deputy MD	CFO	CPO	Export Sales	Observer
Distribution effectiveness in general	Better	Worse	Worse	Same	Better	Worse
Importance of distribution strategy	Very	Very	Very	Extremely	Very	Very
Margins for dealers	Same	Same	Lower	Same	Higher	Same
Dealer profit	Higher	Same	Lower	Same	Same	Same
Sales support to dealers	Higher	Same	Lower	Lower	Higher	Lower
Short distribution chain used	More often	More often	Less often	Less often	Same	Same

Limitations

Several limitations in the present study should be noted. Longer periods of data collection in the field are necessary for deeper understanding and thick descriptions of what is actually happening in an enterprise. In-depth interviews at several layers of management and among production workers would have improved the study. The results of the present study are limited to one successful IJV having one manufacturing site. Representatives of the parent enterprises were not interviewed in the present study. Additional data collection from interviews of executives representing parent organizations, suppliers, customers, and leading governmental agency representatives knowledgeable about the enterprise is recommended in future strategic audits.

Table 3.9. Superiority of Polifoam's Marketing Mix Strategy Compared to Main Competitors

Marketing Mix Factor	Respondent					
	MD	Deputy MD	CFO	CPO	Export Sales	Observer
Product quality (reliability, main-tenance free)	Same	Supe-rior	Supe-rior	Supe-rior	Supe-rior	Superior
Product range	Broad-en	Broad-en	Broad-en	Broad-en	Same	Broaden
Product innova-tions	Newer	Same	Older	Same	Same	Same
Product perfor-mance (output, effi-ciency)	Same	Worse	Same	Same	Worse	Worse
Prices to customers	Same	Higher	Higher	Higher	Higher	Higher
Advertis-ing bud-get	Less	Less	Less	Less	Less	Less
Personal selling effort	Higher	Same	Same	Same	Same	Lower

Table 3.10. Contact with Customers/Dealers at Polifoam

	Respondent					
Contacts	MD	Deputy MD	CFO	CPO	Export Sales	Observer
Customer/ dealer contact very im- portant?	Yes	Yes	Yes	Some- times	Yes	Yes
Contact with cus- tomers on long-term continu- ing basis	Yes	Yes	Some- times	Some- times	Yes	Some- times
Sales calls are made by Polifoam salesper- son	No	Yes	No	No	Some- times	No
Sales on customer calls are made by top exec- utive	No	No	Some- times	Some- times	Yes	Some- times
Top exec- utives visit cus- tomer/ dealer/ user sites	Some- times	Some- times	Some- times	Some- times	Yes	Some- times
Custom- ers/ dealers invited to Polifoam	No	Some- times	No	No	Yes	Some- times

Table 3.11. Planning at Polifoam

Planning Actions	Respondent					
	MD	Deputy MD	CFO	CPO	Export Sales	Observer
Formal long term plans	Yes	Yes	No	No	Yes	Yes
Formal medium to short-term plans	Yes	No	Yes	Yes	Yes	Yes/No
Explicit but in-formal statement of goals	No	Yes	No	No	Yes	Yes
No for-mal plans	No	No	No	No	No	No
More action than planning oriented	Some-times	Yes	Some-times	Some-times	Some-times	Some-times

IMPLICATIONS AND SUGGESTIONS FOR FUTURE RESEARCH

No one enterprise is likely to match perfectly the profile of the theoretically, very highly successful enterprise. A strategy audit of an enterprise, with comparisons to both theoretical propositions on success factor profiles and empirical reports on such factors (see Clifford and Cavanaugh 1985; Doyle, Saunders, and Wong 1992; Doyle, Shaw, and Wong 1993), is likely to provide useful assessments of strengths and weaknesses of the firm's current strategy.

Table 3.12. New Product Development (NPD) at Polifoam

NPD Activity		Respondent				
	MD	Deputy MD	CFO	CPO	Export Sales	Observer
New product ideas can emerge from any source within the company	Yes	Yes	Yes	Yes	Yes	Yes
A lot of concept research and business analysis takes place before investing in the new idea	No	No	Sometimes	Sometimes	Yes	No
Product and/or market testing are always done before launching a new product	No	Sometimes	Yes	Sometimes	Yes	Sometimes

A set of theoretical propositions on how highly successful enterprises differ specifically from less successful firms provides a ground for testing and generalizing results from case studies (see Yin 1989; Campbell 1975). The results for Polifoam indicate that the firm does not fit the proto-typical cases of either the more or less successful enterprise. The results of the strategy audit indicate that Polifoam's executives are frustrated at trying to fulfill both ambitious market and financial objectives. Some greater amount of focus on market growth, and reduced emphasis on short-term profits, would increase the degree of fit of the firm with the success factor profile of the more successful enterprise.

The use of a triangulation research approach provides multiple and overlapping views in a strategic audit of a firm. Key facts, strengths, weaknesses, threats, and opportunities can be confirmed only by the use of multiple data collection methods. The use of single-informants to learn the strategic focus and strengths of firms may provide unrealistic views and be dependent on the functional position of the respondent. Interviews with multiple executives and employees with different job responsibilities are needed to really understand what is going on, and what is likely to happen, in an enterprise.

REFERENCES

"Accountancy" (1992), *The Economist, 325* (7781), October 17, 19-20, 23.

Buzzell, Robert D., and Bradley T. Gale (1987), *The PIMS Principles*, New York: Free Press.

Campbell, Donald T. (1975), "Degrees of Freedom and the Case Study," *Comparative Political Studies, 8* (July), 178-193.

Clifford, Donald K., and Richard E. Cavanaugh (1985), *The Winning Performance*, Toronto: Bantam Books.

Conant, Jeffrey, S., Michael P. Mokwa, and P. Rajan Varadarajan (1990), "Strategic Types, Distinctive Marketing Competencies and Organizational Performance: A Multiple Measures-Based Study," *Strategic Management Journal, 11* (5), 365-383.

Dean, Richard (1990), Interview in Bill Keller, "Capitalism: Big Macs in Moscow," *The Times-Picayune*, January 28, A-18.

Denzin, Norman K. (1978), *The Research Act*, 2d Ed., New York: McGraw-Hill.

Dess, Greg S., and Richard B. Robinson, Jr. (1984), "Measuring Organizational Performance in the Absence of Objective Measures," *Strategic Management Journal, 5* (3), 467-488.

Dougherty, Deborah (1992), "Interpretive Barriers to Successful Product Innovation in Large Firms," *Organization Science, 3* (2), 179-202.

Doyle, Peter, John Saunders, and Veronica Wong (1992), "Competition in Global Markets: A Case Study of American and Japanese Competition in the British Market," *Journal of International Business Studies, 23* (3), 419-442.

Doyle, Peter, Vivienne Shaw, and Veronica Wong (1993), "International Competition in the UK Machine Tool Market," *Journal of Marketing Management, 9* (4), 383-391.

Dyson, Esther (1989), "IJVs Realities versus Fiction," *Forbes, 144,* (December), 114-116.

Franko, Lawrence G. (1989), "Use of Minority and 50-50 Joint Ventures by United States Multinationals during the 1970's: The Interaction of Host Country Policies and Corporate Strategies," *Journal of International Business Studies, 20* (1), 19-40.

Geringer, J. Michael, and Louis Hebert (1989), "Control and Performance of International Joint Ventures," *Journal of International Business Studies, 20* (2), 235-254.

Glaser, Barney G., and Anselm L. Strauss (1965), "Discovery of Substantive Theory: A Basic Strategy Underlying Qualitative Research," *American Behavioral Scientist, 8*, 5-12.

Harrigan, Kathryn R. (1987), "Strategic Alliances: Their Role in Global Competition, "*Columbia Journal of World Business*," Summer, 67-69.

Howard, John A., James M. Hulbert, and John U. Farley (1975), "Organizational Analysis and Information System Design: A Decision Process Perspective," *Journal of Business Research, 3* (April), 133-148.

Howard, John A., and William M. Morgenroth (1968), "Information Processing Models of Executive Decisions," *Management Science, 14,* (March) 416-428.

Hulbert, James M. (1981), "Descriptive Models of Marketing Decisions," in *Marketing Decision Models*, edited by R. L. Schultz and A. A. Zoltners New York: North-Holland, pp. 19-54.

Jick, Todd (1979), "Mixing Qualitative and Quantitative Methods: Triangulation Methods in Action," *Administrative Science Quarterly, 24* (4), 602-611.

Kogut, Bruce (1988), "Joint-Ventures: Theoretical and Empirical Perspectives," *Strategic Management Journal, 9*, 319-332.

—— (1989), "The Stability of Joint Ventures: Reciprocity and Competitive Rivalry," *The Journal of Industrial Economics, 38* (2), 183-198.

Lee, Allen S. (1991), "Integrating Positivist and Interpretive Approaches to Organizational Research," *Organization Science, 4* (2), 342-365.

Miles, R. E., and C. C. Snow (1978), *Organizational Strategy, Structure and Process*, New York: McGraw-Hill.

Miller, Danny (1992), "Environmental Fit versus Internal Fit," *Organization Science, 11* (2), 159-178.

Mintzberg, Henry (1988), "Generic Strategies: Toward a Comprehensive Framework," *Advances in Strategic Management, 5*, 1-67.

Morrison, Allen J., and Kendall Roth (1991), "A Taxonomy of Business-Level Strategies in Global Industries," *Organization Science, 13* (6), 399-417.

Patton, Michael Quinn (1990), *Qualitative Evaluation and Research Methods*, Newbury Park, CA: Sage.

Perlmutter, H.V., and D. A. Heenan (1986), "Cooperate to Compete Globally," *Harvard Business Review* (March-April), 136-174.

Pettigrew, Andrew M. (1983), "On Studying Organizational Cultures," in *Qualitative Methodology*, John Van Maanan, ed. Beverly Hills, CA: Sage, pp. 87-104.

Woodside, Arch G., and Jozsef Kandiko (1991), "Decision-Process in Strategic Alliances: Designing and Implementing International Joint Ventures in Eastern Europe," *Journal of Euro-Marketing, 1* (1/2), 151-212.

Woodside, Arch G., and Piroska Somogyi (1993), "Creating International Joint Ventures: Strategic Insights from Case Research on a Successful Hungarian-Japanese Industrial Enterprise," in *The Economics of Change in East and Central Europe: Its Impact on International Business*, Peter J. Buckley and Pervez N. Ghauri, ed. London: Academic Press, pp. 169-183.

Woodside, Arch G., Daniel P. Sullivan, and Randolph J. Trappey III (1991), "Assessing Relationships Among Strategic Types, Distinctive Marketing Competencies and Organizational Performance," Working Paper, Freeman School of Business, New Orleans: Tulane University.

Yin, Robert K. (1989), *Case Study Research*, Newbury Park, CA: Sage.

Part II

RESEARCH ON KEY SUCCESS FACTORS FOR INTERNATIONAL JOINT VENTURE STRATEGIES

4

Key Issues in the Creation of International Joint Ventures with China

Guo-Liang Xuan
Gunnar Gräf

THE ECONOMIC REFORM PROCESS IN CHINA

The main objective of Chinese development is to catch up to the leading industrial nations in terms of industrial production technology and output. The complete modernization of the economy is necessary to attain this objective by the middle of the twenty-first century. China's development strategy is to reform the national economy and to improve economic cooperation with foreign countries.

Reform of the National Economy

The reform is generally referred to the "four modernizations." The "four modernizations" is development of agriculture, industry, science and technology, and national defense. The development of the economy and a higher living standard will be reached through a linkage of market and plan. There is, however, no specified plan for economic reforms; the lack of time and experience, conflicting interests, and the need for compromise are main reasons for the absence of such a plan.

The Chinese economy has overcome the crises of 1989 and 1990 and had a strong growth rate over the last three years. In the spring of 1992, Deng Xiaoping visited the southern provinces to promote a new reform initiative. Since Deng's historical visit, the concept of the "Chinese Socialism" has developed.

The development and implementation of the "socialist market system" is not only an economic strategy but a direct consequence of previously stagnating reforms. (See Table 4.1.)

The concept of Chinese socialism is related to the following four reforms:

1. Privatization of state-owned companies
2. Development of the market and reform of prices
3. Creation of a social insurance system
4. Separation of business and governmental functions.

Table 4.1. Chronological Overview of Industrial Development in China

1979-1984	First reforms in agriculture. 80% of the population is living in the countryside; a higher living standard would therefore create a basis for other reforms.
1984	First success in agriculture—reforms are expanded to the state industry.
1988-1991	General slowdown of reforms. The main reasons are the high inflation rate and the student demonstrations in 1989.
1992	Since the spring of 1992, the government is following new reform politics. In October 1992, the XIVth Congress of China's Communist Party approved Deng Xiaoping's concept of the "development of the Chinese Socialism."
1993	In March 1993, the concept of the "socialist market economy" is adopted in China's legislation. Decision of transformation to a market economy. Reformation of the financial and the tax systems.
1994	Theoretical development of Deng's ideas.

To prevent an economic crisis such as that which occurred in 1988-90 depends on several points: success of the central government in adopting its economic programs to the individual interests of the provincial governments; efficiency of the economic instruments; consideration of energy, transport, and raw materials in the development process.

Table 4.2 shows an important divergence in economic development between different sectors. Economic growth is followed by a change in economic structure, typical of a rapidly industrializing country.

Industry, commerce, and services have been growing in China's countryside, especially in the period from 1982-87. The main reason for this trend is the migration of unemployed farmers in nonagricultural sectors to urban centers. Today about 10% of the nonurban population is working in a countryside industry. The foreign economy is another factor to influence the developments in the People's Republic of China. Foreign direct investment is considered in the concept of socialist market economy as a success factor in the development of China's economy.

Table 4.2. Economic Growth (in %) of Key Industries

Year	GNP	Agri-culture	Industry	Con-struc-tion	Transport	Commerce
1978	11,7	3,9	17,1	-0,9	11,3	22,5
1979	7,6	6,4	8,1	1,8	2,5	6,9
1980	7,9	-1,8	10,9	29,7	4,1	0,6
1981	4,4	7,1	1,7	1,6	4	19
1982	8,8	11,7	6	4,8	12,2	4,8
1983	10,4	8,5	9,8	18,3	10,9	13
1984	14,7	13	14,9	i7,7	12,9	11,2
1985	12,8	2,7	19,6	24	20,1	18,9
1986	8,1	3	9,6	17,5	11,3	7,2
1987	10,9	4,5	13	13,3	11,4	12,4
1988	11,3	2,2	17,4	8	11,3	9
1989	4,4	3,2	6	-8,5	10,2	-5,8
1990	4,1	7,5	5,5	0,5	4,8	-3,7
1991	7,7	2,3	11,4	15,7	6,4	5
1992	12,8	3,7	20,8	nn	nn	nn

Source: Zhongguo Tongji Nianjian (Statistical Yearbook China) 1992, S. 21, 31 and 34.

JOINT VENTURES IN CHINA

A General Overview

In 1979 the Chinese government decided to expose its stagnated and isolated markets to foreign investors. Foreign investors are now considered to be the "motor of the economy's modernization."

Development of Foreign Direct Investment

In the early days of the reform, the economic situation in China was characterized by a strict adherence to the maoist doctrine of "self reliance." This implied absolute economic independence without any economic interchange with other countries. Not surprisingly foreign trade under Mao was minimal. China's Foreign trade has experienced enormous growth rates (an average of 17%) since its opening. With the fast growth of its exports, China's share in global trade has risen from 0.9% to 2% between 1980-1991.

After a period of high import rates for industrial goods, Chinese leaders realized the potential of modernization because of the high outflow of hard currencies. This can be seen as a main reason for not succeeding in the technology transfer. Low technical and managerial skills in China do not provide the needed know-how. Therefore, China's foreign policy is now focused on exports and more cooperation with foreign companies (see Table 4.3).

The Chinese government actively encourages foreign investment, particularly in priority industries and in the designated special investment zones. In order to acquire foreign technology, equipment, and know-how, China utilizes a number of methods of attracting investment; these include barter trade, compensation trade processing arrangements, joint ventures, and wholly foreign-owned enterprises.

There are different options of cooperation. To attract foreign investors, China now offers many investment incentives. Preferential treatment in the form of tax benefits and other incentives are available to foreign investors in the Special Economic Zones, in designated coastal cities, and in other special investment zones, as well as to approved export-oriented and technologically advanced enterprises.

In general, foreign investment refers to equity joint venture, cooperative joint ventures with limited liability, and wholly foreign-owned enterprises. Over the last years joint ventures have been the preferred form of foreign investment. Foreign investors still regard the joint venture as an investment option for a very good reason: through cooperation the partners can expect better results.

An *equity joint venture* is a separate legal entity and takes the form of a limited liability company registered in China. The partners have joint management of the company, and the profits and losses are distributed according to the ratio of each partner's capital contribution. Equity joint ventures are governed by the Law of the People's Republic of China on Joint Ventures Using Chinese and Foreign Investment, promulgated in 1979, and the implementation regulations, promulgated in 1983. Although a *contractual joint venture* would normally operate under a structure similar to that of Western-style partnership, the parties to the venture may apply for approval to have the company structured as a separate legal entity with limited liability. The profit and loss distribution ratio is established in the contract and can vary over the contact term. Contractual joint ventures are governed by the Law of the People's Republic of China on Chinese-Foreign Cooperative joint ventures, promulgated in April 1988.

Table 4.3. Foreign Direct Investment in the P.R. China 1988-1992

Year	Investment Volume (in millions U.S. $)	Number of Contracts (1000)
1992	$58	48
1991	13	14
1990	8	9
1989	8	7
1988	8	8

Source: Developed from FAZ Frankfurter Allgemeine Zeitung, April 1993.

Wholly foreign-owned enterprises are established exclusively with the foreign investors' own capital. They are normally limited liability companies, the profits and losses of which are borne solely by the foreign investor. Wholly foreign-owned enterprises are governed by the Law of the People's Republic of China on Enterprises Operating Exclusively with Foreign Capital. Wholly owned foreign enterprises are companies that are 100% owned by the foreign investor. Therefore, this form of foreign investment can not be considered as a cooperation. See Table 4.4. It is possible to choose that option of investment in China, but it is necessary that the foreign companies are "conducive to the development of China's national economy." In addition they should use advanced technology and equipment or export all or most of their products.

PROBLEMS AND SUCCESS FACTORS OF JOINT VENTURES IN CHINA

The problems and success factors of Sino-European Joint Ventures have been analyzed by Köhler/Wäscher, Beamish and Schuchardt, and by a research team of the joint research project of the Technische Universität Berlin and the Shanghai Jiaotong University (Trommsdorff and Wilpert 1991) in 1986-1989. Based on a first analysis of Sino-German Equity Joint Ventures and Contractual

Joint Ventures (12 EJV and 4 CJV), the research team focused on 8 equity joint ventures, visiting companies in Germany and the Chinese officials in charge of the given joint venture in China. While the number of Chinese-German joint ventures is small compared to the total number of joint ventures in China, Sino-German Joint Ventures are often considered to be successful and profitable.

The factors that determine most success or failure of a joint venture are summarized in Table 4.5.

Table 4.4. Joint Ventures and 100% Enterprises 1979-1990 (excluding CDAs)

	EJV	CJV	WFOE	Total	Cumulated
1979	7				
1980	27		9		
1981	30	793	16	909	909
1982	19		8		
1983	107	330	15	452	1361
1984	741	1089	29	1856	3217
1985	1412	1611	46	2230	6286
1986	892	582	18	1492	7778
1987	1395	789	46	2230	10008
1988	3900	1580	410	5890	15898
1989	3663	1179	932	5784	21682
1990	nn	nn	nn	6259	27941

EJV = Equity Joint Venture
CJV = Contractual Joint Venture
CDA = Cooperative Development Agreement
WFOE = Wholly Foreign-Owned Enterprise

Source: Trommsdorff/Wilpert: Deutsch-Chinesische Joint Ventures, Gabler Verlag, Wiesbaden 1991.

The following factors deserve attention in particular for Chinese-foreign enterprises:

1. Feasibility Study

Before setting up a joint venture, the two partners must complete a feasibility study. The feasibility study is the most important step in the negotiation of a joint venture; through this study the partners can determine terms that are reasonable and that will lead to a viable project. The World Bank has developed a very convenient system of indices to analyze the feasibility of an investment project. This system has been adopted by China's Governmental Planning Department. The foreign investment projects financed by the World Bank usually get good results in the indices method. The success rate of those projects

Table 4.5. Success Factors: Results of an Expert Panel (Delphi-Method)

Rank	Success factor	Score (1-6)
1.	true cooperation	5,7
2.	both sides have the same cooperation objectives	5,65
3.	management with good leadership skills	5,62
4.	good environment	5,47
5.	competition	5,42
6.	right business decision	5,42
7.	products adapted to market	5,42
8.	quality and productivity	5,42
9.	rational management	5,26
10.	feasibility study	5,2
11.	organization of company	5,17
12.	development strategy	5,1
13.	human resources	5,05
14.	communication of information (intern & extern)	5,05
15.	use of advanced technology and equipment	4,95
16.	foreign exchange balance	4,89
17.	complete accounts	4,78
18.	management has responsibility for joint venture success	4,65
19.	number of foreign sides	4,11
20.	coincidence with international business rules	3,79

1 - not important at all
2 - not important
3 - middle
4 - important
5 - very important
6 - most important

Source: Trommsdorff/Wilpert 1991.

is nearly 90%. The content of a feasibility study of a joint venture is characterized by:

   market study,

calculation of the investment volume,
type of investment,
financing,
stocksharing,
choice of the manufacturing system,
supply of materials,
supply of energy,
analysis of the location,
analysis of the partner,
lifecycle of the joint venture,
return on investment calculation,
risk analysis,
organization of the company and
influence of joint venture on Western partner.

2. Selection of the Right Partner

When investing in China it is important to know about the economic, legal, and the sociocultural environment in the country. There is a general and a specific environment. The partnership figures in the specific environment. It is possible that the right partner can compensate for the problems of the bigger environment. But who is the "right" partner? China is characterized by its bureaucracy and hierarchies. Therefore, it is important that the Chinese partner has:

good "buanzi," which means network in the government and in other
  institutions,
good knowledge of the international management habits,
good understanding of culture, corporate culture and the mentality of the
  counterpart,
an optimistic attitude to come into the market and to get a big market share,
  and
language skills.

3. Coordination of investment objectives of the Chinese and the foreign part-
    ner

The principal objectives in the creation of a joint venture are almost the same as the motives of other investment types (coproduction, wholly foreign owned enterprises, etc.). Generally, European companies have four different motives:

market access,
supply of raw materials,
low cost sourcing, and
environment.

The main objective of foreign companies is, in fact, the Chinese market. The opportunity to conduct business in China means to obtain China's market and other Asian regions as well. The Western partner has access to the Chinese know-how in terms of market knowledge, and understanding of the Chinese language, culture, and mentality, and "Guanxi." Guanxi is very important when doing business in China. The term stands for friendly network. Business people need to know representatives of institutions and governmental bodies to get the most efficient information.

Other motives of European companies for a joint venture are:

stability of the joint venture, possible since 1979 because of the existing joint venture legislation in China,
local investment incentives, especially for joint ventures,
becoming a "partner" of the country and getting a better corporate image, and access to governmental projects.

Equity joint ventures have fewer restrictions on project approval than do wholly foreign owned companies. The Chinese partner can assist in such areas as obtaining government approvals, labor recruitment, sourcing raw materials, and obtaining marketing and distribution channels.   For contractual joint ventures, advantages are subject to approval. Furthermore, investment capital may be recovered and repatriated during the venture period. The partners have the flexibility of operating as either a limited liability company or a partnership. The profit distribution ratio may be varied over different stages of operation. Nevertheless, European investors sometimes feel they do not have enough autonomy in joint ventures. The joint control over operation and management, and the sharing of technology and know-how with the Chinese partner, is often considered a disadvantage.

To modernize about 400,000 companies, China needs the help of the industrial nations. China's main motive for promoting joint venture companies, therefore, is the access to technology and management know-how transfer. In addition, Chinese companies are expecting marketing advantages in the export business. Often, Chinese products can only reach the specification and the quality standard with the help and the reputation of the Western partner.

The principal motives for cooperation of Chinese companies are:

- transfer of production factors that are raw in China,
- transfer of technology, patents, management, and marketing know-how, and
- improvement of the products and introduction of new products.

Marketing

- access to Western markets by using the brand name and the reputation of the foreign partner,
- access to the international distribution network of the partner, and

- improvement of the image and reputation in the Chinese home market.

Education

- training of employees, and
- creation of a local manager upper class.

Economy

- diversification of the regional and sectoral economic structure by governmental control,
- horizontal and vertical integration of the economy, and
- growth of exports and diversification.

Politics

- maintenance of governmental control and coordination of the economy, and
- improvement of the economic independence.

Once a decision to cooperate is made, the different motives of the two partners have to be coordinated. The motives described can be the same for the Chinese and the European partner, such as profit and international export rates. Sometimes difficulties and conflicts exist when, for example, the foreign partners want to sell most of the production in the Chinese market. The Chinese government often will intervene in such a situation. The technology needed by the Chinese partner often is not transferred by the foreign partner or if it is only at high prices. The development of a joint investment project needs time and experience. We found that an average of six months is the time needed to prepare and select the right cooperation partner.

4. Foreign Exchange Balance

Joint ventures need large amounts of foreign currencies to import equipment, materials, technology, know-how, and to pay the salary of the expatriate management. Foreign investment companies may repatriate their profits from China subject to certain restrictions, as follows:

all prior years' losses must first be cleared,
all relevant taxes must be paid, and
the required contributions must be made to the three "funds," namely the staff bonus and welfare fund, the enterprise expansion fund, and the general reserve fund.

Joint ventures usually have their own responsibility to balance exchange income and expenditure. This law follows China's policy to increase the joint ventures' exports. In fact, this law stands in conflict witht he investors' objective to acquire a big share of the Chinese market. During the first years, when the company must still import most of the materials, the law can be very strong in its effects on the joint venture operation. Often companies have to stop their production because of the needed foreign currency.

The problems can be solved as follows:

Distribution on the Chinese market. Joint ventures products sometimes can be sold as import substitutes in the Chinese market. Those products must have a high quality standard and must be "conducive to the development of China's national economy."

Balance of foreign currencies between two joint ventures. Where a foreign investor is participating in different joint ventures, it is possible to balance the losses of one company with the foreign currencies of another joint venture.

Export of other products. Sino-foreign joint ventures can use the distribution system of the foreign partner for the export of other products produced in China. Another possibility is the purchase of Chinese products in Chinese currency and the distribiton in foreign currencies.

Increase the local content. The needed amount of foreign currencies when buying the material overseas may be very inconvenient. Therefore, it is important to find a suitable Chinese supplier to increase the local content of the product. Some companies even ask suppliers from overseas to invest and to produce directly in China.

Use of swap-centers. It is possible to exchange currencies in one of the "swap centers" in Shanghai or in Shenzhen. However, the prices are very high.

Decrease number of expatriates. The number of foreign management personnel should be limited to the lowest possible level where the joint venture still can operate. At Shanghai Volkswagen, the cost of about 45 expatriates is almost the same as the cost for the 2,000 Chinese employees.

5. Management

Conflicts can occur when the management of the joint venture does not have enough responsibility. The parent companies should stay behind and should not intervene in the decisionmaking of the joint venture executive. The objectives, the rules, the stratgies, and the concerns of the different parent companies have been fixed in the joint venture contract; therefore the joint venture managers should have complete rights and responsibilities in the independent management of the company. The two companies should avoid intervening in the joint venture's activities. There was one joint venture manager in Beijing who had to fire a Chinese vice-manager employed by the German parent company. Later, he even had to dismiss a German director from his job. The manager was acting under his own authority, without following the concern of one of the parent companies. That is one reason for the respect he received in running the joint venture.

6. Organizational Structure

Most of the joint venture companies have either a "board" structure, where the board of directors is responsible for management and control, or they adapt a dual organization like companies in Germany do. The board of directors has the task of a supervisory board, and the executive management committee is managing the company. Misunderstandings between the investor company and the joint venture can be avoided the nearer their linkage. Shanghai Volkswagen, for example, uses the dual organization model to prevent conflicts. See Figure 4.1 below.

Figure 4.1. Shanghai Volkswagen Organization

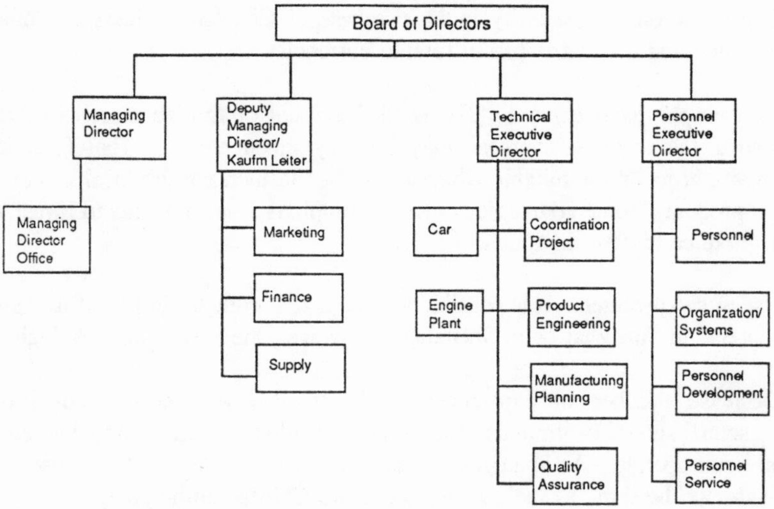

REFERENCES

Beamish, P.W. (1985), "The Characteristics of Joint Ventures in Developed and Developing Countries," *Columbia Journal of World Business* (Autumn), 181-189.

Braun, Inge, and Heike Sspielvogel (1991), "China's 'zweite Revolution'-Anspruch und Wirklichkeit der Wirtschafts- und Gesellschaftsreformen der Nach-Mao-Ära," *Oberender: China auf dem Weg zur Marktwirtschaft*, Hamburg: Springer-Verlag.

Bronder, Christoph (1993), *Kooperationsmanaement: Unternehmensdynamik durch Strategische Allianzen*, Frankfurt-New York: Campus.

Bronder, Christoph, and Rudolf Pritzl (1992), "Developing Strategic Alliances: A Conceptual Framework for Successful Co-operation," *European Management Journal, 10,* (4), 14-21.

Goldenberg, Susan (1990), *Management von Joint Ventures: Fallbeispiele aus Europa, USA, China und Japan,* Wiesbaden: Econ Verlag.

Hax, Herbert (1989), "Ownership and Management in the Chinese Firm— The Agency Problem," *Trends of Economic Development in East Asia,* W. Klenner, ed., Berlin-Heidelberg: Springer-Verlag.

Hirsch, Georges, and Frederick Swierczek (1993), "Multicultural Perspectives on European and Asian Management," *European Management Journal,* 91-103.

Hofstede, Geert (1992), "Die Bedeutung von Kultur und ihren Dimensionen im internationalen Mangement," *handbuch der internationalen Unternehmenstätig keit. Erfolgs- und Risikofaktoren, Märkte, Export-, Kooperations- und Niederlassungsmanagement,* Kumar and Haussmann, eds., Munich: Servic Fachverlag.

Newman, William H. (1993), "Joint Venture II: Erfolgsfaktoren für China," *Harvard Business Manager 3.*

Oppenländer, Heinrich (1992), "Direktinvestitionen und Internationalisierung der deutschen Wirtschaft, *Handbuch der internationalen Unternehmenstätigkeit Erfolgsund Risikofaktoren, Märkte, Export-, Kooperations- und Niederlassungs management,* Kumar and haussmann, eds., Munich: Servic Fachverlag.

Reinhold, Gerd (1992), Wirtschaftsmanagement und Kultur in Ostasien—Soziokulturelle Determinanten wirtschaftlichen Handeln in China und Japan, Munich.

Reinshagen, Peter (1993), Interkulturelles Personalmanagmeent am Beispiel sinoeuropäischer Joint Ventures, European Research Project, EAP Berlin.

Schuchardt, Christian (1994), Erfolgsfaktoren und Interaktionen deutschchinesische Joint ventures, Ph.D. Diss., Technische Universität Berlin, Berlin.

Trommsdorff, Volker, and Bernhard Wilpert (1991), Deutsch-chinesische Joint Ventures, 1. Aufl., Gabler Wiesbaden: Springer-Verlag.

5

Joint Ventures in Hungary:
Criteria for Success

Jim Hamill
Graham Hunt

Joint ventures with local partners have long been used as a foreign market entry and development strategy in countries difficult to enter through either imports or the establishment of wholly owned subsidiaries. British companies, in particular, have a long history of entering into joint ventures, especially in developing countries given past colonial ties with many of these nations. As recently as the late 1970s, almost two-thirds of the total stock of British direct investment abroad remained in developing host countries, most of which was in the form of joint ventures. The geographical focus of such investment changed markedly during the 1980s as a consequence of the wave of British acquisitions abroad; first in the United States, and then in Continental Europe in the run-up to 1992 (Hamill 1988). In the last few years, there has been a reawakening of interest in joint venture formation with the radical political and economic reforms that have taken place in Eastern Europe.

This chapter examines the contrasting experiences of three British companies in attempting to establish joint ventures in one East European country, Hungary. The cases examined are:

- United Biscuits (UB) purchase of an 85 percent stake in Gyori Keksz Hungary's largest biscuit manufacturer,
- Thorn-EMI's unsuccessful attempt to establish a joint venture with the state-owned music company Hungaroton, and
- APV's longer term and incremental approach to the Hungarian food and agricultural machinery market.

An important aim of the chapter is to integrate the three case studies with the extensive volume of literature that exists on planning, negotiating, implementing, and controlling joint ventures. The cases highlight some of the important "do's

and don'ts" of setting up joint ventures in previously centrally planned economies. In the UB case, joint venture negotiations proceeded smoothly, and the
basis has been laid for a successful long-term venture due to the company's
willingness to satisfy Hungarian demands for the transfer of technology,
marketing and management skills. Similarly, APV experienced few problems
given the mutual trust built up in Hungary over a ten-year period. The proposed
Thorn-EMI deal, by contrast, broke down due to a major conflict between the
partners over the ultimate goals of the venture.

The chapter comprises four main sections. Section 1 presents a brief review
of the relevant literature covering both joint venture strategies and joint venture
management. This provides the conceptual framework around which the three
case studies have been written. Section 2 contains a brief summary of the
economic and political reform process in Hungary, focusing mainly on the
privatization program of the last few years. The three case studies are presented
in Section 3; with the final section establishing a number of management
guidelines on negotiating joint ventures in Eastern Europe.

LITERATURE REVIEW

There is extensive literature on the role of joint ventures in international
business covering both the strategic dimension, i.e., the use of joint ventures as
a foreign market entry and development strategy, and their advantages and
disadvantages compared to the alternatives available such as exporting, licensing,
wholly owned subsidiaries, etc.; and the managerial dimension, covering the
problems involved in planning, negotiating, implementing, and controlling joint
venture agreements (see Young, Hamill, Wheeler, and Davies 1989).

Joint Ventures as a Foreign Market Entry and Development Strategy

Joint ventures are sometimes viewed as a second (or even third) best option
for supplying foreign markets—being used only when government regulations
(e.g., ownership and import controls, restrictions on royalty payments, etc.)
prevent the establishment of wholly owned subsidiaries, exports, or licensing.
Indeed, as will be shown later, there are major problems that arise in the
planning, negotiation, and management of international joint ventures that often
result in a high failure rate.

Despite such difficulties, it is widely recognized in the literature that there are
important strategic and competitive advantages that may be derived from
successful joint venture agreements, and that such collaboration may be a first
best option in certain circumstances. Connolly (1984), for example, argued that
the assets of developed-country multinational enterprises (capital, foreign
exchange, technology, management, and marketing skills, etc.) and developing-
country firms (lower costs, greater familiarity with local markets, etc.) are
complementary, and that the combination of these assets in a joint venture results

in mutual benefits. Similarly, Contractor (1984) argued that the loss of control and the sharing of profits inherent in equity joint ventures is more than compensated for by the expertise and capital contribution of the local partner; contacts with government officials;   faster entry into the market;   and risk reduction. Harrigan (1984, 1985) argued that joint ventures should not be seen as a hiding place or as a sign of weakness. Rather, if organized properly, joint ventures can be a source of competitive advantage, a means of defending existing strategic positions against forces too strong for one firm to withstand itself or as a means of implementing changes in strategic postures (e.g. diversification access to technology).   Joint ventures allow each partner to concentrate their resources in areas of expertise, while enabling diversification into attractive but unfamiliar business areas. Overall, Harrigan (1984, 1985) concludes that joint ventures are an important strategic weapon in responding to the challenges of global competition.

A paper by Beamish and Banks (1987) used the internalization and transaction-cost paradigm of Williamson (1981) to explain the conditions under which joint ventures may be more efficient than wholly owned subsidiaries. According to internalization theory, firms would have a strong economic incentive to avoid joint ventures (as well as contractual arrangements such as licensing, management contracts, etc.) because these are inferior to wholly owned subsidiaries in exploiting the firm's ownership-specific advantages.   Some of the problems associated with joint ventures (and contractual arrangements) include strategic risk, especially the problem of opportunism whereby the local partner may take advantage of the MNE's lack of complete knowledge;   the transactions costs associated with writing, executing, and enforcing the joint venture contract;   and dealing with future uncertainty. In order to remove such difficulties, the firm should internalize the activity through the establishment of a wholly owned and controlled subsidiary.   The authors argue, however, that joint ventures that conform to certain preconditions and structural arrangements can provide a better solution to these problems than wholly owned subsidiaries. Although there will be transaction costs associated with contract writing, execution, and enforcement, these will be more than offset by the enhanced revenue potential deriving from the joint venture.   These arise through the potential synergistic effects of combining the complementary assets of the MNE with those of the local partner. While the MNE provides firm-specific knowledge regarding technology, management, and capital markets, the local partner provides location-specific knowledge regarding host-country markets, infrastructure, and political trends. The pooling and sharing of know-how also reduces the information costs of foreign investment, thereby allowing the MNE to reduce the problem of uncertainty at a lower long-term average cost than in the case of wholly owned subsidiaries. The realization of these advantages depends on the establishment of an effective joint venture agreement that encourages mutual trust and the long-term commitment of both parties (in order to reduce opportunism);   and supportive inter-organizational linkages covering mechanisms for the division of profits, joint decision-making processes, reward and control systems, and the effective pooling of resources.

The discussion above has identified some of the major advantages of joint ventures as a foreign market entry and development strategy; these are summarized in Table 5.1. Closely related to this work, there have been several empirical studies that have examined the reasons why firms enter into international joint ventures (Beamish 1985; Killing 1982; Janger 1980; and UNCTC 1987). Three main groups of factors have been identified as being important: a) government suasion or legislation, b) one partner's needs for the other partner's skills, and c) one partner's needs for the other partner's attributes or assets. Government suasion or legislation has been the most important influencing factor in terms of joint ventures in developing countries. For developed country joint ventures, the partner's needs for the other's skills has been the most important factor. The UNCTC (1987) study emphasized the importance of both government legislation and the complementarity of partner's contributions to the formation of joint ventures by developed country firms in industrializing nations. Two types of government policy have been important: a) ownership controls whereby foreign multinationals are allowed to establish local production operations only in joint ventures with local partners; and b) fade-out agreements whereby foreign owned companies are required to reduce their ownership of local subsidiaries to a minority position within a given period of time. In addition to government suasion, the UNCTC argues that the complementary contribution of resources by the partners provides a firm basis for a viable joint venture between developed and developing country firms. The relative contributions of both partners are listed in Table 5.2.

Planning, Negotiating, and Managing International Joint Ventures

The previous section highlighted the strategic advantages of joint ventures as a way of entering and developing foreign markets. Inevitable tensions will arise, however, in the operation of such ventures that often result in failure. The estimated failure rate in joint ventures is extremely high—30% to 61%—with the incidence of failure being highest in joint ventures with developing countries and those involving government partners (see Young, Hamill, Wheeler, and Davies 1989).

The causes of joint venture failure have been extensively discussed in the literature. Tensions arise from the simple fact that there is more than one parent company and culture. This may lead to disagreement and conflict with respect to issues such as the setting of strategic objectives; the distribution of decision-making power; and day-to-day operational control. Holton (1981), for example, identified two main reasons for joint venture failure: a) attempts by one of the partners to retain centralized control, and b) disagreements over operating strategies, policies, and methods. As regards the former, the retention of centralized control may be necessary to integrate the joint venture into the

Table 5.1. Advantages of Joint Ventures as a Foreign Market Entry and Development Strategy

- foreign market expansion with reduced financial commitment

- potential for synergy in the value chain activities of partners leading to cost savings, greater efficiency, and enhanced international competitive ness

- foreign market expansion with reduced management commitment due to the contribution of local partners

- reduced political risk through involvement of local partners

- joint ventures allow a greater degree of parent company control com pared to other forms of foreign market entry such as licensing and non-equity contractual agreements

- joint ventures may result in greater long-term penetration of foreign market, e.g., promotion of local image, proximity to markets, etc.

Source: Derived from Young, Hamill, Wheeler, and Davies 1989.

MNE's global strategy. (In two of the cases presented later—UB and APV—the Hungarian joint venture had an important role to play in the overall global/European strategy of the British partner.) The failure to delegate decision-making power, however, will be resented at the local level and will create pressures for decentralization. The MNE, on the other hand, will be reluctant to delegate such power because of the interdependencies that exist between operating units in different countries.

Several empirical studies have attempted to test the control-performance relationship in joint ventures. Killing (1982), for example, argued that most successful international joint ventures occur when one partner is willing to accept a "passive" role, i.e., dominant-parent ventures perform better than shared-management ventures. Independent joint ventures (in which the venture management team were highly autonomous of both parents) had the highest performance level of the three main types of venture. This conclusion, however, has been criticized in other studies. Janger (1980) and Kogut (1988), for instance, found little relationship between control and performance in comparing shared and dominant joint ventures; however, Tomlinson (1970) concluded that higher levels of return were obtained in joint venture investments with a relaxed attitude toward control.

Apart from disagreements over control and decision-making power, conflicts may arise between partners over venture objectives, strategies, and management.

Table 5.2. Contributions of Foreign and Local Partners to a Joint Ventures

<table>
<tr><th colspan="2">Contribution of</th></tr>
<tr><th>Foreign MNE</th><th>Local Partner</th></tr>
<tr>
<td>

●Technology
●Product know-how
●Patents
●Business & marketing expertise
●Technical training
●Management development
●Finance
●Access to international distribution channels
●Increased exports
●Increased employment
●Improved competitiveness

</td>
<td>

●Knowledge of local political situation, economy, and customs of the country
●General management
●Access to markets
●Marketing personnel and expertise
●Local capital
●Contacts and relationships with host country governments
●Plants, facilities, and land of local partners
●Recruitment of local labor and trade union relationships
●Access to local financial institutions

</td>
</tr>
</table>

Source: Derived from UNCTC (1987).

Holton (1981) lists nine major areas of potential disagreement: strategy; management style; financial management; accounting and control methods; marketing policies and practices; production policies and technology transfers; personnel and industrial relations policies; R & D; and government and trade relations.   In addition, there may be other differences of opinion over the contributions of each party; the distribution of rewards and their composition (e.g., profits, royalty fees, etc.); and the time "scale" of the venture.

It is worth noting at this point, that there is a growing literature on the risks and costs associated with strategic alliances, as a special type of joint venture, which is relevant to the discussion in this section (see, Porter 1986; Jain 1987; Lorange 1988; Hamel, Doz, and Prahalad 1989). Table 5.3 provides a summary of the potential pitfalls of strategic alliances according to leading authors in the field.

The problems associated with joint ventures and their high failure rate implies that great attention needs to be paid to the effective planning, negotiation, and management of such deals. While effective management of the joint venture process will never guarantee success, it will considerably reduce the likelihood of failure. As stated by Holton (1981), "the rather dismal history of international joint ventures could be improved by more efficient planning, negotiation and management."

There is an extensive volume of literature on the management of the joint venture process that has been written both from a conceptual and a practical "do's and don'ts" perspective. One of the most comprehensive analytical models of joint ventures is that developed by Harrigan (1984, 1985). The model, which is shown in Figures 5.1 and 5.2, covers all stages in the joint venture process from first contemplating cooperation to the eventual dissolution of the venture, including the costs and benefits of cooperating; the bargaining agreement; the

Table 5.3. Strategic Alliances: The Costs

Porter (1986):	Coordination costs
	Erosion of competitive position
	Creation of an adverse bargaining position
Jain (1987):	**Costs**
	Mutual dependency
	Uncertainty re-outcomes
	Division of authority and decision-making power
	Top management time and effort
	Risks
	Imbalance in benefits
	Imbalance in commitment and motivation
	Difficulties in achieving an agreement
	Communication problems
	Conflict between partners
	Retaliation from governments and competition
Lorange (1988):	Resource generation and redistribution
	Adjustments to environmental changes
	Developing new business to meet emerging growth opportunities
	Delaying with internal conflict
Hamel, Doz, Prahalad (1989):	Competitive compromise
	Dependency spiral
	Distrust and conflict

Source: Derived from the literature

viability of the venture; the relationships between the two parent companies, parent and child, and the child and its environment; and the evolution of the venture over time.

The starting point in the model is to determine the circumstances under which joint ventures will be formed and how they will be structured. According to

Harrigan, firms should undertake a cost/benefit analysis at the outset before deciding on whether to enter into a joint venture (see Figure 5.1).   As previous sections have shown, firms derive a number of potential benefits from collaborating.   Equally, there are costs associated with forming partnerships, and a joint venture will be formed only if each firm believes that there is greater advantage in cooperating than there will be costs.

The negotiation of the bargaining agreement determines the structure of the joint venture, i.e., the child's domain of activities (see Figure 5.2).   Important components of the bargaining agreement include the determination of outputs (products, markets supplied, etc.); inputs (capital, materials, technology, human resources, etc.);   control mechanisms (distribution of decision-making power, performance evaluation systems, etc.);   and the duration and stability of the agreement. The form of the child (i.e. the bargaining agreement) is the net result of the bilateral bargaining power of its parents, which in turn is determined by six factors: benefits;   costs;   the resources contributed by the parent;   the alternatives available for achieving their objectives;   the need to cooperate;   and barriers to cooperation (costs and other disadvantages). The greater the firm's resources and alternatives for achieving their objectives, the greater their bargaining power. On the other hand, as their bargaining power is reduced, the greater is the need to cooperate and the higher are the barriers to cooperation. Finally, the model covers the dynamic aspect of joint ventures with a number of change stimuli precipitating either the renegotiation of the bargaining agreement or an end to the agreement itself. Harrigan's model is then applied to a detailed analysis of the three relationships crucial to the success of joint ventures, namely, the relationships between the two parents, between parent and child, and between the child and its external environment.

Whereas Harrigan's model covers most aspects of the joint venture, Contractor's (1984) "negotiations planning paradigm" is concerned mainly with the calculation of rates of return to the parent company from joint ventures with local partners in foreign (mainly developing country) markets. Rather than negotiating the joint venture agreement and then computing the extractable or repatriable cash flow (as is the practice in most companies), Contractor proposes a reverse procedure—targeting a particular compensation level and then working backwards to establish the mix of arrangements ("the bargaining agreement") that would provide this. The planning of joint ventures should involve three main steps. First, estimate the value to the joint venture partner and the host country of the transfer of technology and expertise. Second, determine an appropriate or reasonable rate of return from the host country for the transfer of technology, expertise, and investment.   Third, determine the mix of ownership and contractual arrangements best suited to achieve the target compensation level. This will determine the mix of repayments as between dividends, royalties, and mark-ups on traded items. As regards the third stage, Contractor argues strongly that the joint venture agreement covering equity shareholdings should be

Figure 5.1. Partner-to-Partner Relationships Creating a Joint Venture

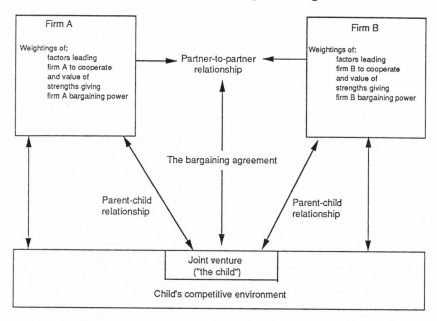

Source: Harrigan (1985).

supplemented by other agreements such as licensing or product supply/purchasing agreements.

Practical recommendations regarding the "do's and dont's" of formulating, implementing and managing joint ventures have been suggested by several authors (Walmsley 1984; Harrigan 1984, 1985; UNCTC 1987; Holton 1981; Connolly 1984; Contractor 1984; Beamish and Banks 1987; Killing 1982). Although there is some disagreement regarding points of detail, broad consensus exists on the various stages necessary for the establishment of successful joint ventures, and these are shown in Table 5.4.

Joint Venture Objectives

A clear understanding of the objectives to be achieved by the joint venture is a necessary prerequisite for the implementation of successful partnerships. Is the joint venture expected to result in major competitive/strategic advantages or is the focus more narrow, e.g., access to restricted foreign markets? A specified time period for the achievement of objectives should be established in order to evaluate joint venture performance.

Cost/Benefit Analysis

Once objectives have been established, the costs and benefits of entering into a joint venture should be assessed, especially in relation to the alternatives avail-

Figure 5.2. Model of Joint Venture Activity

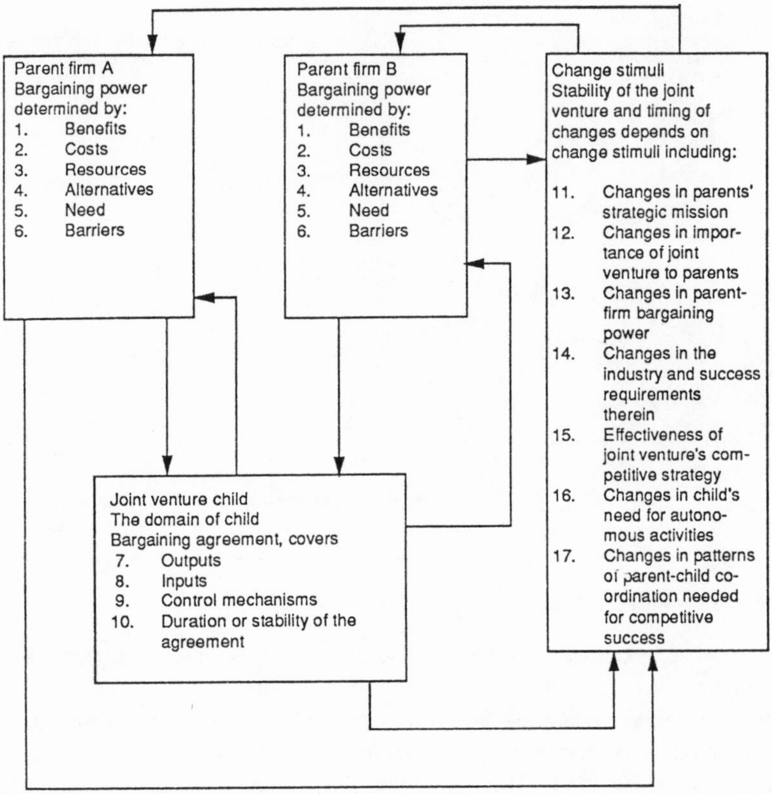

| Parent firm A
Bargaining power
determined by:
1. Benefits
2. Costs
3. Resources
4. Alternatives
5. Need
6. Barriers | Parent firm B
Bargaining power
determined by:
1. Benefits
2. Costs
3. Resources
4. Alternatives
5. Need
6. Barriers | Change stimuli
Stability of the joint
venture and timing of
changes depends on
change stimuli including:

11. Changes in parents' strategic mission
12. Changes in importance of joint venture to parents
13. Changes in parent-firm bargaining power
14. Changes in the industry and success requirements therein
15. Effectiveness of joint venture's competitive strategy
16. Changes in child's need for autonomous activities
17. Changes in patterns of parent-child coordination needed for competitive success |

Joint venture child
The domain of child
Bargaining agreement, covers
7. Outputs
8. Inputs
9. Control mechanisms
10. Duration or stability of the agreement

Source: Harrigan (1985).

able for achieving the same objectives (licensing, etc.). Such analysis should be based on the criteria set out earlier, i.e., financial and management commitment; risk and control; synergy; long-run market penetration; etc.

Selecting Partners

If it is accepted that a joint venture is the superior method of achieving the firm's objectives, the next stage is the selection of the venture partner. This would normally involve at least four separate stages as shown in Table 5.4. Harrigan (1984, 1985) recommends three criteria for the selection of appropriate joint venture partners. First, the firm should consciously select its own partners rather than rely on requests from outsiders. Second, partners with previous experience of joint ventures should be chosen since there is a "learning-curve" effect in cooperation. Experienced partners may be more flexible in negotiations than new ventures. Third, partners should be selected not simply in terms of their financial commitment. Rather, the choice of partner should be based on the complementarities that exist between the two enterprises in order to maximize potential synergies.

The Business Plan

According to most authors, the fourth stage in formulating successful joint ventures is the negotiation of the formal joint venture agreement. Holton (1980), however, argues that the formalization of the joint venture agreement should be postponed until the prospective partners have reached broad agreement on a business plan for the joint venture. The premature involvement of lawyers in the writing of legal contracts has been identified by both Holton (1981) and Harrigan (1984, 1985) as a major reason why many joint venture proposals never go beyond the discussion stage. If the full implications of the potential joint venture have not been fully explored and agreed to by the partners, this will become exposed during the formalization of contracts. Although the legal aspects of contract agreements need to be left to lawyers, problems at this stage can be reduced if company executives have reached prior agreement on a business plan—which may be recorded in a memorandum of agreement or based on mutual trust and understanding. At a minimum, the business plan should provide agreement on the issues listed in Figure 5.6. As Holton (1981) argues, "the business plan should not be viewed as a legal document, but rather as a discussion paper, or a series of discussion papers, in which every effort would be made to bring to the surface the expectations of the parties so that any inconsistencies in those expectations can be revealed and, if possible, resolved."

Negotiation of the Agreement

Agreement on the broad business plan for the joint venture will be followed by negotiations between the partners on the precise details of the joint venture agreement, which will cover similar issues to the above. As Harrigan (1984, 1985) has shown, the eventual format of the agreement will be determined by the relative bargaining power of both prospective partners.

Contract Writing

Once the agreement has been negotiated, it needs to be incorporated into a formally written and legally binding contract that should clearly specify the relationship between the two parents and between parent and child. In addition to covering the issues discussed previously, the formal contract should allow scope in at least three other areas. First, joint venture agreements should be designed not only as marriage contracts but also as divorce contracts, specifying the conditions under which the venture can be dissolved. Second, contingency planning should be built into the business plan and the contract in order to take

Table 5.4. Stages in Planning, Negotiating, and Managing Joint Ventures

1. **Joint venture objectives**
   Establish strategic objectives of the joint venture and specify time
   period for achieving objectives

2. **Cost/benefit analysis**
   Evaluate advantages and disadvantages of joint venture compared with
   alternative strategies for achieving objectives (e.g., licensing) in terms
   of:
   - financial commitment, •synergy, •management commitment
   - risk reduction, •control
   - long-run market penetration
   - other advantages/disadvantages

3. **Selecting partner(s)**
   - profile of desired features of candidates
   - identify/screening of candidates and draw up short-list
   - initial contact/discussions
   - choice of partner

4. **Develop business plan**
   Achieve broad agreement on:
   - partners' inputs (commitments of finance; technology; management;
     etc.)
   - venture outputs (products and markets supplied; dividend and payout
     policy; etc.)
   - management style and decision-making processes (centralization v.
     local autonomy; reporting relationships; etc.)
   - performance evaluation system (accounting and financial controls)
   - marketing policies and practices (marketing mix)
   - production and procurement policies
   - personnel policies
   - R & D policy

5. **Negotiation of joint venture agreement**
   Final agreement on business plan

6. **Contract writing**
   Incorporation of agreement in legally binding contract allowing for
   subsequent modifications to the agreement

7. **Performance evaluation**
   Establish control systems for measuring venture performance

Source: Derived from the literature

account of underperformance. Third, the contract should allow for changes in the business plan over time to account for unforeseen circumstances.

Performance Evaluation

Finally, agreement should be reached between the two partners regarding an appropriate control system for measuring and evaluating venture performance, especially an advanced warning system to identify emerging difficulties.

The UNCTC (1987) has developed a useful checklist as a guide to establishing effective joint ventures; and this is shown in Appendix 1. It is suggested that the joint venture agreement should be comprehensive and cover all major aspects of the business, including the following:

- the major goals of the partners;
- their contributions, responsibilities, and obligations;
- the equity share of each partner;
- means of financing the venture;
- products, customers, and markets to be supplied;
- the composition of the board of directors;
- procedures for selecting senior and middle management;
- provisions for technical training and management agreements that may be part of the joint venture;
- provisions for safeguarding patents, trademarks, and technical secrets;
- duration of the agreement and ways of modifying it;
- management processes, including strategic and operational planning;
- the control and information system;
- sources of supply for raw materials, intermediates, and components;
- accounting standards;
- reporting requirements;
- the audit and review of financial statements;
- means of settling disputes;
- policy regarding the declaration and distribution of dividends;
- procedures for dissolving the partnership and the distribution of assets.

HUNGARY: TOWARD A MARKET ECONOMY

Although it has been the radical reforms introduced since 1989 that have focused attention on the market opportunities available in Eastern Europe, the issue of economic and political reform has been on the agenda in Hungary for at least two decades. Four main phases in the evolution toward a market economy can be identified as summarized below:

Pre-1968—the period in which Communist ideology and power were at their strongest with the economy being managed by traditional central planning techniques.

1968-80—initial attempts at economic reform through the introduction of the New Economic Mechanism (NEM) which aimed at breaking the monopoly held by large State-owned enterprises in different sectors and to encourage greater competition. Success, however, was restricted mainly to agriculture.

1980-88—the extension of NEM across most sectors of the economy and the gradual dismantling of tight central planning; legislation introduced permitting private and foreign investment; firms allowed to opt out of the central planning process; and the establishment of an economic, political, and commercial framework within which a market economy could operate, e.g., the introduction of limited liability.

1989 and Beyond—the introduction of one of the most radical privatization programs of any East European country with the stated objective of transferring most State owned enterprises to the private sector within five years. The privatization process is controlled by the State Property Agency (SPA). An important feature of SPA policy, and one which is relevant to the case studies presented later, is that price is only one of the criteria used in assessing bids. SPA is also concerned that the joint venture or takeover contributes to the long-term economic goals of the country involving an evaluation of the technology, management, and financial aspects of the deal.

As a consequence of the reform process briefly described above, Hungary is now fully committed to a market oriented, outward looking (export driven) economy. The attraction of inward foreign direct investment plays a crucial role in achieving these objectives, and Hungary has been one of the most successful East European countries in this respect. Between 1972 and 1989, the country received less than $600 million in inward direct investment. This increased to approximately £2.5 billion in the two years 1990 and 1991, accounting for 60 percent of the total flow of foreign direct investment into Eastern Europe as a whole. There are now an estimated 13,000 joint ventures in Hungary involving foreign partners.

Case Studies

This section presents the three case studies covering the contrasting experiences of British companies in attempting to establish joint ventures in Hungary. Each case follows a similar structure covering a brief summary; the partners to the venture; joint venture objectives; the negotiation process; and management structure and implementation. The final section of the chapter pulls the three cases together by presenting a number of management guidelines for the successful negotiation of joint ventures in previously centrally planned economies, derived from the case studies and related to the literature review presented earlier.

UNITED BISCUITS (UB)

Summary

This case covers the purchase of an 85 percent controlling interest in Gyori Keksz—Hungary's largest biscuit manufacturer—by the British company United Biscuits (UB) in 1991. The Hungarian venture plays a strategically important role in UB's overall European operations, as well as providing a platform for entering and developing the Hungarian and other Eastern European markets. The success of the venture can be attributed to the fact that agriculture and food processing has been identified by the Hungarian authorities as a priority development sector and by UB's willingness to invest capital and transfer technology to the venture.

The Partners

UB is one of the largest food companies in the world with an annual turnover of approximately £3 billion (1991). Principal products of the company include biscuits, confectionery, snacks, and frozen and chilled foods. The group has grown consistently over the last three decades or so, mainly through acquisitions. In 1973, UB established a major presence in the U.S. market with the acquisition of the number two producer Keeblers. More recent acquisitions have focused on building brands and market share in Europe in the run-up to the Single European Market. UB uses a number of clearly defined criteria when selecting an acquisition candidate, which are important to note since the same criteria were used in the choice of Hungarian partner. The acquisition criteria used are that

- the target company must be operating in UB's core business,
- UB can bring something to the company, e.g., marketing, technology, etc.,
- the target has good products and management, and
- the target has a large market share being either the market leader or in a strong number two position.

Gyori Keksz is Hungary's largest biscuit manufacturer. By Hungarian standards, it has the reputation of being an efficiently managed company with good products.

Joint Venture Objectives

The joint venture with Gyori Keksz was announced in April 1991 and involved the purchase of a 75 percent (later increased to 85%) controlling interest by UB.

The purchase occurred at a time when the formalized legal framework for the privatization of Hungarian industry was being put into place and this considerably aided negotiations. This contrasts with the more "ad hoc" procedures faced by Thorn-EMI (see later).

In terms of strategic objectives, the joint venture with Gyori Keksz was aimed not only at gaining entry into the Hungarian market but was to play an important role in UB's overall European strategy. The three main objectives underlying the venture were:

Market access. To a large extent, the purchase of a controlling stake in Gyori Keksz was motivated by UB's desire not to miss out on the huge (potential) opportunities likely to arise from the reform process in both Hungary and other Eastern European countries. The purchase secured entry into the Hungarian market and could be used as a launch pad into closely related markets in Eastern Europe. In many respects, it was a "testing of the waters" before undertaking larger investments and more committed operations in the future.

Pan-Europeanization. The European food industry has traditionally been fragmented on a country-by-country basis reflecting national taste and cultural differences. In the last few years, however, the industry has become more pan-European in scope with the growth of Euro-brands and the wave of crossborder mergers, acquisitions, and strategic alliances amongst major producers. This trend has been reflected, too, in food retailing where major companies such as Aldi and Carrefour now operate a European network of stores and have a buying organization that attempts, where possible, to buy for its European operations as a whole. These retailers demand large volumes and bulk discounts.

These trends had a major impact on UB's decision to purchase its controlling interest in Gyori Keksz. Some of UB's products such as "Cream Crackers" and "TUC" biscuits are pan-European. They are also commodity type products that must be produced in very high volumes at low cost. The Gyori Keksz venture is to occupy a strategically important position in this respect acting as a low cost sourcing base for such commodity products for major European retailers that are highly price sensitive.

Brand development. While the initial strategy was to use Gyori Keksz as a low cost production base, the longer term aim is to introduce UB's other snack brands into the highly developed Hungarian and Eastern European markets. Gyori Keksz is seen as an excellent base for such future development.

Negotiations

In identifying Gyori Keksz as a partner, UB used the same criteria applied by the company to any acquisition or joint venture (see earlier). As Hungary's largest biscuit producer, Gyori Keksz was clearly operating in the same business as UB and with a leading market position. By Hungarian standards at least, it was a well managed company with good products. Finally, there was considerable scope for improving value added through additional capital investment and through the transfer of UB technology, marketing, and management skills. A significant capital investment program is to take place involving the setting up of production facilities in five product segments—biscuits, wafers, snacks, peanuts, and confectionery. Although R & D will be centralized at UB, significant technology transfer will occur (e.g. JIT); Hungarian nationals will be trained in marketing planning and brand management; new accounting and financial control procedures will be introduced; and a management information system installed. UB's proposals in these areas were crucial to the deal being accepted by the Hungarian authorities since agriculture and food processing has been identified as a priority development sector requiring the transfer of western technology and skills. This resulted in a relatively lenient attitude being adopted by the principal negotiating body for privatization—the State Property Agency—who were further encouraged by UB's willingness to establish an enterprise agency to help individual private businesses to develop. As a consequence negotiations over the purchase proceeded smoothly with no major problems.

Management Structure

As stated above, UB owns 75 percent of the venture. The residual shareholding is divided between the local council (15%) and the State Property Agency (10%). The local council have a shareholding because they were the landowners on which the facilities were built. The SPA share will be reduced to 5 percent with the residual being offered to employees of the firm. UB has the option to buy the residual 25 percent within a year.

The Board of the joint venture comprises three UB personnel from the United Kingdom; two employees of Gyori Keksz (a requirement of Hungarian law); and one other local Hungarian. The controlling stake of 85 percent allows UB to run the joint venture as a wholly owned subsidiary. Actual decisionmaking will, however, be as decentralized as possible. Gyori Keksz will be granted a high level of autonomy in decisions affecting the Hungarian market only. Decisions with wider implications for UB's overall European strategy will be more centralized.

Implementation

The successful implementation of the joint venture will be supported by the following policies:

R & D. This will be centralized within UB but with the free flow of information and know-how to Hungary. Immediate applications will be on solving existing production problems and introducing new products to the Hungarian market.

Capital investment. A major capital investment program to modernize plant and equipment is to be introduced covering five main areas—a complete biscuit production line; a new wafer production line; a new crisps production line; frying equipment for processing peanuts; and longer term introduction of a confectionery production line. Such investment satisfies the main objective of SPA to modernize the agricultural and food processing sectors.

Marketing. The introduction of Western marketing practices and brand management; and the training of local nationals in marketing.

Technology transfer. The major capital investment program will involve the large scale transfer of technology from the United Kingdom.

Management accounting. Transfer and training in modern management accounting techniques to align Gyori Keksz's accounting system with that of UB.

Management skills. Ongoing training in areas such as negotiations, industrial relations, and personnel management.

Market research. To better assess market potential in Hungary.

THORN-EMI

Summary

Unlike the previous case of a successfully established joint venture, Thorn-EMI's proposal to establish a 50:50 joint venture with Hungaroton was aborted in August 1990. Major conflicts had arisen between the partners over the aims and objectives of the joint venture and their respective contributions. The Ministry of Education and Culture had viewed the venture primarily as a vehicle for promoting Hungarian musicians and culture rather than as a viable business entity in its own right. This proved unacceptable to Thorn-EMI.

The decision not to proceed with the venture attracted considerable publicity at a time when the government's mass privatization program was about to get underway. This led to major doubts being expressed by both western industrialists and Hungarians themselves as to the government's willingness to relinquish control over industry. The feeling was that officially the government was in favor of privatization, but psychologically it was reluctant to accept foreign investment. Clearly UB benefitted greatly from the more formalized privatization scheme introduced subsequent to the breakdown of Thorn-EMI's proposal. The case highlights the fact that it may be better to abort negotiations than to enter a troubled marriage.

The Partners

Thorn-EMI's principal business activities are the rental and retailing of electrical equipment; lighting; security systems; and music. The case presented here covers the music divisions, which accounts for 27 percent of total group turnover of £3.7 billion (1990). EMI music is a globally integrated operation covering artist development and promotion, recording, manufacturing, marketing, and distribution of music. Major performers signed to EMI include Cliff Richard, Paul McCartney, Duran Duran, Kate Bush, Queen, Tina Turner, Stevie Nicks, M.C. Hammer, the Beach Boys, and many others.

Hungaroton is Hungary's largest music company with an 80 percent market share and major exports to other Eastern European countries. Unlike Thorn-EMI, it is mainly a classical rather than popular music concern.

To understand the rationale underlying the proposed joint venture, it is necessary to briefly summarise key developments in the global music industry as they affect both partners. These include:

• *overcapacity*—especially in the production of vinyl records due to consumers switching to audio cassettes and compact discs. In 1991, Thorn-EMI made considerable provisions for the write-off of vinyl record pressing facilities surplus to requirements. Hungaroton is primarily a manufacturer of vinyl records with large pressing facilities.

• *classical/mainstream mix*—classical music sales account for only 8 percent of total worldwide music sales revenue—and the same percentage of Thorn-EMI's total music sales. Hungaroton, on the other hand, earns 80 percent of its revenue from classical music sales.

• *people business*—a music company is only as powerful as the artists it has under contract. Actual manufacturing of the product (vinyl records, cassettes, compact discs) has little effect on competitiveness, and there is an increasing tendency amongst the major music companies to subcontract the production process. In global terms, Hungaroton's artist portfolio is extremely weak compared to Thorn-EMI (see earlier).

• *piracy and counterfeit products*—this is a major problem for the world's leading music companies who invest heavily in promoting and developing artists only for pirate manufacturers to launch cheap, low quality products onto the market. It has been estimated that between 70 and 80 percent of all Western music sold in Eastern Europe is pirated, and there are few legal supports for intellectual property.

Joint Venture Objectives

At least initially, the proposal was a "textbook" example of mutual partner benefits through a joint venture. Major benefits to be derived by Thorn-EMI included:

• the establishment of a major presence in Eastern European markets with Hungaroton having an 80 percent market share in Hungary and well developed exports to other Eastern European countries.

• the growing market potential in Eastern Europe for Western music. Hungaroton would provide a "bridgehead" through which Thorn-EMI could develop its popular music business in Eastern European markets.

• the two companies had a long history of cooperation through the licensing of artists which would be developed further by the joint venture.

• Thorn-EMI would be better able to control counterfeiting of its products in Eastern Europe through a joint venture.

• Thorn-EMI would gain access to Hungaroton's classical music business for world markets.

The Hungarian partner would gain access to Thorn-EMI's worldwide distribution, especially for the development of their large classical music portfolios; hard currency would be earned to invest in modernization of recording facilities and manufacturing operations; and the venture would provide access to Thorn-EMI's huge artist portfolio.

Negotiations

Despite these mutual benefits, the joint venture proposal failed. There was no single event that brought about failure. Rather, a series of actions and periods of inaction resulted in mistrust between the partners and conflicts of interest over the goals of the venture. Major contributing factors included:

• the fact that negotiations were handled by the Ministry of Education and Culture rather than the State Property Agency. The latter had been established to oversee the privatiation of Hungarian industry. Ideologically, it was pro-western and pro-foreign investment. The Ministry, by contrast, was a relic from the past. Its ideology stemmed from the days of strict central planning, and its primary function was to promote Hungarian culture rather than to encourage inward foreign investment.

• one of the main reasons why Thorn-EMI was keen on the joint venture initially was that it had worked previously with Hungaroton's managing director Jenoe Bors and was very confident in his abilities. Two weeks before the deal was finalized, however, Bors was fired and replaced by Istvan Ella, a well-known Hungarian organist, but with no previous business experience.

• with the removal of Jenoe Bors, key elements of the original draft agreement were changed. Ella's main objective was to use the joint venture as a means of promoting Hungarian musicians and culture, rather than as a stand-alone profit organization.

• finally, the original proposal envisaged that £14.8 million would be made available for investment in modernized production and recording facilities, with part going to the Ministry of Education and Culture. With the appointment of Ella, however, there were fears that the venture would become a vehicle for promoting Hungarian culture (e.g., the funding of two new orchestras) rather than as a viable business entity in its own right.

An important footnote to this case is that Quint, a company formed by Jenoe Bors, is rapidly stripping away Hungaroton's 80 percent market share and attracting many Hungarian musicians. Thorn-EMI is negotiating several cooperative ventures with Quint, following the breakdown of negotiations with Hungaroton.

APV

Summary

Of the three cases examined, this one comes closest to the theory of internationalization as an incremental process (stages of development approach), with the increasing involvement of a firm in a particular foreign market over time being accompanied by a shift toward more committed market development modes. APV's involvement in Hungary has evolved over a decade from the supply of plant, equipment, and technical assistance to its current 60 percent joint venture, APV Ungaro. As in the UB case examined earlier, there was a complementarity of interests between APV and the Hungarian government. For the company, APV Ungaro has provided the base for developing the vast potential of Eastern European markets. For the government, APV has provided the required technical know-how in food processing equipment that has been designated a high priority sector.

The Partners

APV is the world's leading supplier of process equipment to the food, beverage, and food-related industries, with an annual turnover of approximately £900m (1990). It is the only company supplying a comprehensive product portfolio to the whole spectrum of dry, liquid, frozen, fresh, and animal food industries. The APV Ungaro joint venture is primarily concerned with the manufacture of equipment related to the liquid food sector of APV's operations which covers breweries, fruit juice plants, and dairy product plants.

There are three Hungarian partners in the joint venture comprising a refrigeration company whose personnel are being trained by APV in the marketing of its products in Eastern Europe; a mining company, which provides buildings and labor; and the Hungarian Foreign Trade Organization, which in the past was responsible for all imports of food processing equipment into the country.

Joint Venture Objectives

For APV, the Hungarian joint venture is the hub of the company's operations in Eastern Europe, acting not only as a manufacturing and service facility, but also as a clear signal to other East European customers of their commitment to the region as a whole. The venture is mainly concerned with manufacturing activities that are labor intensive and require relatively low levels of technical inputs and know-how, e.g., stainless steel pipe manufacturing. The decision to form APV Ungaro was taken within the context of an overall strategic review of APV's worldwide operations involving a major rationalization program. As part of this review, several low-tech, labor intensive component plants in the United Kingdom were closed and production transferred to Hungary. The Hungarian plant has been integrated into APV's worldwide operations, supplying stainless steel components to all divisions of APV and receiving high technology components from the United Kingdom. The main objective of the Hungarian partners to the venture was to gain access to the technical know-how required to modernize the country's food processing industry.

Negotiations

As stated previously, APV has adopted an evolutionary, stages of development approach to its involvement in the Hungarian market. This reflects the company's own increasing confidence in operating in the country, together with the progressive liberalization of the Hungarian governments foreign investment legislation. The main stages in the company's involvement in the country were:

• *International tendering.* In the early 1980s, APV was involved in tendering for the provision of large scale dairy plants to be operated by the State-owned sector. The Hungarian government wanted to acquire Western technology for use in its dairy processing industry.

• *Representative office.* The high level of technical back-up required in international tendering and recognition that agriculture and food processing were going to be key industries in Hungary's long-term development led APV to set up a representative office in the country. The office was headed by a technically qualified executive from the U.K. head office and provided advice to various government customers on the plant and equipment required for a particular job and made tenders on behalf of APV. The office was also used as a sales-representative center for markets in Czechoslovakia, Poland, and the Soviet Union.

• *Minority joint venture (40%).* APV had always viewed its representative office as an intermediary stage toward a greater commitment to Eastern European markets. In addition to its activities stated above, the office also undertook market research to identify possibilities for the establishment of some form of production facility. One of the main findings of this research was that many Hungarian and other East European commercial refrigerators had extremely short product life cycles, due mainly to problems with the compressor. This led APV to the next stage in its development in Hungary, namely, the establishment of a 40 percent owned joint venture concerned mainly with the refurbishment of refrigerators using compressors shipped out from the United Kingdom. At the time, the establishment of a minority joint venture was an ideal choice for APV. It allowed the company to supply a particular market niche without requiring high levels of capital investment that APV felt unwilling to make because majority-owned foreign joint ventures were still prohibited and strict currency regulations controlling repatriation of earnings were still in force. Within a short period of time, however, it became apparent that the low cost labor available in Hungary provided major opportunities for APV in terms of its global strategy. This, combined with the progressive liberalization of foreign investment legislation, led to the final stage—the establishment of a majority owned (60%) manufacturing joint venture.

• *Majority Owned, Manufacturing Joint Venture (60%).* Although in theory it was possible to operate a majority-owned joint venture in Hungary since 1968, the reality of the situation made this extremely difficult in practice. It was not until 1988 that liberalization had gone far enough for APV to feel confident in making a larger investment in Hungary. As stated previously, the new joint venture played an extremely important role in APV's overall global strategy responsible for the production of low tech, low cost components.

Throughout this evolutionary process from initial tendering to the establishment of a majority-owned joint venture, negotiations with the Hungarian government and other joint venture partners proceeded smoothly. This can be attributed to a number of factors—the government's identification of food processing as a priority sector; APV's strategy of sourcing locally whenever possible; the supply of technical assistance; and so on.

Management Structure

In 1988, APV could have opted for 100 percent ownership, but preferred a 60/40 joint venture, believing that the long-term success of the venture required the active involvement of local partners in decisionmaking. As stated earlier, there were three main local partners participating in the venture.

Implementation

The major issues involved in implementing the joint venture included:

Management recruitment and training—Despite considerable efforts to find a local manager to oversee the joint venture, it proved difficult to find anyone with the necessary skills. Start-up operations, therefore, were staffed by APV managers transferred from the United Kingdom. A large scale training program, however, was introduced to develop the necessary skills of Hungarian nationals. APV has been in the forefront of management training and development in Hungary, including training for other Hungarian organizations in Western business methods.

Accounting procedures—Two sets of accounts needed to be produced; one for APV and one to meet the requirements of the Hungarian government. Gradual integration of the two systems, however, will occur as Hungarian accountancy procedures are brought into line with Western standards.

Foreign exchange—Hard currency targets are set for APV-Ungaro; that if met they will, bring a reduction in tax liability. This has been introduced by the government to promote exports.

Local sourcing—Procurement policy of the joint venture is to source locally for low-technology components. Higher technology components such as sensors, thermostats, and control panels are sourced from the United Kingdom. The willingness to source locally was welcomed by the government for stimulating local enterprises and reducing hard currency expenditure on imports.

CONCLUSIONS

The case studies presented in this chapter covered two successful and one aborted joint venture negotiations in Hungary. Although it is difficult to generalize from the small number of cases studied, taken together with the literature reviewed earlier, a number of success criteria can be identified for negotiating joint venture agreements in ex-centrally planned economies (see Table 5.4).

The establishment of clearly defined joint venture objectives is a necessary prerequisite for successful negotiations. Both the UB and APV deals had clearly stated objectives covering the Hungarian market and the role of the joint venture in the groups' overall European strategy. More significantly, there was flexibility in both agreements allowing for an evolution over time in the product and market strategy of the Hungarian operation and for the continuing upgrading of technology and management transfers. In the Thorn-EMI deal, major conflicts arose between the partners over strategic objectives.

Partner selection is a major determinant of joint venture success. In both the UB and APV deals, there was a clear strategic fit between the U.K. and Hungarian partners. This was not the case in the Thorn-EMI deal where the strategic objectives of the partners diverged.

According to Harrigan (1984, 1985), the outcome of joint venture negotiations is determined by the relative bargaining power of partners. Both UB and APV were in a strong bargaining position due to their control over technological know-how and the fact that they were operating in industries identified by the Hungarian authorities as "priority" sectors. Neither company, however, abused this position, being very willing to contribute to the economic development goals of the country through technology transfers, etc. Thorn-EMI was in a less powerful position given that it was negotiating with a government Ministry rather than the market-oriented State Property Agency.

In conclusion, the key to successfully negotiating joint ventures or acquisitions in Hungary is the ability to cultivate good relationships with the authorities and venture partners. The way of achieving this is to match the requirements of the country for foreign currency, modernization, technology transfer, exports, and so on with the need for efficiency and profitability of the joint venture itself. While the latter must remain the ultimate goal of any deal, it will only be possible with sensitivity to the development needs of the host economy.

Political and economic reform in Eastern Europe will continue to create joint venture opportunities for Western companies. The success of these ventures, however, is by no means guaranteed and requires careful planning, negotiation and management.

APPENDIX 1: OUTLINE OF MAJOR ASPECTS
OF A JOINT VENTURE AGREEMENT

The following presents a comprehensive list of factors that could be included in joint venture agreements. It should be pointed out, however, that all of these aspects do not necessarily apply to every joint venture agreement.

1. Purpose and character of a joint venture:

(a)   major goals/strategy of foreign partner;
(b)   major goals/strategy of local partner;
(c)   products/industries/markets/customers served.

2. Contributions of each partner:

(a)   capital;
(b)   existing land, plant, warehouse, offices, other facilities;
(c)   manufacturing design, processes, technical know-how;
(d)   product know-how;
(e)   patents and trademarks;
(f)   managerial, production, marketing, financial, organizational, and other expertise;
(g)   technical assistance and training;
(h)   management development;
(i)   local relationships with government, financial institutions, customers, suppliers, etc.

3. Responsibilities and obligations of each partner:

(a)   procurement and installation of machinery and equipment;
(b)   construction, modernization of machinery and equipment;
(c)   production operations;
(d)   recruitment and training of workers and foremen;
(e)   quality control;
(f)   relationships with labor unions;
(g)   research and development;
(h)   general, financial, marketing, personnel, and other management;
(i)   continuous training of personnel.

4. Equity ownership:

(a)   equity granted to foreign partner for manufacturing and product technology and industrial property rights;
(b)   equity granted to local partner for land, plants, warehouses, facilities, etc.;
(c)   ownership share of foreign partner;
(d)   ownership share of local partner.

5. Capital structure:

(a)   equity capital;
(b)   loan capital, national and foreign;
(c)   working capital;
(d)   provisions for raising future loan funds;
(e)   loan guarantees by partners;

(f)   future increase in equity capital;

(g)   transfers of shares of stock, including limitations.

6. Management:

(a)   appointment/composition/authority of the board of directors;

(b)   appointment and authority of executive officers;

(c)   expatriate managers, technicians, and staff;

(d)   right of veto of appointment of officers and key decisions;

(e)   development of local managers, including time schedule;

(f)   organizations;

(g)   strategic and operational planning;

(h)   information system;

(i)   control procedures.

7. Supplementary agreements:

(a)   licensing and technology agreements;

(b)   management contracts;

(c)   technical service agreements;

(d)   allocation of foreign partner's corporate overhead to affiliate.

8. Managerial policies:

(a)   declaration of dividends;

(b)   reinvestment of earnings;

(c)   source of supply of materials, intermediates, and components, including price, quality, assurance of delivery;

(d)   major marketing programs, including product lines, trademarks, brand names, distribution channels, promotion, pricing, service, and expenditures;

(e)   export markets and commitments;

(f)   executive compensation and bonuses.

9. Accounting and financial statements:

(a)   accounting standards;

(b)   financial statements in currencies of host and foreign countries;

(c)   reporting requirements;

(d)   audit and review of financial statements.

10. Settlement of disputes:

(a)   board of directors and executive committee;

(b)   mediation;

(c)   arbitration.

11. Legal matters:

(a)   relevant local laws, regulations, and policies;
(b)   governmental approvals required;
(c)   articles and bylaws of incorporation;
(d)   anti-trust considerations;
(e)   tax laws and considerations;
(f)   selection of legal counsel;
(g)   use of courts of host country.

Source: UNCTC (1987)

REFERENCES

Beamish, P.W. (1985), "The Characteristics of Joint Ventures in Developed and Developing Countries," *Columbia Journal of World Business, 20* (3), 39-46.

Beamish, P.W., and J. C. Banks (1987), "Equity Joint Ventures and the Theory of the Multinational Enterprise," *Journal of International Business Studies, 18* (2), 22-27.

Connolly, S.G. (1984), "Joint Ventures with Third World Multinationals: A New Form of Entry to International Markets," *Columbia Journal of World Business, 19* (2), 13-19.

Contractor, F.J. (1984), "Strategies for Structuring Joint Ventures: A Negotiations Planning Paradigm," *Columbia Journal of World Business, 19* (2), 81-88.

Contractor, F.J., and P. Lorange, P. (1988), "Competition vs. Cooperation: A Benefit/Cost Framework for Choosing Between Fully-Owned Investments and Cooperative Relationships," *Management International Review, Special Issue, 28,* 127-136.

Dunning, J.H., and J. Cantwell (1982), "Joint Ventures and Non-Equity Involvement by British Firms with Particular Reference to Developing Countries: An Exploratory Study," *University of Reading Discussion Papers in International Investment and Business Studies,* No. 63.

Friedman, W., and G. Kalmanoff, (1961), *Joint International Business Ventures,* New York and London: Columbia University Press.

Hamel, G., Y.L. Doz, and C.K. Prahalad (1989), "Collaborate with Your Competitors—and Win," *Harvard Business Review* (Jan-Feb), 87-93.

Hamill, J. (1988), "British Acquisitions in the US," *National Westminster Bank Quarterly Review* (August), 4-11.

Harrigan, K.R. (1984), "Joint Ventures and Global Strategies," *Columbia Journal of World Business* 19 (2), (Summer), 76-79.

—— (1985), *Strategies for Joint Ventures,* Lexington, MA: Lexington Books, D.C. Heath & Co.

Holton, R.H. (1981), "Making International Joint Ventures Work," in *The Management of Headquarter-Subsidiary Relationships in Multinational Corporations*, L. Otterbeck, ed., Aldershot: Gower, 361-386.

Jain, S.C. (1987), "Perspectives on International Strategic Alliances," in *Advances in International Marketing*, Greenwich, CT: JAI Press Inc., 56-73.

Janger, A.R. (1980), *Organisation of International Joint Ventures*, New York: Conference Board.

Killing, J.P. (1982), "How to Make a Global Joint Venture Work," *Harvard Business Review* (May-June), 121-128.

Kobrin, S.J. (1988), "Trends in Ownership of American Manufacturing Subsidiaries in Developing Countries: An Inter-Industry Analysis," *Management International Review, Special Issue, 28,* 151-171.

Kogut, B. (1988), "A Study of the Life Cycle of Joint Ventures," *Management International Review, Special Issue 8, 28,* 101-111.

Lorange, P. (1988), "Cooperative Strategies: Planning and Control Considerations," Centre for International Management Studies, WP-512: Toronto, Ontario.

Porter, M.E., ed. (1986), *Competition in Global Industries*, Boston, MA: Harvard Business School Press.

Stopford, J.M., and L. T. Wells, Jr. (1972), *Managing the Multinational Enterprises*, New York: Basic Books.

Sukijasovic, M. (1970), "Foreign Investment in Yugoslavia," in *Foreign Investment: The Experience of Host Countries*, I. A. Litvak and C. J. Maule, eds., London: Praeger; quoted in Artisien, P. (1985), *Joint Ventures in Yugoslav Industry*, Aldershot: Gower.

Tomlinson, J.W.C. (1970), *The Joint Venture Process in International Business: India and Pakistan*, Cambridge, MA: MIT Press.

United Nations Centre on Transnational Corporations (UNCTC) (1987), *Arrangements Between Joint Venture Partners in Developing Countries*, UNCTC *Advisory Studies*, No. 2, Series B, New York: UN.

Walmsley, J. (1982), *Handbook of International Joint Ventures*, London: Graham & Trotman.

—— (1984), "International Joint Ventures," paper presented at U.K. Academy of International Business Conference, Bradford, April, 4.

Williamson, O.E. (1981), "The Economics of Organization: The Transaction Cost Approach," *American Journal of Sociology, 87* (3).

Young, S., J. Hamill, C. Wheeler, and J. R. Davies (1989), *International Market Entry and Development: Strategies and Management*, Harvester-Wheatsheaf, Englewood Cliffs, NJ: Prentice-Hall, Hemel Hempstead.

6

Parent Company Characteristics and International Joint Ventures' Success in England and the U.S.A.

Barbara Parker
Yoram Zeira

There is growing practical interest in how to establish and maintain an effective international joint venture (IJV), but it is not clear that parents will succeed with IJVs by drawing on principles learned from other international experiences. Unlike the wholly owned subsidiary over which parental authority is clear, the IJV is a separate legal entity representing partial holdings of two or more legally and economically independent organizations for which the headquarters of at least one is located outside the host country (Shenkar and Zeira 1987). Parent firms accustomed to a competitive model of organization evidently find it difficult to cooperate when establishing joint control over the IJV (Geringer 1988), to understand each other when cultural differences arise, or to introduce mechanisms appropriate for IJV operations (Perlmutter and Heenan 1986). IJV failure rates are high (Killing 1983; Kogut 1987), and to date these failures have been attributed to any number of reasons, including differences in the size of the parents (Geringer, 1988) their reputation (Janger 1980), as well as managerial problems with task (Lane and Beamish 1990).

Since the numbers of IJVs are growing, it is imperative to understand in greater depth why failures occur and when IJV effectiveness is achieved. Factors antecedent to or developed at the point of partner selection are believed to have an important effect on IJV outcomes (Geringer 1988; Perlmutter and Heenan 1986). Matching the results of phenomenological research with emerging empirical research suggested 10 major characteristics affecting IJV outcomes. These are stated as hypotheses and tested in U.S. and U.K. joint ventures. Results from hypotheses testing provide insight into the relative importance of each characteristic, and they are also used to develop a model that includes pre- and post-incorporation variables.

LITERATURE REVIEW

The literature on IJVs reveals a number of parent-company characteristics that are likely to influence IJVs effectiveness. A brief description of those measured in the present study follows.

Number of Parent Companies

Bivens and Lovell (1966) found that an increased number of parent companies increases the magnitude of internal conflicts, and impedes communication and coordination between parents. Killing (1982) found that a greater number of parents blocks communications for venture staff and complicates the decision-making process for parents and venture alike, and Hladik (1985) also concluded that coordinating the differences between partner goals becomes more difficult as the number of partners increase.

Satisfaction with Equity Distribution

Researchers have identified relatively few relationships between equity position, degree of control, and effectiveness (Gullander 1976; Lane and Beamish 1990; Schaan 1983). Rather, the more important relationship with effectiveness appears to be how satisfied partners are with equity distributions. Forced equity relationships are shown to be less successful than voluntary equity relationships for some IJVs (Lane and Beamish 1990; Lyles 1987), suggesting that it is not the amount of equity but rather partner satisfaction with it that affects outcomes.

Ownership Types, Reputations, Goals, and Industry Similarities

In the case of IJVs, ownership type usually refers to how parents are themselves owned, e.g., private, public, state-owned, or some combination of these three. Raveed and Renforth (1983) suggest that the IJV is more likely to become entangled in internal politics when one parent is state-owned and another is privately owned, and Beamish (1985) found that the government partner contributed to some measure of IJV instability when matched with public manufacturing firms. Janger (1980) notes that the state-owned parent may be more interested in national development goals, e.g., providing jobs, where the private firm may be more interested in profits.

Reputation is important to parents and venture alike. For parents, their partner's reputation in a country is likely to affect their own status (Janger 1980), while similarity in partner reputation is believed to be one basis for the trust and cornerstone of IJV stability (Killing 1983; Schaan 1983). Inasmuch as past performance is believed to be a valid predictor of future performance, the past success implicit to a good reputation may help realize success with the IJV. A partner's international reputation is believed to help local firms achieve growth objectives (Datta 1988), and the local partner's reputation may help partners attract competent local managers (Lane and Beamish 1990).

Research shows that reasons to joint venture can differ (Geringer 1988; Harrigan 1984), and these differences sometimes impede IJV effectiveness (Habib and Burnette 1989). Goal incongruity enhances the potential for conflict frequently realized in the IJV (Geringer 1988; Janger 1980), can impede policy implementation (Datta 1988), and may affect subsequent performance. As was true for other similarities, industry similarity reduces the potential for conflict between venturing parents. The potential for conflict is reduced because similarity in industry means parent managers know one another (by name or reputation) and have the experience needed to judge the other partner's competence (Zeira and Shenkar 1990).

Degree of Autonomy

It is not yet clear whether IJV autonomy is an antecedent or a consequence of IJV effectiveness (Holton 1981; Killing 1982), but current research indicates that autonomy ensures the flexibility important to many IJVs (Harrigan 1987), letting the IJV adapt to environmental change (Lorange and Roos 1990).

Documents of Incorporation

Western firms, particularly those from the United States, almost always prefer to institute formal controls of the rational/legal type in IJVs (Janger 1980), and this preference is most often reflected in detailed documents of incorporation (Berg and Friedman 1980; Martinez and Ricks 1989; Schaan 1983). While detailed documents may not prevent disagreements, they may reduce the potential for misunderstandings, and this is one reason why detailed documents of incorporation are considered important by policymakers in multinational corporations (MNCs).

Fit Between Personnel Policies of Parent Companies and Host Country

IJVs are complex organizations harboring many opportunities for miscommunications and misunderstandings. Similarities of several sorts are believed to be useful in improving fit and reducing the likelihood that misfired messages will disrupt IJV performances. When this fit is tight, managers and personnel alike have fewer problems developing and conforming to control systems, rewards are consistent with expectations, and expectations do not undergo radical changes. All these factors suggest that a closer fit between personnel policies and host country policies tends to reduce the potential for dysfunctional conflict at work (Zeira and Shenkar 1990).

METHODOLOGY

The approach in the first stages of our research was phenomenological in nature. Over the course of the two-year period from 1986-1988, top executives of IJVs and their parent companies in Israel, Western Europe, the Far East, and North America, as well as others who participated in a number of international executive development programs, were requested to express their views about managing IJVs. The interviewees were asked to freely discuss their feelings about IJVs, to compare IJVs with other types of domestic and international organizations, to assess the factors that contribute to their success, and describe those that hamper ventures' goal achievement. The meetings were completely and intentionally unstructured, took place within and outside the work settings, and were not limited in their length or in any other respect. Some interviewees suggested meeting with the authors to help them think out the issues they themselves raised and to draw a comprehensive picture of their feelings and assessments. Several interviewees stated that the meeting prompted them to make self-assessments and guided their subsequent steps as executives in multinational settings. In addition, several chief executive officers allowed or invited the authors to visit their IJVs, meet with their deputies and other parent and host-country employees, and observe a variety of settings and situations.

Content analysis of more than 100 interviews and meetings was then conducted and three types of questionnaires were developed: two for CEOs of IJVs and one for policymakers of the parent companies of IJVs. The findings presented below are based on the questionnaire tailor-made for CEOs of IJVs. None of the CEOs who filled out this questionnaire participated in any way in the phenomenological stages of the research.

All of the CEOs who participated in the early stages of our research stated repeatedly that the success of an IJV depends first of all on three key and critical factors. First, parent companies establishing an IJV must be convinced that all of them are going to gain equally from running the venture. When one or more feel that they have little to gain but much to lose from this type of joint ownership, the venture will sooner or later encounter major problems and may even fail. Second, the parent companies must implicitly trust each other with regard to their mutual intentions and have complete faith in the competence of the IJV's top managerial team. Third, IJVs cannot achieve competitive advantage unless the parent companies are willing to transfer their technology, know-how, and resources to them on a continuous basis.

Since all the CEOs emphasized these three factors and explained them at great length, we decided not to test them further or validate them on another research population. The content analysis, however, indicated that the majority of the ventures' executives hold 10 basis hypotheses to be true, regarding the relationships between the parent companies and IJV effectiveness, even though consensus was lacking and a minority made contradictory assessments. The 10 hypotheses were tested in the 1991 study reported below:

Hypotheses

1.   The greater the number of the parent companies—the more effective the IJV.

2.   The more satisfied the parent companies with the equity distribution among themselves—the more effective the IJVs.

3.   The greater the similarity of ownership type among the parent companies—the more effective the IJV.

4.   The more similar the core industry of the parent companies—the more effective the IJV.

5.   The more similar the goals of the parent companies—the more effective the IJV.

6.   The greater the degree of autonomy accorded to the IJV by the parent companies—the more effective the IJV.

7.   The more detailed the legal arrangements signed by the parent companies—the more effective the IJV.

8.   The more similar the reputation of the parent companies—the more effective the IJV.

9.   The closer the fit between the personnel policies of the parent companies and those of the host country—the more effective the IJV.

10.   The more responsibilities shared among the parent companies—the more effective the IJV.

THE RESEARCH POPULATION

The Respondents

The data presented in this section compare 40 IJVs operating in the United States with 35 IJVs operating in England. All respondents, in both the United States and England, are males. In England, 91.4% of the 35 respondents are the CEOs of the venture and 8.6% are acting CEOs. In the United States, 85% are the CEOs, 10% are acting CEOs, and 5% occupy somewhat lower positions.

As for nationality: 60% of respondents in England are British citizens, 25% are expatriates with the same citizenship as one of the parent companies (that is, they are citizens of Australia, Belgium, Canada, Holland, Norway, the United States and Switzerland), and 14.3% are third-country expatriates, that is, they are not British citizens, and they do not have the same citizenship as one of the parent companies.

Of the 40 respondents in the United States, 67.5% are American citizens, 27.5% are expatriates sharing the citizenship of a parent company (that is, they are citizens of Belgium, Canada, Egypt, France, Germany, Japan, Holland, Norway, and England), and 5% are third-country nationals. The ratio of host-country national and expatriates in top positions is similar in the two countries.

The executives were asked to state their age, level of education beyond high school, and months of experience of working abroad during their career. Table 6.1 summarizes these findings. The T tests indicate that they do not differ in their international experience (P = .38), that the executives in the American IJVs are somewhat older (P = .081) and have more years of higher education (P = 0.05).

Table 6.1. Age, Education, and International Experience

| | Country | | | | | | |
| | England | | | United States | | | |
Respondents	N	M	SD	N	M	SD	P
Age (Years)	34	43.0	7.78	40	46.52	9.13	.081
Education (years of education beyond highschool	35	4.14	1.56	37	4.97	1.95	.05
Experience (months of working abroad)	35	65.69	52.52	32	80.66	83.85	.380

N = number; M = mean; SD = standard deviation; P = probability

The IJVs

The executives were requested to specify the core industry of their IJVs and to state whether their venture tended to focus its efforts on one main area or to diversify. Table 6.2 indicates that the ventures in both the United States and England operate in a wide variety of fields, although only few (classified under "other") maintain diversified operations.

Table 6.3 indicates that most ventures in England and the United States have two or three parent companies. A high number of parent companies seems to be uncommon. In the United States, 28 of the 40 IJVs have only two parent companies, whereas in England 17 out of the 35 have three parent companies. The difference in parent-company distribution is significant (P = .015).

The executives who filled out the questionnaires were requested to state whether their ventures are public, private, or state-owned, and also to clarify whether their parent companies share the same type of ownership or differ in this respect. Table 6.4 presents the ownership structure in England and the United States. In both countries the majority of parent companies prefer to share ownership with partners who have a similar ownership structure. The difference between England and the United States is insignificant (X^2 = 1.44; P = .230).

Table 6.5 shows that there is no significant difference between England and the United States in either the size of the IJVs or in their ages. However, ventures operating in the United States are owned by parent firms that are much larger than the ventures operating in England (P = .006).

The data presented in Table 6.6 reveal that in the ventures operating in the United States, the phenomenon of a "dominant parent" (that is, a parent firm re-

Table 6.2. Main Industry of the IJVs

Main Industry	Country	
	England (35)	United States (40)
Finance	4	1
Food and beverages	6	3
Electronics	4	3
Computers (software)	2	2
Transportation	3	3
Pharmaceuticals	1	3
Small consumer products	5	5
TV and mass communications	1	2
Petroleum and chemicals	4	2
Heavy industry	2	8
Others	3	8

Table 6.3. Number of Parent Companies

Number	Country	
	England	United States
2	11	28
3	17	8
4	6	3
5	-	-
6	1	1
Total	35	40

Table 6.4. Ownership Type

Ownership type	Country			
	England		United States	
	N	%	N	%
Identical Ownership:	26	74.3	26	57.6
Public	11		16	
Private	14		10	
State-owned	1		0	
Combined ownership:	9	25.7	14	42.4
Public and state-owned	3		1	
Public and private	5		12	
Private and state-owned	1		0	
Private, public, and state-owned	0		1	
Total	35		40	

sponsible for running the venture, regardless of its equity ownership) is more prevalent than in the ventures operating in England (P = .035). Also, the domestic reputations of the parent companies of the British ventures are more similar to each other than are the domestic reputations of parent companies for American ventures. The difference is significant (P = .007). Finally, the data suggest that goals of the parent companies in establishing the British IJVs were similar, whereas the goals the parent companies of the American IJVs expected to achieve were dissimilar (P = .085).

The data indicate that in all other respects the IJVs in England and the United States are similar. Their CEOs have similar degrees of freedom regarding the formulation and implementation of their strategic business plans; their documents of incorporation are quite detailed; they are free to develop human resource management practices based on the host-country characteristics; their parents have similar international reputations and engage in the same industry. Even the levels of satisfaction with the equity distribution of minority parents are similar (see Table 6.6).

Table 6.5. Ventures' Size and Age

Charac-teristics	Country	N	M	SD	T	df	P
Number of em-ployees on the IJV pay-roll	England	35	1,962.31	2,933.69	0.78		.440
	United States	40	1,515.70	2,014.18		73	
Years of operation	England	35	10.80	7.62	1.15	73	.253
	United States	40	8.52	9.25			
Number of em-ployees on parent company payroll	England	34	9,193.04	11,738.22	-	68	.006
	United States	36	35,446.80	52,709.79	284		

N = number; M = mean; SD = standard deviation; T = student t value; df = degrees of freedom; P = probability level

HYPOTHESES TESTING

Six of the questions in our research tool aimed to measure levels of IJV effectiveness. The executives were asked to state (on a 5-point Likert-type scale) to what extent their IJVs (1) achieve their goals as specified in the documents of incorporation; (2) meet the expectation of their stakeholders; (3) have a growing market share; (4) are financially profitable; (5) meet targeted growth objectives; and (6) meet targeted profit objectives. The internal consistency of these six items was found to be quite high (Cronbach alpha = 0.84), suggesting that they all measured the same factor.

The general picture that emerges from the data is that the IJVs in both England and the United States are quite effective. For example, in England, 67.6% of the IJVs achieve all or most of their goals as specified in the documents of incorporation. In the United States, the responses indicate 75% do so, (X^2 insignificant). The remaining ventures achieve about half their goals. None of the respondents feels that the ventures achieve only some or none of their goals.

Table 6.6. Parent-Company Characteristics Which Impact the Ventures

Characteristics	Country	N	M	SD	T	df	P
Ventures having a dominant parent	England United States	34 40	1.06 1.34	.181 .212	- 2.15	72	.035
Ventures formulating their strategic business plan independently of the parent firms	England United States	35 40	3.31 3.10	1.34 1.24	0.72	73	.475
Ventures implementing their strategic business plans independently of the parent firms	England United States	35 40	4.14 3.90	1.24 1.13	0.88	73	.377
Ventures having detailed documents of incorporation	England United States	35 39	4.11 3.87	.832 .932	1.18	72	.241
Ventures having autonomy to develop HRM practices based on the host culture characteristics	England United States	35 40	4.09 4.10	.951 .810	-.07	73	.944
Ventures having parent companies with similar international reputations	England United States	35 40	4.03 3.75	.923 .899	2.77	73	.190
Ventures having parent companies with similar domestic reputations	England United States	35 40	4.09 3.5	.887 .934	2.77	73	.07
Ventures having minority parent(s) satisfied with the equity distribution	England United States	26 13	4.08 4.31	1.09 0.63	- 0.70	37	.487
Ventures having parent companies primarily engaged in the same industry	England United States	35 40	3.63 3.82	1.37 1.06	- 0.70	73	.487
Ventures whose parent companies established the IJV to achieve similar goals	England United States	34 39	4.56 4.31	.50 .69	1.75	71	.085

Table 6.7. IJV Effectiveness

Hypothesis	Country	
	England	United States
H_1 Number of parent companies	$x^2 = 1.47$ -.04 $P = 0.225$	.25o
H_2 Equity distribution	.77***	.33*
H_3 Ownership type	.28o	
H_4 Similarity of industry	-.33*	.00
	$x^2 = 0$	
H_5 Similarity of goals	.42** $P = 1.0$ .82***	.23o
H_6 Autonomy: formulation implementation	 .67***	.34* .09
H_7 Legal agreements	.54*** .47**	 .37*

H_8 Reputation:
    international
    domestic
	
	 .69***
		
		 .12
		 .30*

H_9 Personnel policies	-.10	.31*
H_{10} Dominant parents		-.12

o = $P < .10$; * = $P < .05$; ** = $P < .01$; *** = $P < .001$

The T test suggests that the executives in the United States assess their ventures as being slightly more effective than do the executives in England. Although the difference is not significant at the .05 level, the direction is clear (England: Number = 34, Mean = 3.53, Standard Deviation = .75; United States: Number = 40, Mean = 3.87, Standard Deviation = 1.88; P = .076).

Table 6.7 presents the correlations (Pearson and point bi-serial tests) among the 10 variables suggested by the CEOs who participated in the phenomenological research stages as major predictors of success and venture effectiveness.

H_1—Number of parent companies: The CEOs claimed that the larger the number of parent companies—the more effective is the IJV. Indeed, the findings in the United States point in this direction (P < .10). However, the British data do not.

H_2—Equity: The CEOs stated that IJVs are more effective when the minority partners are satisfied with the equity distribution and do not attempt to change the ownership structure; any such attempt makes it extremely difficult for them to run the IJVs effectively. The data from England strongly support this hypothesis (P < .001), as do the American data (P < .05).

H_3—Ownership type: Similarity in ownership type does not seem to affect the performance of the ventures (England: X^2 = 1.47, P = 0.225; U.S.A. X^2 = 0; P = 1.0). In both countries, ventures whose parent companies have a similar ownership type are as effective as ventures whose parents differ in their ownership type.

H_4—Similarity of industry: The British data offer some support for the CEOs' claim that similarity in the core industry of the parent companies positively affects the IJV's performance (P < .10). The American data are inconclusive.

H_5—Goals: The findings regarding the goals of the parent companies are contradictory. In England, when the parent companies have dissimilar goals—the ventures are more effective (P < .05), whereas in the United States the ventures seem to be more effective when the goals of the parent companies in establishing them are similar (P < .10).

H_6—Autonomy of ventures: The hypothesis concerning this variable relates to the level of autonomy the ventures have in formulating and implementing their strategic business plans. In England, both activities are highly and positively related to effectiveness (formulation: P < .01; implementation: P < .001), whereas in the United States the data suggest a positive correlation between effectiveness and autonomy in formulation of strategy (P < .10) but no relationship between effectiveness and autonomy in implementation.

H_7—Legal agreements: The findings reveal strong and positive correlations between the level of detail of the legal documents of incorporation and IJV effectiveness in both England (P < .001) and the U.S.A. (P < .05).

H_8—Reputation: The hypothesis concerning this variable relates to both international and domestic reputation of the parent companies. In England, both international (P < .001) and domestic (P < .01) reputation are correlated with effectiveness. In the United States only the domestic reputation of the parent companies affects the venture's effectiveness (P < .05), the international reputation apparently being irrelevant.

H_9—Personnel policies: The findings support the hypothesis concerning this variable in both England and the United States. Ventures in England (P < .001) and the United States (P < .05) are more effective when IJV executives are allowed to depart from the personnel policies of the parent companies and implement policies that fit the host-country culture.

H_{10}—Dominant parent: The data provide no support for the hypothesis concerning this variable. Ventures with a dominant parent and ventures without a dominant parent are equally effective, in both England and the United States.

DISCUSSION

Analysis of the data demonstrates that most of the hypotheses were corroborated in both England and the United States; however, the support was stronger in the case of the British IJVs (9 out of 12 assessments compared to 7 out of 12 of the American ventures), and the correlations were more significant.

The direction of support was also identical, except for the item regarding the goals of the parent companies. In England, IJVs are more effective when the goals of the parent companies in establishing the venture are dissimilar ("very dissimilar" or "completely dissimilar"), whereas for the United States the data suggest that the ventures are more effective when the goals of the parent companies in establishing the ventures are similar ("almost completely similar goals" or "very similar goals"). In other words, the findings indicate that IJVs can be effective as long as the parent-company goals are compatible and each parent is able to achieve its own objectives. It is neither essential nor necessary for parent-company goals to be identical or congruent, but they must be compatible.

The findings make it possible for us to present a model of desirable parent-company characteristics that increase the chances of forming and running effective joint ventures. We argue that in the absence of these characteristics, the probability that the IJV will succeed and achieve competitive advantage is low. The model can also serve as a checklist for companies planning to establish IJVs. The more closely they are able to adhere to the model—the greater their chances of establishing and running effective IJVs.

Our model (see Figure 6.1) has two dimensions. The first relates to six essential characteristics that should be evident in the pre-incorporation stage, and the second relates to three essential characteristics that should be evident after incorporation.

The First Dimension—Pre-Incorporation

Trust

Companies considering the establishment of an IJV should be convinced first of all that they can trust their potential partners with regard to their intentions toward and expectations from the partnership. A partnership should not be formed if the parties harbor doubts concerning each other's motives or suspect that one or another of the potential partners has or even may have a hidden agenda and latent goals.

Equity

Potential partners should be completely satisfied with the proposed equity distribution structure. Any discontent before incorporation, or any latent intent to change the ownership structure and deprive any given partner of some or all of their equity, predicts difficulties, and conflicts, and increases the possibility of failure.

Legal Agreement

Potential partners must make sure that the legal arrangements and all the documents of incorporation are sufficiently detailed and that all eventualities are properly covered, insofar as this is possible. It is extremely important to specify in the documents which potential conflicts are to be dealt with, how, when, and by whom.

Compatibility of Goals

It is strongly recommended that potential partners check the compatibility of their goals. Our studies reveal that congruency of goals is not a prerequisite. Compatibility, however, is essential. Under no circumstances should the idea of a partnership be entertained when the achievement of goals (through the IJV) by one parent company may harm another parent company. Thus, the goals of all potential partners have to be thoroughly analyzed. If conflicting goals are revealed, an IJV should not be established.

Industry Compatibility

An IJV should not be established if potential parent companies feel that they will be competing with each other in the venture's planned fields of operation. Such competition will make collaboration and technology transfer impossible, and without cooperation among the partners, IJVs cannot prosper.

Reputation

Potential partners must check their level of international and domestic reputation in the host country. The levels should be as similar as possible. Disparity of reputation may distort the delicate balance of power among the parent companies, as the venture's employees may not be as loyal as they should be to parent companies of lower repute. This in turn may lead to technology, know-how, advice, or instructions being ignored. The equity structure may also be changed and parents of lesser repute may be pushed aside.

The Second Dimension—Post-Incorporation

Technology Transfer

Following the establishment of an IJV, its parent companies have to transfer all the different types of technology agreed upon in the documents of incorporation in an ongoing manner. Depriving a venture of promised know-how andresources can trigger serious and unexpected reactions from the venture's staff, as well as from other partners. No parent company can expect to gain continually from an IJV if it evades its responsibilities regarding technology transfer.

Figure 6.1. A Model of Parent-Company Characteristics Essential for IJV Success

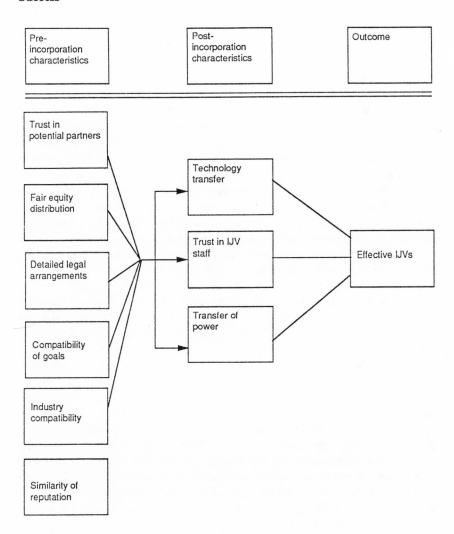

Trust

Confidence in the competence of the top managerial team of an IJV is a must. This team operates in a host country with rules, regulations, and norms, not to speak of the political and economic contexts, that usually differ from (and sometimes even contradict) those of the parents' countries. If trust is not complete, conflicts among parent companies and disagreements between the venture's staff and the parent companies will be inevitable.

Transfer of Power

The success of an IJV depends on its ability to fit its outputs to the expectations of its main stakeholders, especially those in the host country. Achieving this fit depends on the transfer of power by the parent companies to the IJV. This transfer is essential in three areas: 1) policy formulation—the IJV staff must be permitted to formulate its strategic business plans as they see fit; 2) policy implementation—the staff should be able to implement the strategic business plans free from daily intervention on the part of the parent companies; 3) HRM policy—the IJV must be allowed to formulate and implement personnel policies that fit the characteristics of the host country, even if these policies deviate from those that prevail in the parent countries or are recommended by the parent companies.

Apart from serving as a checklist for parent companies, our model also seems to provide one possible way to explain why so many companies hesitate to establish IJVs, see this form of joint ownership as the least preferred structure, or decide to avoid it altogether. The model also suggests why the failure rate of IJVs is so high. Our theoretical explanation is based on a close look at our data, which reveal two conflicting processes with regard to companies' power.

If companies are to form IJVs and run them effectively, according to our findings, in the pre-incorporation stage, the potential partners need to focus their efforts on six activities aimed at ensuring that in forming an IJV, they will not be losing their power but rather decreasing their risks and increasing their gains. Top executives are advised to check the intentions of their potential partners to assure that a hidden agenda does not exist, and that the partner will not harm their companies in any way. They must also make sure that the equity distribution will be fair and commensurate with their investment, and that it will not enrich the partners disproportionately to their investments. They are also required to formulate the legal agreement so that their interests will be promoted and not impaired. They must check the industry compatibility, as well as the compatibility of the partners' goals, to make sure that they will not conflict with their own goals and cause them to lose their competitive advantage. They also need to check the level of reputation of their potential partners, to make sure that no gap exists that will prevent their advice and orders from being strictly followed by the venture's staff.

In other words, our study suggests that executives in organizations considering the formation of IJVs should focus their attention on six complex and uncertain issues, all of them aimed to ensure that the formation of an IJV will increase the power of the organization and its ability to achieve a competitive advantage. When the final decision to form an IJV is reached, internal stakeholders must be convinced that the incorporation of the venture will bring about substantial gains that are otherwise unattainable.

However, in the post-incorporation stage, the same policymakers who worked so hard earlier to make sure that no power will be lost in the formation of an IJV are now requested to transfer substantial amounts of power to their partners and to the IJV staff to ensure that the venture will succeed. The continuous transfer of technology, the delegation of authority to the venture's staff, the authority given to the venture to act according to unfamiliar rules and regulations, and the willingness to let the IJV formulate and implement its strategic business plans—all these mean the transfer of considerable power to the venture.

This transfer may well be perceived as a disaster by the policymakers whose business it had been in the pre-incorporation stage to make sure that no power will be lost in establishing the IJV. They, therefore, take all necessary steps to see that it does not happen. However, in so doing, they bring about what they tried so hard to avoid—they bring about failure.

Our study suggests that companies desiring to form effective IJVs must carry out these two processes in tandem. We argue that when company policymakers are convinced that the six pre-incorporation requisites have been fully met, they logically have every justification to change direction and carry out the three post-incorporation requisites (as indicated by the arrows in our model.) However, this "package-deal" may be perceived by many experienced top executives as containing built-in contradictions, since the post-incorporation activities imply undoing of activities that are an integral part of the pre-incorporation stage. Clearly, it can be extremely difficult for executives to ensure, in the pre-incorporation stage, that no power will be lost and that uncertainty will be minimized, and then, immediately after incorporation, to decentralize, to delegate crucial authority, to release their grip on the venture, and to increase their level of uncertainty. We maintain, therefore, that companies that cannot fully carry out these two processes should avoid forming IJVs. Those that can will have an increased chance of owning effective IJVs.

REFERENCES

Beamish, P.W. (1985), "The Characteristics of Joint Ventures in Developed and Developing Countries," *Columbia Journal of World Business, 20,* 13-19.

Berg, S.V., and P. Friedman (1980), "Corporate Courtship and Successful Joint Ventures," *California Management Review, 22,* 85-91.

Bivens, K.K., and E. B. Lovell (1966), *Joint Ventures with Foreign Partners, International Survey of Business Opinion and Experience,* New York: National Conference Board.

Datta, D.K. (1988), "International Joint Ventures: A Framework for Analysis," *Journal of General Management, 14,* 78-91.

Geringer, J.M. (1988), *Joint Venture Partner Selection,* New York: Quorum Books.

Gullander, S.O. (1976), "Joint Ventures and Corporate Strategy," *Columbia Journal of World Business, 11,* 104-114.

Habib, G.M., and J. J. Burnette (1988), "An Assessment of Channel Behaviour in an Alternative Structural Arrangement: The International Joint Venture," *International Marketing Review, 6,* 7-21.

Harrigan, K.R. (1984), "Joint Ventures and Global Strategies," *Columbia Journal of World Business, 19*, 7-17.

—— (1987), "Why Joint Ventures Fail," *Euro-Asia Business Review, 6*, 20-26.

Hladik, K. (1985), *International Ventures: An Economic Analysis of US-Foreign Business Partnerships,* Lexington, MA: Lexington Books.

Holton, R.H. (1981), "Making International Joint Ventures Work," in *The Management of Headquarters-Subsidiary Relationships in Multinational Corporations* L. Otterbeck, ed., pp. 255-267. New York: St. Martin's Press.

Janger, A. (1980), *Organization of International Joint Venture Work,* New York: The Conference Board.

Killing, J.P. (1982), "How to Make a Global Joint Venture Work," *Harvard Business Review, 60*, 120-127.

—— (1983), *Strategies for Joint Venture Success,* New York: Praeger.

Kogut, B. (1987), "Joint Ventures: Theoretical and Empirical Perspectives," *Strategic Management Journal, 9*, 319-333.

Lane, H.W., and P. W. Beamish (1990), "Cross-cultural Cooperative Behavior in Joint Ventures in LDCs," *Management International Review special issue*, 87-102.

Lorange, P., and J. Roos (1990), "Formation of Cooperative Ventures: Competence Mix of the Management Teams," *Management International Review special issue*, 69-86.

Lyles, M.A. (1987), "Common Mistakes of Joint Venture Experienced Firms," *Columbia Journal of World Business, 20*, 465-487.

Martinez, Z.L., and D. A. Ricks (1989), "Decisions of Affiliates: U.S. Firms in Mexico," *Journal of International Business, 20*, 475-487.

Perlmutter, H.W., and D. A. Heenan (1986), "Thinking Ahead: Cooperate to Compete Globally," *Harvard Business Review March-April*, 136-152.

Raveed, S.R., and W. Renforth (1983), "State Enterprise-Multinational Corporation Joint Ventures: How Well Do They Meet Both Partners' Needs?" *Management International Review, 23*, 47-57.

Schaan, J.L. (1983), "Parent Control and Joint Venture Success: The Case of Mexico," Unpublished Ph.D. dissertation. University of Western Ontario.

Shenkar, O., and Y. Zeira (1987), "Human Resources Management in International Joint Ventures: Directions for Research," *Academy of Management Review, 12*, 546-557.

Zeira, Y., and O. Shenkar (1990), "Interactive and Specific Parent Firm Characteristics," *Management International Review, special issue*, 7-22.

Part III

ASSESSING SUCCESS AND FAILURE OF CROSS-HEMISPHERE INTERNATIONAL JOINT VENTURES

7

Where Have the U.S.-Dutch Joint Ventures Gone? In Search of Dimensions That May Bring Down Untimely Dissolutions

Theo Roebers

U.S.-DUTCH JOINT VENTURES

Within the framework of strategic alliances, the joint venture has no doubt been able to arouse the interest of management and academic literature (Lyons 1991). This type of partnership has a variety of formats and ways of implementation, and could serve diverse purposes. In essence this alliance involves two or more legally distinct organizations (the parents), each of which actively participates, beyond a mere investment role, in the decision-making activities of the jointly owned entity (Geringer 1991). An international joint venture is a partnership between an international company (in this study headquartered in the United States) and a firm that (in principle) is native to the country where the venture is located. As this study deals with joint ventures located in the Netherlands, the other parent is a Dutch company.

ADVANTAGES AND DISADVANTAGES OF THE JOINT VENTURE

Reduction of risk can also play a role without considering development projects. This is especially true of ventures that were established more than thirty years ago (e.g. the partnership between Cyanamid and the AKZO subsidiary, Ketjen, that ended in 1989), which began in a period when American partners were anything but sure about the European economic and business future. Financing the whole investment in a local production was avoided by a partnership.

Looking for overseas production facilities, the international company in the present climate prefers to prevent creating capacity and employing new staff if an overseas unit can be found with excess capacity. The owner of that unit is a candidate partner. In a less developed country, a local partner may be a compulsory route. In newly capitalizing countries, complete ownership of a local company is normally not permitted. The obligatory way, through a joint venture, creates the same token good relations with the host country's governmental bodies and secures local assistance to overcome the "foreignness" in a xenophile market (Kuiper 1988; Roebers 1985). Our study deals with U.S.-Dutch partnerships, where the motive of pleasing authorities may be of less importance; but notwithstanding the fact that the market in the Netherlands, or on a wider scale in Europe, has a certain resemblance to the U.S. home market, in many of the examined cases the foreign partner decided to avail himself of the expertise of his overseas partner in the local area of local business conditions. Xytel Corp., for instance, is using superb technology in its successful venture with Tebodin Engineering Consultants; but for process development consultancy, one has to be in touch with the customer and that is what the Dutch partner—well introduced in the European process industry—takes care of.

However, the joint venture is not without its problems. Parent companies may have different perceptions of management, control, and financial systems; national characteristics, even in the western hemisphere, vary in terms of such factors as attitude toward customers and suppliers. Such differences between American and Dutch managers have been noticed. Nomination of a manager of one the two partner firms as the joint venture general manager could represent a mean of exercising managerial control (Geringer and Hebert 1989). If the manager of the joint venture located in the Netherlands is a Dutch citizen, dominance of the local firm's culture may be expected; that is not necessarily synonymous with dominating the decisionmaking. The U.S. parent could control through reporting systems, actively joining the planning and budgeting process. Schaan (quoted in Geringer and Hebert 1989) drew up a table of positive and negative control mechanisms, which unfortunately does not specify any form of control or initiative in the field of product development; this may implicitly be included in participation in the planning process; contextually, however, it may be outweighted by the budgeting side. Differences in management style and product orientation might be an obstacle for development; these differences could be weakened in effect by giving the joint venture autonomy in product development. Such autonomy does not exclude the international partner from remaining a potential voice in management; nevertheless, quite a few cases reveal that in this way the local partner gets a "free ride."

CRITICAL DIMENSIONS WORTH BEING CONSIDERED

Alliances can generally be categorized into those intended to "facilitate access to a technological capability" and others primarily relating to "market access" (Nueno and Oosterveld 1988). The former includes cooperation between partners that are both competent, but who—although competitors—join forces for innovation. After completion of the project, they do the market launch individually. A collaboration of that kind did not turn up amongst the joint ventures in research. In all but one of the cases, the interest taken by the Dutch partners was in technical know-how, already existing in the U.S. firm. Next to the acquisition of technology, the local partner was in search of rights to use a well-known U.S. corporate logo and brand or trade name.

"Market access" was the motive for more than half of the U.S. companies. If companies are to compete in a foreign market against firms possessing local knowledge and the advantages of local nationality, they must possess some form of quasi-monopolistic advantage. From this very general proposition, Davies (1977) posits: whether or not the advantage resides in the ability to differentiate a product or in knowledge gained through successful research and development, its use involves the transfer of that technical information from market to market. The options then become exporting or local production. If the former is unattractive for reasons of costs, the decision to employ the latter will be forced. For Neville Chemical Corp., the transport costs on their resins were prohibitive in view of low prices prevailing for that commodity. So they had to seek cooperation and located Cindu Chemical Industries. The Cindu plant could manufacture Neville's products, and Cindu's sales staff was well introduced to European and Middle East buyers. Neville's technical expertise has been complemented through this venture by Cindu's local marketing know-how that is a firm-specific asset. Complementariness of Cindu's product lines and similarity of application areas are the specific assets that could not be acquired separately from the firm. For American companies, even the bigger ones, it appears under the circumstances that the risk of go-it-alone is too big. It is not only the financial aspects, that have to be considered. A full takeover of the firm holding the know-how will involve substantial management costs if the firm to be acquired is large, if it operates in a different industry, or if it is foreign-based. Taking over will sometimes mean buying a collection of other businesses and a labor force that is foreign and/or employed in fields unknown by the buyer. In that case a joint venture is desirable, as it reduces management costs (Hennart 1988).

The transfer of technical know-how to a partner has been explained in the literature as meeting the requirement of product diversification when entering a new market. The local expertise to understand and meet customers' requirements can effectively be ensured by creating a joint venture that is given the permission to use the foreign partner's production know-how. Stopford and Wells (1972) found that when product adaptations were to be expected, joint ventures were more likely than wholly owned subsidiaries. This long existing experience would indicate that the joint ventures examined in the Netherlands would have been directed at product development. Results of the study about the ventures in question will show, however, that the international companies do not believe the idea that the technology can be applied without adaptation and that the jointly established company does not need to be involved in product development or modification. As an example, we mention Cyanamid (under pressure of Esso

U.S.A. at that time) which had to create a modus to provide Esso Europe locally
with the identical catalysts provided elsewhere in the world.

From that line of argument follows naturally the make or buy decision of the
Dutch partner when considering product line extension. Avoiding expensive
R&D work, accelerating time to market, and obtaining certainty in regard to the
functionality of an existing product are three reasons to try and find a licensor
or technology transferring co-venturer. In several cases, the identified U.S.
partner was by no means considering internationalization of their marketing.
Robishaw Engineering Inc. would never have entered the European market on
their own initiative. It was the Dutch partner who was interested in the
introduction of Robishaw's pontoons in Western and Eastern Europe—which led
to the joint venture Flexifloat Systems BV at Rotterdam.

A local partner will have planned how to shape his product offering to meet
customers' needs prior to entering into a joint venture. Opting for collaboration
implicates that the partner should provide adequate technical know-how leading
to such line extension. The rejection of the manufacturing decision implies a
purchase route through a partner furnishing know-how, dismissing the necessity
for local variation. The joint venture as an external substitute for internal R&D
has already been validated by Friedman, Berg, and Duncan (1979). They dealt
with domestic ventures; in international ones, the technology could be hypothe-
sized less universally. However, although this study is not dealing with
specifically global or standard "state of the art" products, the Dutch partners were
for the most part not expecting either to have to adapt the basic or conceptual
characteristics. Flexifloat may again serve as an example: over the total duration
of the partnership (which ended in 1989), there was no need for development or
modification as the technology transferred appeared to be fully meeting market
requirements.

TRACING U.S.-DUTCH JOINT VENTURES IN THE NETHERLANDS

There is no governmental body or statistical bureau that keeps records of
interest on joint ventures. In common parlance, contract manufacturing, toll
processing, and licensing are joint ventures of a sort. These cooperations, that of
the exporter working with a foreign distributor, as well as minority participations
may get the same label and appear on the listings. From the data bank of "Het
Financiëel Dagblad" (the Financial Daily) focusing on the totality of alliances,
a pretended joint venture may easily have to be skipped after inspection of firm-
specific documentation or publications. The American Chamber of Commerce
in the Netherlands had no specific listing in its data bank either. Out of all U.S.-
Dutch cooperations listed by the Chamber, thirty-two have been identified as
joint ventures in our study. The sample included only ventures located in the
Netherlands, but neglected those few that are engaged in professional services
(auditing and real estate for instance).

The research was primarily conducted through a series of interviews with Dutch CEOs and Vice Presidents Marketing or Operations of twenty-seven U.S.-Dutch joint ventures. The managers of three joint ventures refused participation, and in two others the proper information could not be obtained. The reader should realize that respondents, although the formal executives of the joint venture, were not all on the payroll of the separate entity. Part of them were employed full-time by the Dutch parent firm to the joint venture, others part-time. In the useable sample, all respondents appeared to be Dutch citizens. In a few cases a delegate of the U.S. partner had presided previously over the joint venture. In view of the period that the actual respondent was in charge of either the joint venture itself or of the Dutch parent company, the foreign managers must have been repatriated long ago. The dominance of the local partner's culture, if not of the decisionmaking—even though it is not the subject of this research—was noteworthy. This potential onesidedness is negligible in view of the objectively verifiable answers. The results four categories of industry are given in Table 7.1.

Apart from two companies, one in food and one in miscellaneous, the examined firms were in industrial marketing, in which, by definition, the products are less susceptible to the "people differences" that usually change when crossing borders. Local partners interviewed were as a matter of fact considering the acquired product line extension to be uniform internationally. That underlies their opinion that line stretching would be realized by acquisition of adequate technical know-how. This would free the jointly owned entity from R&D work.

Table 7.1. Industry Categories of Sample Joint Ventures

			No.
Metal work-ing/electrical			11
Chemical			5
(Micro)Electronics			4
Agro, Food	5	}	
		}	7
Miscellaneous	2	}	—
Total Sample			27

BENEFITS GAINED BY EACH OF THE PARTNERS

Various obvious motives for the partnership such as reduction of costs, proximity to the customer, increase of global market share, and avoidance of overcapacity that were brought up by the respondents during the discussions will not be used as explanatory factors per se. They are in principle supporting the major motives under examination, namely market entry, acquisition of adequate technology, and the extension of the product line.

With respect to "market entry," the global customer base of the U.S. parent company versus the one of the Dutch parent, as well as the fact of whether current joint venture customers were already buying from either partner before the alliance started, were examined. Also investigated was whether the local partner—prior to entering into the joint venture—already had marketing experience with the *new product line* or with a substitute to it. In regard to the *sufficiency of the technology transferred,* each company surveyed was asked details about the dynamics of the industry and its impact on customer needs in comparison with those in the United States. The respondent was asked to indicate whether or not the technology transferred had been adjusted to modify the product in order to meet local requirements. If local requirements did not allow a 100% identical product version, the basic conceptual changes of the product were clearly distinguished from marginal adaptations such as a change-over to the metric system or replacement of a component to comply with local regulations. The former implied *joint product development work,* whereas the latter was sometimes left to the customer service technicians as a trivial deviation on a day to day basis. Table 7.2 adds joint R&D work to the three objectives as the inverse of sufficiency of technology.

The importance of the objective to *stretch the product line* is obvious. It is particularly important for the chemical companies because all of them received a novel addition to their range; this is not completely surprising taking into consideration that Dutch or European technology was still behind that of the United States.   Positive answers in the metalworking/electrical and agro/food/ miscellaneous groups were 64% and 57%, respectively.   In the electronic companies, the establishment of which are more recent, three out of the four have been trying successfully to lay their hands on a developed overseas product.

Almost all the firms that experienced no product line extension at the start of the joint venture were already involved in the distribution of the product of the eventual co-venturer, or they were handling a similar product from another source. Just one respondent, in a venture for seed growing, had as its only objective doing local research (as the Western European climatical conditions cannot be duplicated or simulated in the United States); it does not touch the parents' products— the Dutch partner still is acting independently as a distributor for its ally in research.

There is a fair number of respondents who answered that the joint venture has had no need to look for *additional technology.* In contrast, the chemical companies could not live without updating technology through joint research work, apparently because of the older technology transfer. A company in mineral powders could not answer the question positively. It was liquidated before having an opportunity to get a fair notion about the sufficiency of know-how.

A number of companies equal to the ones that received adequate technology, twelve, indicated the need for joint development work in the joint venture. Stertil BV., for instance, applied the dock levellers techniques that were appropriate for the United States and Europe were appropriate in the 1970s. In that company, market distribution systems differed from those overseas, rendering another dock

Table 7.2. Profiles of 27 U.S. - Dutch Joint Ventures

	Yes	No
Product line extension for the Dutch partner	19	8
Efficaciousness of technology transferred	12	15
Joint development work required at a later stage	12	15
Market entry for the U.S. partner	15	12

board concept necessary. In this case, like in several others, there was feedback of the innovations to the U.S. partner; however, the new concept was not of interest to the American customers. The opposite holds for resins for which Cindu could make a development laboratory and staff available. Cindu, as the Dutch partner, brought its R&D laboratory in as part of the equity. The development results are imperatively shared with the U.S. partner, in view of the required interchangeability of the products of the joint venture with those of the U.S. partner on the world market.

At first sight the outcome with regard to sufficiency of technology transferred and the outcome with respect to the need for joint R&D at a later stage are mutually exclusive. If it should have become clear that the technology transferred is inadequate to meet customer's needs in the long run, the venture's policy goals would be for new product development. Actual development work on top of the received technology would evidence a negative sufficiency. A few exceptions teach us that these variables are not necessarily antagonistic.

De Jong-Coen BV., which wished to add high performance burners to the line, received the know-how from the United States, and it continues the same policy for further needed additions. It certainly has insight in customers' needs, but it has no staff or pilot facilities to design the required new types. So the jointly owned entity continues to rely on the expertise of Coen Inc. through technology updated in the United States. Another example is TDF Tiofine BV. that happily used the technology received for pigments from Cyanamid International Development Corp. Four years ago it had to conclude that the U.S. parent's know-how was insufficient to manufacture the products meeting transforming environmental standards. The Dutch company itself had no research capacity either, so that technology had to be sourced from a third party. Both investigated variables were consequently negative. A venture in high tech computer peripherals, Black Box Datacom BV., could surely do with the technology supplied; however, it developed a lap top computer that goes with the peripherals better than any other PC. The U.S. parent, Black Box Corp. Inc., and its international subsidiaries have filled their lines with the Dutch (contracted out) lap top. The remaining fifteen respondents are in joint ventures of which the Dutch parent already distributed the products from the U.S. partner and had no signals from the market to take up any study for change of design or concept.

In the total sample, the U.S. companies that had a first market exposure are slightly outnumbering the ones that were already on the Dutch or European market; in the different industry groups, however, the variances are remarkable. For example, whereas only one U.S. food company achieved an introduction to the Benelux market (out of the group of seven in agro, food, and miscellaneous), each of the five chemical companies reported an entry, as did the majority of the electronic firms.

THE LIFE SPAN OF THE JOINT VENTURE; IN SEARCH OF INFLUENCING VARIABLES

As was written in the chapter introduction, half of the examined ventures are no longer existing—fourteen out of twenty-seven. In Table 7.3 the lifespan of twenty-seven joint ventures are indicated. The number of joint ventures that broke up are in parentheses. For those existing less than ten years, a relatively high number have been terminated. Hennart (1988) characterizes the mean life of a joint venture as short on average. In this study, I find another confirmation— there are ten entities in the first category with an average life span of 5.5 years. The all-over average lifetime of the sample joint ventures is 16.4 years, which is no doubt pushed upward by three chemical firms that have existed for a period of 32 years.

Is there any relationship to be found between the scope and the objective of the joint venture on the one hand and the life span and its success on the other hand? In search of explanatory factors, I will use the four dimensions discussed above.

Table 7.3. Life Span of Twenty-Seven U.S.-Dutch Joint Ventures

Number	On-going	Terminated
00-09 years	10	(7)
10-19 years	7	(3)
20-29 years	5	(2)
30 years and over	5	(2)

The figures in parentheses represent the number of terminated partnerships.

ADDITIONAL ITEMS TO THE PRODUCT LINE
OF THE LOCAL PARTNER

The extension of the product line of the Dutch partner does not prevent a high proportion of mortality, but the same is true for those of twenty and thirty-plus years. If the joint venture survives the first ten years, that may impart a longer life expectancy see Table 7.4.

Table 7.4. Influence of Extension of Product Line for the Dutch Partner

	Extension		No Extension	
00-09 years	8	(6)	2	(1)
10-19 years	4	(1)	3	(2)
20-29 years	3	(1)	2	(1)
30 years and over	4	(1)	1	(1)
	—	—	—	—
	19	(9)	8	(5)
average life span	16.3 years		16.6 years	

The figures in parentheses represent the number of terminated partnerships.

Prima facie a relationship between age and life expectancy may be assumed, but nevertheless no statistical reliability is resulting. The Kolmogorov-Smirnov 2-sample gives too low values to have a reliable result.

THE IMPORTANCE OF ACQUIRED TECHNOLOGY
FOR THE LOCAL PARTNER

Does the dimension of adequate technology give a better indication of stability for the joint venture? More likely, after analyzing Table 7.5, the opposite is true. Reckoning with five companies of thirty years plus, we see that they survived notwithstanding the inadequate know-how transferred. If the joint venture undertakes product development, exploiting one partner's technology but expanding it through joint research work, this variable could be studied as an explanation for the shared equity stability of the joint venture. Kogut (1989) reports, as a statistical result of a test in R&D intensive industries, that research and development in the joint venture tend to make it less vulnerable to untimely termination. If the industry requires expending a relatively high degree of resources on research and development, this interaction evokes a greater willingness of the partners to endure in their cooperation.

Table 7.5. Influence of Efficaciousness of Technology Transferred

	Adequate		Not Adequate	
00-09 years	6	(4)	4	(3)
10-19 years	2	(0)	5	(3)
20-29 years	4	(2)	1	(0)
30 years and over	0	(0)	5	(2)
	12	(6)	15	(8)
average life span	13.4 years		18.7 years	

The figures in parentheses represent the number of terminated partnerships.

U.S.-DUTCH JVs PRONE TO UNTIMELY DISSOLUTION EVEN WHEN R&D IS UNDERTAKEN

In the examined ventures, that were not meant to undertake joint R&D activities, it seems that *un*intentional product development, indicative of an ad hoc approach increases stability. However, our findings do not support this supposition (see Table 7.6).

Although joint R&D for product innovation in most cases has not been the initial goal of the partnerships, it sometimes appeared to be indispensable for the local marketing strategy. Even if the technology transferred was state-of-the-art and is still fully applicable in the United States, the perception of the customer base in Europe may be different, as occurred with the dock levellers at Stertil BV. Another example is a catalyst manufacturing unit of Cyanamid-Ketjen: the U.S. partners in that venture thought it could satisfy the needs of European oil refiners (subsidiaries of their U.S. customers) with the same products, based on the same technology. However, "think globally, act locally" is applicable. Exxon Europe required proprietary catalysts not available in the product line of Cyanamid. One year after the start of the joint venture, the Dutch staff had developed a new series of catalysts without their partner knowing in detail what was happening. In the semi-conductor industry, I examined the case of Xycarb BV., where the Dutch partner would only be responsible for production and marketing, the technology being brought in by Ultra Carbon Inc., the U.S. partner. However, the process could not be run on that basis; with a subsidy of the Dutch Innovation Board, the joint venture succeeded in making the process work for local conditions. Neither need nor details were communicated to partners. At the first contractual opportunity, the Dutch partners easily bought out

Table 7.6. Influence of Joint Development Work for Product Modification

	Factual R&D		No R&D	
00-09 years	4	(2)	6	(5)
10-19 years	5	(2)	2	(1)
20-29 years	0	(0)	5	(2)
30 years and over	3	(1)	2	(1)
	—	—	—	—
	12	(5)	15	(9)
average life span	17.4 years		15.5 years	

The figures in parentheses represent the number of terminated partnerships.

their U.S. co-venturers as did the Dutch partners in the other two cases described in this paragraph. The importance of systematical feedback by means of reporting to the international partner, and of control over product management by means of joint planning and budgeting, is clearly demonstrated by the these three cases. A table of positive and negative control mechanisms for that purpose (Schaan, quoted in Geringer and Hebert 1989) is recommended.

MARKET ENTRY FOR THE INTERNATIONAL FIRM

The relationship between "market entry," as the last of the four dimensions, and the stability of the venture can be deduced from Table 7.7. A tendency to a higher stability, on average as well as outcome, in the majority of age categories may be observed. The differences are nevertheless negligible and are not reliably significant.

KEEPING IN TOUCH WITH THE DUTCH AS LOCAL PARTNER

A correlation finds a certain degree of correlation exists between the dimension "joint R&D work" and the buying out by Dutch partners of the American parent company. Out of the fourteen terminated partnerships, there were five buy-outs by the Dutch partner after the joint venture had undertaken joint research work into product development. The fact that the Dutch partner—being local—had a better insight into the value and potentiality for growth of the jointly owned entity did no doubt predispose the local partner to be the buying out party. Three acquisitions of the U.S. participation have taken place, however, without the joint venture having undertaken any (joint) product development.

Table 7.7. Influence of an Effected Market Entry for the U.S. Partner

	Effected entry		No market entry	
00-09 years	6	(4)	4	(3)
10-19 years	2	(0)	5	(3)
20-29 years	3	(1)	2	(1)
30 years and over	4	(1)	1	(1)
	—	—	—	—
	15	(6)	12	(8)
average life span	17.7 years		14.6 years	

The figures in parentheses represent the number of terminated partnerships.

The inverse is also worth mentioning: four Dutch partners were bought out—all of them participating in entities that were not involved in any development activities. Johnson-Hamstra BV, now 100% American owned, may serve as an example. The joint venture was for Johnson Inc., the long arm for production and service; all development and updating of technology was for Johnson's account. At Dutch American Plantbreeders BV. R&D was neither the goal nor practice, because of the small size of the Dutch partner. The latter was bought out the moment that the jointly owned entity became less important to the U.S. parent which was channelling its marketing in a new fashion.

THE ROUTE TO EUROPE IS NOT PAVED WITH JOINT VENTURES

Unlike the possibilities in newly capitalizing countries, where the joint venture is normally the only mode of entry, the opportunities for entry and investment in the Netherlands are numerous. So numerous that U.S. companies are not often selecting that route. Most of the thirty-two identified cases—a modest percentage of hundreds of U.S.-Dutch alliances—appear to be of a transitory nature: one of the few results of this study confirming earlier findings in literature.

Widely known motives for considering a joint venture have been examined in identified U.S.-Dutch cases: product line extension for the Dutch partner, acquisition of U.S. know-how and technology to commence production in the Netherlands, joint R&D activities to customize a U.S. product (line) for the European market, and market entry strategy for the U.S. partner. Accomplishment of any of these four objectives does not result in certainty about the success or stability of the partnership. At the most, this study reveals that not achieving the goals as represented by the four dimensions will lead to a higher percentage of untimely terminations. Apart from the four dimensions, respondents indicated a variety of opportunistic reasons to dissolve the venture that have not been categorized. Some can always been foreseen in managerial decisionmaking with regard to entering into a strategic alliance, whereas the four examined dimensions —notwithstanding their unpredictable influence—will continue to be of great importance.

REFERENCES

Davies, Howard (1977), "Technology Transfer Through Commercial Transactions," *The Journal of Industrial Economics, 26* (2), 161-175.

Friedman, Philip, Sanford V. Berg, and Jerome Duncan (1979), "External vs. Internal Knowledge Acquisition: Joint Venture Activity and R&D Intensity," *Journal of Economics and Business, 31* (2), 103-111.

Geringer, Michael J. (1991), "Strategic Determinants of Partner Selection Criteria in International Joint Ventures," *Journal of International Business Studies, First Quarter*, 41-62.

Geringer, Michael J., and Louis Hebert (1989), "Control and Performance of International Joint Ventures," *Journal of International Business Studies, Summer*, 235-254.

Hennart, Jean-Francois (1988), "A Transaction Costs Theory of Equity Joint Ventures," *Strategic Management Journal, 9*, 361-374 .

Kogut, Bruce (1989), "The Stability of Joint Ventures: Reciprocity and Competitive Rivalry," *The Journal of Industrial Economics, 38* (2), 183-198.

KPMG Klijnveld Management Consultants (1991), *Joint Adventures*, Utrecht: KPMG.

Kuiper, W.G. (1988), *Joint Ventures: A Special Phenomenon in International Tax Law?* Ph.D. Dissertation, Leiden University.

Lyons, Michael P. (1991), "Joint Ventures as Strategic Choice—A Literature Review," *Long Range Planning, 24* (4), 130-144.

Nueno P., and J. Oosterveld (1988), "Managing Technological Alliances," *Long Range Planning, 21* (3), 11-17.

Roebers, Th. J. (1985), *International Private Law and the Joint Venture Regulations of the P.R. of China,* Unpublished Masters thesis, Leiden University.

Stopford, M, and L. Wells (1972), *Managing the Multinational Enterprise,* New York: Basic Books.

8

European Ventures in China: Characteristics and Entry Strategies

David K. Tse
Kevin Y. Au
Ilan Vertinsky

INTRODUCTION

The integration of the European countries into a single market has changed how we perceive its market characteristics. Such changes also affected the firms. To capture the enlarged market in Europe and new global markets, many European companies engage in acquisition, mergers, and other forms of interfirm alliances. As a result we may be seeing the emergence of a new generation of firms. These firms may bear some of the conventional country characteristics (e.g., United Kingdom, Germany, France), but at the same time they seem to exhibit some unique characteristics of being "European" enterprises. This chapter compares firms from various European countries to firms of other regional groupings (e.g., Japanese, American, and/or Asian). It differs from previous approaches that emphasize finding unique characteristics of British, French, and/or German firms.

To understand behaviors of European companies, this chapter used firm specific data on how companies entered one of the largest markets in the world—China. The choice of China as a context offered some advantages. First, as one of the first planned economies to experiment freely with the market system, the China experience may provide some insights as to how the Eastern European countries, in which many European companies are active, may develop. Second, since its modernization, China has gone through a number of critical economic and political changes, so that the data set (from 1979 to 1991) may offer some insights as to how European firms adapted their strategies to this changing host environment. Third, China has attracted an unprecedented number of foreign businesses. Accordingly, the data offered a rich array of business strategies adopted by the investing firms from various countries.

This chapter focuses on how European companies venture into China. Four dimensions of their operations are examined. They include entry mode (export of commodities, export of technologies, licensing, and direct investment), interactions with different levels of the host governments, location of the ventures, and the various forms of strategic alliances. Other characteristics, such as the venture size, industry type and different phases China went through in its development, are also considered. How the European companies behaved are compared to the American, Asian, and Japanese firms.

Characteristics of European Ventures

Until recently there has been a general lack of understanding as to how European firms as a group behave because previous studies concentrated more on country-specific firm behaviors. For example, in the auto industry, the Swedish firm Volvo was particularly strong (Quelch, Buzzell, and Salama 1990) in designing pan-European and global strategies to advance their global competitiveness. Their German counterpart, VW, chose to operate in comparatively low wage regions as a strategy for growth (Avishai 1991). In the insurance industry, it was suggested that U.K. and Swedish firms were more liberal than U.S. companies with regard to captive formation (Richardson 1992). Swiss insurance firms were said to be prepared to compete globally (Studer 1991).

Compared with firms from other regions of the world, European companies were found to be most active in joint ventures in Eastern European countries and the Soviet Union (Pettibone 1991; Rock 1990). They also led in forming strategic alliances among themselves and with other countries as Europe merged into single market (Quelch, Buzzell, and Salama 1990). In expanding to international markets, European firms tended to introduce existing products to new markets, while U.S. firms concentrated on new products. Beyond these general perspectives, existing effort in understanding how European firms behave has not matured to offer more insightful generalizations.

The Changing Chinese Environment

A large volume of work has reported on how the Chinese business environment has changed since the country modernized its economy. During the last 13 years, China has increased her GNP more than four times, attracted $16.11 billion in foreign investments (Beamish and Wang 1989), and expanded trade activities by five times; as of 1991, it was among the top 20 trading nations in the world (*Country Report* various issues; Sung and Lee 1991). Underlying these amazing achievements, China's business environment has gone through the following important phases, due largely to changes in the country's national foreign business policies and political events.

The first phase, often regarded as the initial stage of growth, was from 1979 to September 1983 (Pearson 1991). During this period, the Chinese government promulgated the Joint Venture Law (1979) that established principles and procedures for foreign investments. China also joined important international organizations including the International Monetary Fund, the World Development

Bank, and the United Nations. The Chinese government began to experiment with Special Economic Zones in Guangdong Province (to which Hong Kong belongs), where foreign enterprises had more freedom in their operations (such as hiring and firing employees), as exemplars of development (*China Statistic Yearbook* various issues). This move stimulated tremendous interest from foreign investors, but the major growth of investments was yet to come. The investors were still doubtful whether the Chinese government was truly committed to opening the economy, and they were waiting for China to clarify her policies concerning foreign ventures.

The second phase, characterized by phenomenal growth of foreign investments, was from October 1983 to October 1986. This was the period during which the Chinese government declared the Joint Venture Implementing Regulations (1983) in which policies on patents, profit repatriation, and foreign exchange for investors were clarified. The Chinese government's commitment to the open door policy was also reflected in the opening of her 14 coastal cities in 1984 (*China Statistic Yearbook* various issues). Many firms felt optimistic about the business environment and jumped on the China wagon creating what Pye (1982) called the "Westchester Country Syndrome." At the same time, some side effects began to surface. In particular, the economy was overheating, numerous incidences of corruption broke out (which later led to the movement against "spiritual pollution"), and the government's foreign reserves dipped. These events led to a readjustment period.

From November 1986 until June 1989, the Chinese government endeavored to regulate her economic growth more tightly. On the one hand, demand for consumption goods—especially those imported—were capped, breaking the continuous drop in external accounts and the decline of the foreign reserve (*Country Report* various issues). Concurrently, in response to potential worries by foreign investors, the Chinese government further reduced regulatory controls over foreign investments. The Provisions for the Encouragement of Foreign Investment were further enhanced. These provisions granted tax incentives, delegated power to provinces to deal with foreign investments, and deregulated limits on ownership and span of investment. This allowed foreign investments to continue to grow. Investments from economies that had not been active in China before, such as Taiwan and South Korea, began to pour in (see Pearson 1991).

Events in June 1989 dramatically changed the Chinese business environment. It cast a great shadow on her growth path. A number of key industries were devastated. In particular, the tourist industry lost many of its customers, and even after three years, the country's hotel occupancy rate was far below the level it had been before. While many economic factors were unchanged, the enthusiasm foreign investors held dimmed. Political risks and uncertainties about the country resurfaced (Keck 1989). In international circles, previous support gave way to pressure. As the second most important importer for Chinese products, the United States demanded that the Chinese government improve her human rights conditions in order to retain its Most Favored Nation status. While the Chinese government had clearly sweetened its conditions to lure foreign businesses, the drop in foreign business ventures was obvious (Shenkar 1990).

Entry Mode

Different types of entry modes are known to represent varying levels of control, commitment, and risks for the investing companies. To firms entering into new and/or unstable markets, such concerns would likely be of significance (for a review, see Dunning 1988; Shenkar 1990). In addition, the choice of entry modes may depend on other factors including a firm's resources and its global strategies.

Export of commodities, for example, is regarded as the simplest way and least risky option to enter a market. On the other hand, joint ventures may represent more profitable options as they combine the firm's specific advantages and the host country's location advantages.

In China, joint venture is of particular interest. It is the most actively researched topic. From the previous 12 studies, it was suggested that joint venture is the oldest form of business venture in China (Beamish and Wang 1989), and this form of entry is popular among foreign investors and has proven to be reasonably successful (Pearson 1991; Shenkar 1990). A number of factors made this mode most popular. First, the Chinese government encouraged joint ventures because they were very effective in generating employment and in transferring advanced technologies while demanding less investments from the country. To the investors, joint venture allows more control of the product quality and at times, access to the huge Chinese market. Third, location advantages, such as lower labor costs, were available for the joint venture firms.

Interacting with Different Levels of the Chinese Governments

As in other countries, there are various levels of the government a firm can choose (and at times is obliged) to deal with. In China there are roughly three levels: the state, the provincial, and the municipal governments. The choice of the levels of government may bear greater significance in China than in other market economies because they represent different risks to the investing firms. Generally speaking, the higher the level of government involved, the more secure the ventures. This is because higher level governments have more authority in approving projects, interpreting government policies, and exercising controls. As suggested by studies in negotiating with the Chinese, Pye (1982; Hendryx 1986a) has observed the importance of such government guarantees.

Operating in a planned economy with low incentives to do the jobs right, foreign ventures have encountered obstacles that required strong bureaucratic support, and in this case, different levels of the Chinese government. Thus the higher the level in the government with which a firm dealt, the more opportunity a firm would have in removing these obstacles. Nike, for example, had problems in securing raw materials from China, and the management faced difficulty in negotiating with the factory managers at the municipal level (Aguilar 1988). The firm brought the matter to the chairman of the people's council (officially the highest governing body in the country) and resolved most of the problems. The results may have been different if other levels of the government had been involved.

At the same time, however, firms may have to invest more time and energy in order to work with the state rather than local governments because the state government is generally overwhelmed with such requests. On the other hand, Asian firms (mostly from Hong Kong) seemed to be quite effective in overcoming hurdles in their ventures with lower level governments. This may been due largely to the strong ethnic ties owners of these Hong Kong firms have with people in the municipal and/or provincial governments. Relationship ("Quanxi", that is, knowing some insiders) has been known to be a key to success in China.

As China progresses, investors gain experience and expertise. It is expected that an increasing number of ventures will interact with lower levels of the government. The Chinese state government also encourages such decentralization of economic decisions, delegating more authority to the provincial and municipal governments. It will be of interest to see how changes in the country's stability affect the firms' choices of governments to deal with.

Location

One cornerstone in China's modernization has been the creation of Special Economic Zones (SEZ) where market-oriented policies have been systematically adapted. Four SEZs were designed in 1980 (at Shenzhen, Zuhai, Shantou, and Xiamen), a fifth, Hainan Province, has been added since then. The SEZs have proven to be extremely successful in attracting foreign investors and activating China's export economy. By 1990, the number of foreign investments totalled more than 6,600 worth US \$4.5 billion in these SEZs (*China Statistical Yearbook* various issues). The volume of manufactured products exported accounted for 60% of the SEZs' total production.

The success in the SEZs was extended to a lesser degree to the 14 coastal/open cities in China (including Guangzhou, Shanghai, and Tianjin) in 1984. As ports and regional industrial centers, these cities received similar concessions as the SEZs, but they did not have strong budget support for infrastructure. By 1991, 45 cities along the coast were designated open/coastal cities.

The SEZs, the coastal cities, and the rest of China, therefore, represent varying degrees of control and incentives for the foreign investors. Some ventures (e.g., Nike) that have problems in non-SEZ and non-coastal cities did much better in the plants they later set up in the SEZs. It is, therefore, of interest to see how firms from different regions chose their locations in China and whether their locational strategy changed as China went through different economic and political changes.

Strategic Alliances

Faced with rapid technological advances, changing market structure, and increasing global competition, strategic alliance has become the corporate buzz-word in the 1990s. There are many forms of alliances ranging from contractual agreements to acquisitions. The advantages are numerous: lowering risk, sharing technology, learning from other firms, increasing efficiency, quickening market access (as in Europe and Asia), enhancing global mobility, and, of course, improving global competitiveness. In this chapter we concentrate on the choice of different countries as partners as firms formed their strategic alliances.

Foreign ventures in China face a number of options in forming partnerships. First, the firms can form partners with those from their own country. In particular, it is likely that many Japanese companies adopt this way of strategic alliances. Such a strategy is most reasonable given the many inter-firm linkages and interlock directors in Japanese trading "keiretsus" (Gerlach 1992). As a result, strategic alliances among the members of the "keiretsus" would be easier to form and have better chance to succeed because of greater confidence and less suspicion among the alliance members. For firms from Europe, the United States and/or Asia, the lack of a higher level institutional structure and the aggressive inter-firm competition often discourage the firms from forming alliances with firms within their own country firms.

Second, the investing firms may form partnerships with those from Asian countries. This strategy is especially appealing given the lack of understanding of how the Chinese governments, firms, workers, and consumers behave. Asian partners may prove to be extremely useful to entering, managing, and operating joint ventures in China because they understand the Chinese environment better.

Last but not the least, the firms can form partnerships with those from non-Asian countries. This is especially attractive if the investing firms are looking for partners who have complementary expertise in the venture. Such international alliances may be motivated to share the risks of the venture.

RESEARCH METHOD

To compare how European, Asian, American, and Japanese ventures enter China, a database on Chinese foreign investments was developed. Two research assistants coded information on foreign ventures published in the *China Business Review* (a major professional publication on China) from 1979 to 1991. The published information contained the news releases from the Chinese Government. The coders were Chinese. One of them was born in Hong Kong while the other worked in the provincial government office in China for more than five years. The coders were interested in the topic but were not aware of the underlying propositions of the study. The coding scheme was first developed by the researchers and was modified after the coders tried the scheme. The inter-coder reliability was very high (higher than 98%) because most of the items coded were factual and little subjective judgement was needed.

These firm-specific ventures were the ones contracted, and as mentioned in previous literature (Beamish 1992; Sung and Lee 1991), the number of ventures contracted were higher than those actually carried out. One may argue that these intended ventures represent a more robust database because they were not affected by the operational and/or bureaucratic difficulties the ventures later encounter and hence were not carried out. The database complemented most of the earlier attempts on this topic (e.g., Beamish 1985; Shenkar 1990) where in-depth analyses of selected joint venture cases were reported.

Variables Coded

The entry modes of ventures were grouped into four categories: export of commodities, export of technologies, licensing (including turnkey operations and other contractual agreements), and direct investment. The ventures' country of origin (by country name), timing (month and year of the venture), size (in U.S. dollars), location (whether the venture was in Special Economic Zones, open/coastal cities, or other places), and the level of government involved (state, provincial, and municipal) were also coded. To code the type of business, a coding scheme based on Standard Industrial Classification codes was adopted. For the purpose of this chapter, the agricultural and mining ventures were excluded and all business ventures were classified into manufacturing or service ventures. To understand the strategic alliances in the ventures, whether the ventures involved the same country partner, other country partner (aside from the Asian), or the Asian partner were also coded. The database contained 3,432 firm specific ventures from 1979 to 1991 that have the full set of information described above.

FINDINGS AND DISCUSSION

Overall Pattern

Table 8.1 compares the overall characteristics of the ventures by region in China. In terms of the entry mode, European ventures had the highest percentage of export of commodities compared to the other regional groups of ventures (44.6%, row 1, column 4), while the Asian ventures had the highest percentage of ventures using the direct investment mode (67.7%, row 4, column 1). Similar to their U.S. and Japanese counterparts, the European ventures dealt more with the state government (38.3%, row 5, column 4), while the Asian ventures dealt more with the municipal government (52.9%, row 7 column 1). In terms of the choice of locations, the European, Japanese, and the U.S. ventures had similar patterns (rows 8 to 10), while the Asian ventures had the highest percentage in Special Economic Zones (19.4%, row 8 column 1). In terms of strategic alliances, the European ventures seemed to favor going in alone, as these firms had the lowest percentage of companies forming alliances among the four regional groups (rows 11 to 13); nevertheless, more of them

formed partnerships with Asians (5.3%) than with firms of their own country
(1.5%) or of non-Asian countries (1.8%).   In contrast, the Asian and the
Japanese ventures had higher percentages in forming strategic alliances. As ex-

Table 8.1. Characteristics of Foreign Business Ventures in China, by Region

	Asian Companies	Japanese Companies	US Companies	European Companies
Entry Mode	(n = 524)	(n = 905)	(n = 950)	(n = 1008)
Export of Commodity	16%	29%	37%	45%
Export of Technology	5	15	11	11
Licensing	11	22	17	23
Direct Investment	68	35	35	21
Level of Government				
State Government	18	38	41	38
Provincial Government	30	24	28	24
Municipal Government	53	37	31	36
Location				
Special Economic Zone	19	7	7	54
Open coastal cities since 1984	42	51	53	49
Others	39	43	40	46
Strategic Alliances				
Same country partner	2	13	2	2
International partner	7	3	5	2
Asian partner	7	3	4	5
Period of Ventures				
(in number of ventures)	89	210	190	198
Initial opening	269	496	487	533
Growth	101	136	207	195
Readjustment	65	63	66	82
Post June 4th				

pected, the Japanese had the highest percentage of intra-country partnerships
(12.9%), confirming the influence of "keiretsus" in Japanese corporate culture.
The Asian ventures, perhaps trying to compensate for their general lack of
advanced technologies, had the highest percentage of international partners
(7.1%).
    To further understand the phenomena, each strategic dimension was discussed
one by one with the help of more detailed tables. For the Entry Mode, results
from Table 8.2 confirmed the common belief: most of the ventures (40%, row
10, column 1) adopted export of commodities in Phase 1 and direct investments
took over in later phases of China's growth (65.9%, row 5, column 4). These

two modes of entry became increasingly dominant as time went on, growing from 64% (row 15, column 1) of all ventures in Phase 1, to 87.3% (row 15, column 4) in Phase 4. The firms' strategy was likely caused by the changes in Chinese government policy and the growth in experience firms achieved. Interestingly, however, the European ventures seemed to display the slowest

Table 8.2. Entry Mode, by Region and Phase

		Phases		
	1	2	3	4
A. Direct Investment				
Asia	52%	68%	70%	85%
Japan	18	33	49	81
United States	23	34	40	64
Europe	19	17	24	42
All Regions	24%	34%	42%	66%
B. Export Commodities				
Asian	24%	13%	23%	9%
Japanese	37	28	26	10
United States	47	34	42	18
European	44	47	41	43
All Regions	40%	33%	35%	21%
C. Direct Investment &				
Export Commodities				
Asian	75%	81%	93%	92%
Japanese	55	61	75	91
United States	70	62	65	82
Europe	63	64	65	84
All Regions	64%	67%	77%	87%

The percentage in the Table represents the percentage of all Asian ventures that use direct investment as a way to enter the Chinese market in Phase 1.

Phase 1 - Initial Opening, 1979 - June 1983
Phase 2 - Growth, July 1983 - June 1986
Phase 3 - Readjustment, July 1986 - June 1989
Phase 4 - Post June 1989, July 1989 - December 1991

change in their entry strategies. They consistenty had the highest (or close to the highest) percentage of ventures in exporting commodity and the lowest percentage in direct investments among the four regional groups in all phases. Nonetheless, their percentage in direct investment increased from 19.2% to 41.5% in Phase 4.

Table 8.3 displayed the locational choice of the foreign ventures. In this strategic dimension, the European ventures also displayed some unique characteristics. They had the lowest percentage of ventures in SEZs (3.0% in Phase 1 and 3.1% in Phase 4). While the other ventures increasingly chose to operate in open cities, the share of European ventures in these cities declined (from 56.7% in Phase 1 to 46.9% in Phase 4). There could be two alternative ex-

Table 8.3. Locations, by Region and Phase

	Phases			
	1	2	3	4
A. Special Economic				
Zone	29%	16%	18%	25%
Asia	4	7	8	6
Japan	6	6	8	9
United States	3	6	5	3
Europe	10%	8%	9%	10%
All Regions				
B. Open Cities	35%	39%	53%	46%
Asian	46	50	50	63
Japanese	51	52	56	61
United States	57	51	40	47
European	47%	49%	49%	53%
All Regions				
C. Others				
Asian	36%	46%	29%	30%
Japanese	50	43	42	32
United States	44	42	36	30
Europe	40	43	55	50
All Regions	43%	43%	42%	36%
D. A + B				
Asian	64%	54%	71%	70%
Japanese	51	57	58	69
United States	57	58	64	70
Europe	60	57	45	50
All Regions	57%	57%	58%	64%

planations. First, their experience might have given the European firms more confidence to operate in inner regions of China. Alternatively, they might choose to operate in regions of less competitive pressure.

Table 8.4 displays how foreign ventures worked with different levels of Chinese governments. Here again the European ventures adopted a different strategy—they had the highest percentage of ventures dealing with state governments (47.1% in Phase 1, 36.8% in Phase 4). Their unique strategy was well reflected in Phase 4, in which the percentage of European ventures dealing with state government increased while the percentage in all three other regional

Table 8.4. Government Levels Involved, by Region and Phase

	Phases			
	1	2	3	4
A. State Government				
Asia	16%	15%	29%	13%
Japan	31	42	38	19
United States	43	40	44	28
Europe	47	41	31	37
All Regions	36%	36%	36%	25%
B. Provincial Government				
Asian	26%	34%	22%	28%
Japanese	36	23	25	19
United States	27	28	29	23
European	22	22	30	28
All Regions	28%	26%	27%	25%
C. Municipal Government				
Asian	59%	52%	49%	59%
Japanese	33	35	37	62
United States	30	32	27	49
Europe	31	37	39	35
All Regions	36%	38%	36%	50%

groups dramatically declined. This further confirmed their risk-aversive strategy in China.

In terms of forming strategic alliances, Table 8.5 displays the percentage of firms who invited others in venturing into China. As the China market expanded, its size and complexity would likely demand more investment, and as a result, one would expect more and more firms forming alliances in China. This general belief is confirmed in Table 8.5: more and more ventures formed alliances as time went by. In Phase 1 around 10% of all ventures had alliances; the percentage jumped to 15.9% during China's readjustment period. After June 4, 1989, the percentage almost doubled to 30.7% (last row, last column). The political uncertainty in China may not be the only cause, but it is certainly an obvious contributing factor.

The European firms again displayed some unique strategies. From Phases 1 to 3, the European ventures maintained a more solitary approach in China—they had the lowest percentage in forming alliances. Even when partners were needed for potential higher risks (as in Phase 4 in China), they still had the lowest per-

Table 8.5. Strategic Alliances, by Region and Phase

	Phases			
	1	2	3	4
A. Country Partner				
Asia	2%	1%	3%	5%
Japan	18	11	16	18
United States	3	1	2	6
Europe	9	1	2	12
All Regions	4%	4%	5%	10%
B. International Partner				
Asian	6%	6%	6%	11%
Japanese	2	2	4	6
United States	2	4	5	5
European	3	2	7	24
All Regions	40%	3%	6%	12%
C. Asian Partner				
Asian	6%	6%	6%	11%
Japanese	1	2	4	6
United States	2	4	5	5
Europe	4	2	7	24
All Regions	3%	3%	6%	12%
D. All Partners				
Asian	13%	11%	20%	30%
Japanese	19	15	27	32
United States	6	11	13	18
Europe	6	4	10	42
All Regions	11%	10%	16%	31%

centage of firms forming alliances with international partners (row 9). Interestingly, more European firms seemed to join with Asian partners (row 14) than U.S. and Japanese ventures (rows 12 and 13). The change in Phase 4 was very dramatic (row 14, column 4). The percentage of European firms forming alliances jumped more than three times after June 4, 1989.

SUMMARY AND CONCLUSION

As an attempt to understand how European firms behave, the study has revealed some interesting findings. European firms seemed to follow a more risk averse strategy. They preferred the less risky export options to the higher risk and higher return direct investment option. When dealing with host governments, they tended to favor higher level governments even though such strategies sometimes demanded more time and energy. They were found to be conservative in forming strategic alliances, whether within their own group or with non-Asian international partners. When faced with potential instability, they were the quickest to react, reducing potential risks by forming alliances with other firms. These observations may be interesting inputs for future research efforts.

To investigate beyond the current study, the next step in understanding how European firms function is to classify the firms into meaningful strategic clusters (e.g., Scandinavian, Northern Continental Europe, Southern Europe, etc.). Grouping firms from 14 countries into a single unit may not be the most effective way to study how European firms behave. As Europe emerged as one of the four global trading blocs (Ohmae 1985), an in-depth understanding of how the European companies behave is needed.

In this longitudinal investigation into how foreign business ventures have entered the Chinese market, the study confirmed the significance of public policies, investment incentives, and political stability to foreign investors. The gradual introduction of free market policies (especially in SEZs and coastal cities) has been the foundation stone for the phenomenal Chinese economic growth. Together with strong commitment to modernization and guaranteed investment incentives through public regulations, many firms were motivated to enter China seeking potential markets and sources of low labor costs. Furthermore, the data showed how a single political event (June 4, 1989) could greatly change how firms behave.

REFERENCES

Aguilar, Francis J. (1988), *General Managers in Action*, New York: Oxford University Press.

Avishai, Bernard (1991), "A European Platform for Global Competition: An Interview with VW's Carl Hahn," *Harvard Business Review, 69*(4), 102-113.

Beamish, Paul W. (1985), "The Characteristics of Joint Ventures in Developed and Developing Countries," *Columbia Journal of World Business* (Winter), 13-19.

—— (1992), "The Characteristics of Joint Venture in PRC," Working Paper, Western Business School, University of Western Ontario.

Beamish, Paul W., and John C. Banks (1987), "Equity Joint Ventures and the Theory of the Multinational Enterprise," *Journal of International Business Studies, 17* (1), 1-16.

Beamish, Paul W., and H. Y. Wang (1989), "Investing in China via Joint Ventures," *Management International Review, 29* (1), 57-64.

China Statistical Yearbook, various issues since 1981.

Country Report on China, The Economist Intelligence Unit, London, various years from 1982 to 1992.

Daniels, John D., Jeffrey Krug, and Douglas Nigh (1985), "U.S. Joint Ventures in China: Motivation and Management of Political Risk," *California Management Review, 27* (4), 46-58.

Davidson, William H. (1987), "Creating and Managing Joint Ventures in China," *California Management Review, 29* (4), 77-94.

Dunning, J. H. (1988), *Explaining International Production*, London: Urwin Hyman.

The Economist (1992), "Deng Prepares China's Future" (June 22), 36.

Gerlach, Michael L. (1992), "The Japanese Corporate Network: A Block Model Analysis," *Administrative Science Quarterly, 37* (1), 105-139.

Hendryx, Steven R. (1986a), "Implementation of a Technology Transfer Joint Venture in the People's Republic of China: A Management Perspective," *Columbia Journal of World Business* (Spring), 361-374.

—— (1986b), "The China Trade: Marketing the Deal Work," *Harvard Business Review* (July/August), 75-84.

Keck, E. (1989), "Covering all the Bases: Political Risk Insurance No Longer Seems Like `Optional' Coverage," *The China Business Review* (September/October), 20-21.

Ohmae, K. (1985), *Triad Power*, New York: The Free Press.

Pearson, M. M. (1991), *Joint Ventures in the People's Republic of China*, Princeton, NJ: Princeton University Press.

Pettibone, Peter J. (1991), "Negotiating a Business Venture in the Soviet Union," *Journal of Business Strategy, 12* (1), 18-23.

Pye, L. (1982), *Chinese Commercial Negotiation Style*, Cambridge, MA: Oelgeschlager.

Quelch, John A., Robert D. Buzzell and Eric R. Salama (1990), *The Marketing Challenge of 1992*, Reading, MA: Addison-Wesley Publishing Company Ltd.

Richardson, John D. (1992), "U.K., Sweden Leading Way in European Captive Scene," *National Underwriter, 96* (10), 9, 33, 42.

Rock, Stuart (1990), "Volkschairman," *Director, 44* (3), 68-73.

Shenkar, Oded (1990), "International Joint Ventures' Problems in China: Risks and Remedies," *Long Range Planning, 23* (3), 82-90.

Studer, Margaret (1991), "Swiss Insurance Policy for European Integration," *Multinational Business, 3* (Autumn), 37-44.

Sung, Yun-Wing, and Lee Ming-Kwan, ed. (1991), *The Other Hong Kong Report 1991*, Hong Kong: Chinese University Press.

Young, S., J. Hamill, C. Wheeler, and J. R. Davies (1989), *International Market Entry and Development*, Englewood Cliffs, NJ: Prentice Hall.

Part IV

RESEARCH ON INTERNATIONAL JOINT VENTURE STRATEGIES IN WESTERN AND CENTRAL EUROPE AND RUSSIA

9

Development of International Joint Ventures in Russia: Risks and Opportunities

Vladimir L. Kvint

For 74 years of Soviet history, foreign economic activity was a monopoly of the state. Even state enterprises and industrial ministers were not authorized to have direct business relationships with foreigners. All foreign trade and foreign business cooperation belonged exclusively to two state executive bodies, the Ministry of Foreign Trade and the State Committee for Foreign Economic Ties. The former was responsible for all export and import activities, while the State Committee was responsible for Soviet investment abroad, such as construction of a cement plant in Iraq, a ferrous metallurgical facility in India, and a nickel plant in Cuba. The great majority of this activity is now in the form of unpaid debt to Russia from these countries. The total amount of debt to Russia is $64 billion, while Russian debt to foreigners is $80 billion. All activity of the state, however, was the result of political, not economic, decisions. Thus, in terms of economic implications, it was not until 1986 that foreign bodies were permitted to own property within the Soviet Union, with the exception of embassies and some foreign government trade representative offices. When foreign investors like FIAT went to Russia in 1966-1970, this was not a true form of foreign investment, but rather a trade transaction, as the USSR government bought the plant.

Inefficient economic mechanisms virtually exhausted all the natural resources that were easily extractable or harvestable. More and more inputs were required to extract the same output, which led to diminishing returns. In the USSR and its satellite countries, it was necessary to garner resources from an ever expanding geographic area; to exploit the East and North; to dig deeper to try to maintain output. The industrial structure of the USSR was based on the extensive economic model. Even Western European countries came to this meadow; Germany, France, and Italy started to drink from the river of natural gas flowing through the Siberian pipeline. Finland continued to receive its energy blood from Russia. But, the natural surface resources were depleted. The development of new oil and gas fields, and new non-ferrous metal and diamond pits required more investment and more resources, which Russia did not have. It required more workers and more equipment, neither of which Russia had. As a result, the of GNP in Russia declined every year, from 1970 through 1985. The cumulative decline was over 250%. Moreover, this economic mechanism did not stimulate the introduction of Russian scholars', scientists', and technologists' discoveries and innovations into practice. Russian achievements were more widely and more quickly put into practice in other countries. For example, the Russian invention of the continuous steel casting method for steel production is used for 90% of steel production in Japan and the United States, while in Russia, it is only used for 30%. Seventy percent of steel production in Russia is based on older, outdated methods. The same happened with Russian laser technology, for which they won the 1965 Nobel Prize, as well as with other technologies.

By the end of the 1970s, Soviet non-military plants had a technological base that was 15–20 years behind that of developed countries. While President Reagan encouraged modernization of equipment by decreasing the amortization schedule from 7 to 5 years, the rate at which Russia upgraded its own equipment was only 2% per year. As a result, the gap in levels of technical modernization between Russia and the United States and other developed countries continued to grow. The situation continued through the mid 1980s, and continues even today.

Computerization of Russian industry only began on a wide scale in the 1980s and is still essentially in the introductory stage, especially in services. It became clear that without industrial and technical cooperation with the world business community and the world market, the USSR would continue to regress compared to the rest of the developed world. This became obvious even to the bureaucrats from the Central Committee of the Communist Party, and these factors combined to bring about the birth of "perestroika" and the new winds of freedom. As a result, 1986 was the first time that the 2 state monopolies for foreign economic activity were destroyed. Industrial ministries like the Ministry of Machinery Building, the Ministry of Non-Ferrous Metals, and the Ministry of Communication and Post won the right to create foreign trading companies. Through these companies, they were authorized to sell part of their output abroad and to keep part of the export proceeds for technology development. Also, they were authorized to buy new equipment abroad.

In 1987, the 500 largest state industrial companies were accorded the same right. Finally, on January 13, 1987, a historical decision was made to permit joint ventures with the participation of foreign companies. But, ideology was so central to this decision that Gorbachev signed two decrees that day; one concerning joint ventures with participation of organizations from *socialist* countries, and one concerning joint ventures with participation of organizations from *capitalist* countries. The decrees said that up to 49% of the joint venture could belong to the foreign partner, but the foreign partner could not have its representative as the Chairman or the Director General of the joint venture. The result was that *during all of 1987, only 23 joint ventures were created, 2 of which were U.S./Russian.*

The disappointing outcome of all the changes in the USSR, and the rapid disintegration of the national economy, made it possible for market-oriented economists to prepare a draft of a new, more liberal joint venture regulation, which became law on December 2, 1988. The Communist Party bosses were kind enough to sign this decree, because they were faced with the reality that by the end of 1988, only 192 joint ventures had been established. The party bosses were amazed that more foreign companies had not come to take advantage of the Socialist Paradise. From that point forward, foreigners could occupy any position in the joint venture, and the percentage of investment was not limited. The liberalized regulations immediately gave rise to an increase in joint ventures— 1,274 by the end of 1989. Companies from Germany, Austria, and Finland, countries that had long experience and long-time economic relationships with the Soviet government, led the way.

The year 1990 saw continued growth in joint ventures which reached 2,905 by the end of the year. I started my analysis of joint venture experiences in 1988. These seven years have shown trends and problems in the creation of joint ventures. This growth is shown in Table 9.1. It was important to me because in 1988 I had participated in drafting the joint venture regulations that still form the basis of current regulations in all the former Soviet Republics. Of course, as usual, all the drafts developed by scientists, scholars, and lawyers from academic institutions were duly changed by the bureaucrats from the Central Committee of the Communist Party and the USSR Council of Ministers. Nonetheless, the final decision in December 1988 was a substantial improvement, and I felt some responsibility for it. The following are the initial conclusions of this study.

THE REASONS FOR FAILURE OF THE JOINT VENTURES IN 1988-1992

28%—inappropriate or no joint venture partner. The majority of failures result from a lack of connections and understanding of Russian business. In transitional times, it's very difficult to find a reliable partner. When foreigners cannot find a partner, they cannot create a joint venture. But, if the partner is inappropriate, weak, or not ready for international business, it is even worse. Foreigners spend considerable money for trips, negotiations, etc., and then unexpectedly find that the partner cannot solve the problems of the new enterprise in Russia or can't establish a good relationship with the local and central governments (necessary in most cases). To solve the problem, American firms can now use the services of any of the Big Six accounting and audit firms, all of which have come to Russia. KPMG was the latest to come, in 1993.

20%—financial problems. The second important point centers on the problem of a quasi-convertible ruble. Many people make this issue the cornerstone of negotiations, but this approach is incorrect. After July 15, 1992, when the Russian Central Bank organized regularly held dollar/ruble exchange auctions in Moscow, inconvertibility became less of a problem. The experience of companies that are operational in the Eurasian market shows that convertibility is not a serious issue. Rather, it is the share of initial capital investment each party

Table 9.1. Growth Rate of Joint Ventures in the Former Soviet Union

	Russia	All Republics	Total Number of Ventures
1988	NA	1.0	< 500
1989	NA	12.7	< 500
1990	NA	29.0	< 500
1991	NA	43.0	< 500
1992	31.0	37.0	500 - 1000
1993	NA	NA	NA
1994	170.0	110.0	2905

contributes to the joint venture that is the most important negotiating point. This division of investment and ownership lasts for the life of the joint venture, and parties will divide all profits according to the percentages of initial capital investment.

16%—bureaucratic problems, usually ignorance of which government officials have required authority. This problem stems from a misunderstanding of the functions and scope of activity of various government bodies, state companies, and private companies in Russia. It is very important to know when, for what reason, and to whom in government it is necessary to go, or if it is necessary to go at all. This varies according to the industry and function of the joint venture. It illustrates the importance of knowing the structure of the Russian government and the functions of various central and local government bodies.

10%—legal problems. During these transitional times, Russian law has continued to move in a positive direction, changing from totalitarian law without rights for companies to being increasingly market oriented. Legal problems in establishing joint ventures are related primarily to the format of the legal document and not to its content. For example, the Russian Ministry of Finance, which registers all joint ventures, cannot approve joint venture agreements that are written in a format other than that adopted by the Russian government. The best way to solve this problem is to use the services not only of American lawyers, but also of Russian lawyers (who are likely to be cheaper), or to use the services of American law firms that have representatives and experience in

Russia. Some of these firms are Baker and McKenzie, Debevoise and Plimpton, White and Case, and Mudge, Rose.

10%—unfavorable negotiation results, usually due to differences in mentality. Unfortunately, we must attribute 10% of failures to differences in mentality. This shows how absolutely necessary it is to have consultants with strong involvement in Russian business or Russian persons on hand who have executive experience.

Another 5% fail because of an unfavorable feasibility or market study, and other miscellaneous reasons account for the final 3%.

Effects of Changes in the Operating Environment on Joint Ventures Established During 1993 and After

Many changes have occurred. Consider the development of a market economy in Russia and the appearance of major capitalist institutions (such as insurance, banking accounting firms, and a regularly working Moscow currency exchange), and Russia's membership in multilateral organizations. Further, consider that Westerners have grown more experienced in establishing and operating businesses in Russia. And, consider that Russian business people themselves have become more experienced. There is a new level of openness in the country, and the situation has substantially changed regarding the creation of companies that have foreign capital or that are wholly owned by foreigners. The level of success of the creation of companies has more than doubled and is now at 17% instead of 8%. The reasons for failure to establish joint ventures in 1993 and 1994 were:

Bureaucratic problems—18%. The character of the bureaucracy in Russia has changed. Foreigners now are more knowledgeable of the structure of the Russian government, but the current bureaucracy is one of the most corrupt. So, now the bureaucratic problems are strongly related to corruption.

Financing problems—16%. Again, the character of financial problems has changed. Now, the issue is not with convertibility of the currency, but rather related to inflation and the devaluation of the ruble.

No partner found—15%. The drop in this reason from 28% to 15% reflects the fact, again, that both Western and Russian business people are growing more adept at working together. In addition, improvements in the communications systems, particularly in data services which are available, has made information more accessible to both Russians and Westerners.

Legal problems—10%. This issue has not changed greatly.

Unfavorable negotiations—13%. While this has increased somewhat, the character of the issue is basically the same.

Unfavorable feasibility/market study and other problems—11%. Again, these issues have not changed greatly.

LOCATION OF JOINT VENTURES WITH FOREIGN COMPANIES' PARTICIPATION (PARTICULARLY FROM CAPITALIST COUNTRIES)

These firms were strongly influenced by their understanding of the risk of investing in Russia, especially the political risks. During 1989, 85% of all joint ventures created were located in Moscow, 10% were in St. Petersburg, and only 5% were scattered over all the other territory of the former USSR! This results from foreigners' perception that the highly centralized Soviet government structure was still very much in place; that the iron curtain was not just an image, but a virtual reality. Companies tried to be close to the government and, as a result, most of the offices were set up in central Moscow. However, there was no economic reason or basis for this decision. Lack of information on other locations prohibited the joint ventures from being set up elsewhere. Foreigners only knew that Moscow was the center for all activity and did not want to be far from it.

At the same time, joint ventures in the Russian Far East and Siberia (a territory larger than the United States or Canada) accounted for only 1% of all joint venture activity (12 of more than 1,200 ventures). This showed that foreigners had no information regarding the social and economic processes that were taking place in the ruined Soviet Union, as it approached its end. The political risk of investment is much lower in the Far East and Siberia than in Moscow and St. Petersburg. The Far East population is very involved in the political struggle and where nationalists and pseudo-patriots have created centers of joint venture activity.

The disintegration of the Soviet Union seriously changed the whole process of the creation of joint ventures. A summary of these changes are shown in Table 9.2. By 1992, 34% of the joint ventures created were in Moscow. During the same period, the percentage of joint ventures in other regions of Russia increased by only 4%. Serious changes in the Baltic States, however, caused the number of joint ventures created there to increase markedly. The Lithuanian Parliament's Declaration of Independence in March 1990 showed the world community that the Baltic States were on their way to a market economy. Investors found that joint ventures in the Baltic States enjoyed a more stable environment. But, the Baltic States lack sufficient economic factors to contribute to the high degree of profitability possible with Russian joint ventures. The Baltic States have no natural resources, the process of privatization is behind Russia's, and the economic conditions are not oriented toward attracting foreign investment, but rather toward development of domestic entrepreneurial business. This became especially clear at the end of 1991, when almost 68% of joint ventures in the Baltic States worked as intermediaries for exporting Russian raw materials or products like non-ferrous metals, although the Baltic States do not produce non-ferrous metals. However, for foreigners, it was the easiest way to receive non-ferrous metals without export licenses from the Russian government. But in 1993, this type of business with Russia decreased greatly because 1) the Russian government established borders with the Baltic States, 2) the Russian government created customs posts with the Baltic States, and 3) it became easier to receive export licenses from the Russian government to sell products in countries *outside* the former Soviet republics, than it to sell in the former Soviet republics. It has at last been understood by Russia that going directly to the world market with its products eliminates the middle man, and higher profits can be made. In 1993, the Baltic States' participation in this type of business decreased to 5% of the total number of joint ventures.

The growth in the number of joint ventures has been very stable in Ukraine, Kazakhstan, Turkmenistan, and Kyrgyzstan. This will continue from 1995-1997, particularly in Kyrgyzstan, Turkmenistan, Kazakhstan, and Belarus. Regulations

Table 9.2. Location of International Joint Venture Former Soviet Republics and Cities

Areas	1990	1991	1992	1994
Russia (Total)	74%	76%	56%	61%
Moscow	54	46	34	NA
St. Petersburg	8	9	3	NA
Ukraine	7	8	10	13
Georgia	4	2	2	1
Baltic States	9	17	16	6
Moldvoa	1	1	1	1
Armenia	1	1	1	1
Belarus	2	1	3	3
Kazakhstan	2	2	5	7
Turkmenistan	NA	NA	NA	4
Uzbekistan	NA	NA	4	5
Other Republics	1	2	6	5

in these states have stimulated foreign investment much more effectively than in other republics. Kyrgyzstan is the first of the former republics to permit foreigners to buy land, and the political situation there is more stable than in the European part of Russia.

The number of joint ventures in Moldova, Azerbaijan, Armenia, and Georgia has been insubstantial until now, and will, in fact, decrease due to the civil war in Moldova, and the strife between Azerbaijan and Armenia, and between Georgia and the Abkhaz Republic. Armenian business leaders living abroad tried to create joint ventures in Armenia, but the war and energy shortage (almost a complete lack of energy) halted any joint venture activity.

In November 1994, 28,000 joint ventures with foreign participation or wholly-owned foreign companies have been established in the former USSR, with 17,000 of these in Russia. Creating joint ventures is more difficult (only 8% of efforts were successful from 1988-1992, and in 1993, only 17% of efforts were successful) than reaching profitability (32%-35% of joint ventures, once created, are profitable, which is much higher than the rate of profitability in the United States).

INDUSTRIES

When Russian joint ventures began, the majority were concentrated in a few industries.

Intermediaries

These joint ventures do what the state can't. They buy raw materials and industrial waste from Russia and sell it abroad. The first legal Russian millionaires came from this business. Companies have played a large role in this industry because they receive money from foreign firms for disposing of industrial waste. Moreover, Russian industrial waste can very valuable. For example, one U.S. company extracted 60 pounds of gold from 10 tons of microelectronics scrap. In 1992, this type of joint venture activity increased considerably. In 1993, 43% of all joint ventures attempted to play an intermediary role as a part of their activities.

Software

Another very profitable area for joint ventures, especially between 1987 and 1991, has been software. All of the giants, such as IBM, Microsoft, and Lotus, came to Russia and created distribution companies. These companies have utilized Russian engineering and scientific achievements. Software has been customized and translated for the Russian market. In addition, joint venture activity in the computer industry, particularly with firms from the United States, Japan, Taiwan, and South Korea, has increased substantially in Russia and has focused mainly on final assembly of computers. The shortage of computers in Russia created an interesting phenomenon regarding payment terms: Russian customers (state, private sector, and cooperatives) agreed to buy computers for hard currency because the locally assembled computers utilized inexpensive Russian labor and therefore, were slightly cheaper than imported computers. However, once the initial urgent need for computers had been satisfied, computers and software were then sold for rubles. In addition, the July 1992 introduction of the currency exchange market enabled the vendors to convert their ruble earnings rather easily.

Heavy Industrial Production

There was a great increase in the number of joint ventures involved in heavy industrial production, particularly in Russia, then in Kazakhstan. In Russia, the majority of industrial joint ventures are connected to the enrichment of natural resources from raw materials from industrial waste, and with the conversion of military plants. Instead of building tanks in Saratov, they now build busses. Likewise, facilities for building military electronics have been converted to TV production, while facilities that produced precision equipment for submarines now produce sewing machines.

Travel and Tourism

More and more joint ventures are appearing in the tourism and hotel industry. Prior to 1991, most of this activity was in the European part of Russia, the Baltic States, the Ukraine, and even Georgia. Now, northern Russia, Siberia, and the Russian Far East see a great deal of activity.

Research and Development

In 1992 and 1993, an explosion of growth in R&D occurred. Foreigners began to understand and take advantage of the great resources to be found in Russian scientists' and scholars' achievements, inventions, and knowledge. The number of joint ventures in this area skyrocketed. Firms, like Bell Labs, are working with Russian scientists to study space, electronics, optics, lasers, and nuclear energy. Some of the joint ventures concentrate solely on the transfer of Russian technology and patents.

Telecommunications

Telecommunications problems were major barriers to the development and internationalization of Russian business. But, because telecom is a very profitable business, because it is easy to develop this business, and because many military communication systems have been and continue to be converted to civilian use, telecommunications has become one of the most internationalized industries.

Other

There has been a significant growth in the development of the insurance, banking, accounting and auditing, and social services industries. For example, many large insurance companies are in the process of creating joint ventures. AIG was the first; it created a joint venture with the Russian military pension fund in October 1994. Only 12 foreign banks, including Credit Lyonnais, Chase Manhattan, and Citibank, have been awarded a domestic license to take deposits. The creation of joint ventures are just beginning in the health industry. Construction is a very attractive industry, with heavy participation from Turkish, Finnish, Austrian, and Polish companies.

SIZE

At the same time, the number of joint ventures with capital of more than $10 million has decreased, as more and more small businesses go to Russia. Because of the limitation on foreign insurance firms' activities in Russia and in all other republics except Belarus and Kyrgyzstan, President Yeltsin signed a decree in February 1993 regarding the creation of the State Investment Company. This company will insure foreign investment in Russia from political risk. It appears that this will increase the size of foreign investments in joint ventures in Russia.

COUNTRIES

Currently, companies from two nations dominate Russian joint venture business—Germany and the United States. A summary of the countries engaged in Russian joint venture business is found in Table 9.3. The growth in the number of German companies has been smooth and steady, while the U.S. growth was spurred on in 1992 by the failure of the 1991 coup. But Germany was strongly involved with investment in East Germany and with new opportunities given to Germany by the creation of the European Union. As a result, the activity of Germany in Russia has slowed somewhat. German companies continue to build joint ventures in Russia, but the rate of growth has declined.

The failed coup attempt also gave U.S. firms more confidence that democracy would reign, that the market would open, and that U.S. firms would become the leading investors in Russia. Italy has also been very active in the European parts of Russia and in the Ukraine. Great Britain is very strong player in Russia and Azerbaijan. But the reality is that Americans and Europeans, because of new opportunities afforded by NAFTA and the creation of the European Union, will face a shortage of capital for investing in Russia.

When the joint venture process first began, Japan was very involved, especially in the Russian Far East. The majority of Japanese companies that came to the Russian market were oriented toward working with their old government contacts and with groups that they had already established contacts with. However, the Japanese suffered the same setback as Occidental Petroleum, an American company. Their approach did not work because most of the old bureaucrats and bribe takers had retired or lost power, something for which the Japanese were unprepared. Then, the Japanese government started to link investment with political decisions regarding the Kurile Islands. Both of these business decisions have combined to substantially lower the influence of Japan and Japanese firms on joint venture activity in Russia. It was not a surprise when, under this pressure, Yeltsin canceled his planned trip to Japan in the fall of 1992. Japan also recognizes now that it faces strong competition in Russia, and especially in the Russian Far East, from South Korea, Singapore, Taiwan, and, beginning in 1993, from China. After Yeltsin's 1993 visit to China, a Russian/Chinese

Table 9.3. International Joint Ventures in the Former Soviet Republics by Investing Country

Country	1990	1991	1993
Germany	15%	14%	13%
USA	10	13	17
Former Comecom Countries	8	7	7
Finland	7	7	5
Italy	9	6	5
Austria	6	6	5
Great Britain	NA	6	6
Switzerland	NA	4	3
South Korea	NA	NA	3
Japan	2	1	2
France	NA	NA	2
China	NA	NA	3
Other EC Countries	17	19	17
Others	19	17	13

business relationship quickly developed. South Korea's position in the Russian Far East and in Kazakhstan, where many ethnically Korean people live, is also quite strong. South Korean firms are building good relationships with the Korean community in Russia, using them as a source of market knowledge and assistance. As a result, in 1993, Japanese leaders revised their policy regarding Russia and reduced the pressure over the Kurile Islands; this resulted in new opportunities for Russian/Japanese business relations. This will enable Japanese to come to the Kurile Islands, at least as joint venture partners. The Kurile Islands became a free economic zone, and I hope some Japanese companies will have special privileges there.

An interesting process began in the Caucuses and in the Russian Central Asian republics, where 50 million Muslims live. One could say that the Muslim business connection grew very quickly. Companies from Iran, Saudi Arabia, Kuwait, and the United Arab Emirates, as well as from Turkey, are fiercely competing in this area. These business relationships also have a political side, and it is clearly very important for the world community to protect this region from strong Islamic Fundamentalist influence. It is, therefore, important to help companies who are in this region for economic reasons, not because of political or religious agendas. From that point of view, the Turkish government plays a very important role.

ROLE OF MULTILATERAL INSTITUTIONS FOR FOREIGN INVESTORS IN RUSSIA

In 1992, an historic event occurred for Russia; it became a member of the IMF and World Bank. This was important not only for monetary reasons, but also because it was a major indication of Russia's movement toward supporting civilized, modern international business and of Russia's readiness to abide by international economic and business conditions. The IMF and the World Bank were created in July 1944, under to an agreement signed at Bretton Woods, New Hampshire. (Later, the International Finance Corporation and Multilateral Investment Guarantee Agency were created.) For 50 years these institutions have been working to coordinate and create cooperation between developed countries and emerging democracies. Of course, conditions are different than they were 50 years ago, but these institutions continue their goal of helping to create a free, market-based economy and a stable economic foundation in third world countries, developing countries, and post-Communist countries. In 1944, the Soviet Union had the opportunity to become a founding member of this organization, and Stalin sent his representatives to several meetings. But then he decided that these institutions were "too imperialist" for USSR participation, and for 48 years the Soviet Union remained outside of the circle of legal international economic and financial institutions. But at the end of the Soviet Union, the Soviet and then Russian leaders found that the IMF and World Bank were two of the major resources for additional out-of-pocket expense money, and they started to use these institutions. In April 1992, leaders of the Western countries, especially Presidents Bush and Kohl, initiated a proposal providing $24 billion in aid to Russia. In July 1992, the IMF met to make a decision whether or not to issue this money to Russia. But the bureaucratic mechanisms of these institutions were not much better than those of the Communist bureaucracy, and so as of March 1995, the money still has not been issued or delivered in full.

Of course, the major problem of these multilateral institutions is their mechanisms. They are oriented toward working only with the governments of countries, not with private companies and entrepreneurial institutions in recipient countries. As a result, money flows to inexperienced governments who have few or no people who understand a capitalist economy. It is like sending money "down a rat hole." Membership in the IMF and World Bank, however, provided a large number of advisors and new conditions to Russia, which had a tremendous influence on the activity of the government there. Especially important has been the role of the IMF and the World Bank in developing an economic and business information system in Russia. They have created a system for calculating economic indicators. Russians representatives and a Russian Executive Director were appointed to work with the agencies, in what was in basically an educational experience. Unfortunately, the IMF and the World Bank, especially during their initial involvement from 1991-1993, had a long-standing, primitive understanding of the processes in Russia. As a result, their recommendations led to negative results along with the positive. One dramatic example occurred in 1992.   The inexperienced Mr. Gaidar was appointed as Acting Prime Minister and inexperienced IMF advisors gave him recommendations. At the urging of Gaidar, who knew little of Russian business and economy, the Russian government made a decision to liberalize prices before demonopolization of the economy, before conversion of the military industry to civilian production, and before privatization.   This policy led, not to the liberalization of prices, but to an immediate dramatic increase in prices. Prices for meat, milk, clothes, and all basic needs jumped sky-high. People were no longer able to feed their own family on their salaries. Executives, including joint venture executives, *had* to increase salaries.

At this moment, IMF "experts" recommended that the Russian treasury not print new ruble bills. As a result, they worsened the situation. In addition to inflation, Russia was also hit by deflation. Due to the IMF recommendations, banks simply didn't have enough currency. For many companies, salaries went unpaid for 6 to 8 months, leading to civil disobedience.   Companies issued billions of rubles of IOUs instead of salaries to employees, and people lost all incentive to work. Finally, the Gaidar government understood that they had to print money, contrary to all the recommendations of the IMF and World Bank. They started to put into circulation new money each month, in amounts far exceeding what was already in circulation. This had a very negative influence on foreign companies which went, or tried to go, to Russia.

This illustrates that not all recommendations pertinent to, for example, Latin America will also be pertinent to former Soviet bloc countries. Moreover, if a recommendation leads to good results in Poland, one cannot assume it will work well in Russia. For example, in Poland, the so-called "shock therapy" has produced results that were bad, but not as bad as the results in Russia. Why? Because in Poland, even in Communist times, almost all agriculture, and almost 40% of the economy, was in private hands in the former Soviet Union; less than 4% of agriculture was in private hands. In general, all generations in Poland remember capitalism, because Communism was only instated 45 years ago. In Russia, Communism reigned for 74 years.

This is one of the examples of the dangerous activity of the IMF and World Bank, which go to each country with standard methods and procedures, without an understanding of how to make recommendations that are specific to the situation at hand. And Western advisors who have spent not even a year or two in Russia, put in their own two cents. This can be dangerous because their understanding of the circumstances, based perhaps on only a few weeks of business trips, is likely to be insufficient. At this point, the situation speaks for itself; it is necessary to change the mechanism of activity of these multilateral institutions.

Time has shown that the world business community needs a new mechanism to solve large-scale economic and business problems. First, this mechanism must be much more flexible. Second, the time between making political decisions and putting the decisions into practice must be shorter. Third, the mechanism must be oriented toward private capital and entrepreneurs, and not toward governments.

The world is giving birth to many institutions that work for a time and then die. Some of the organizations, especially regional groups, are functioning well. But, a global institution is evolving—the regularly scheduled meeting of the leading seven industrial countries of Canada, France, Germany, Great Britain, Italy, Japan, and the United States. In most cases, during the meetings the G7 leaders made good political decisions, but not all of the decisions are implemented. Economic decisions are usually made without input from economists and are not as sound. It would be smart to evaluate the price of the politicians' economic decisions. Unfortunately, most think that they are just as qualified to make economic decisions as to make decisions about soccer or football games, where they are also not professionals. But naturally, this attitude lays the ground work for mistakes to be made and is part of the reason why decisions are not implemented. At the same time, the world may be fortunate that the decisions are not implemented.

How might the G7 meetings be made into a workable global institution? These meetings of the greatest powers in the world have tremendous potential. It is necessary to convert these meetings to a real institution and create a mechanism for implementing the resulting decisions. The leaders allocate money, but it is usually not delivered to the intended recipient countries. Why? Because the meeting is a good forum for political decisions, not for economic decisions. By developing the G7 meetings into an institution, the resulting decisions will benefit from economic input and implementation will be improved. Just as an army has a strategic branch and an operational branch, I could say the difference between institutions with 50 years of experience, like the IMF and World Bank, and the new institutions will be their time frame. G7, as an institution, should be oriented toward short-term goals. But, G7 will try to protect its strategic role, and so the answer to the dilemma of an appropriate mechanism for implementing strategic decisions is simple and already exists; the traditional Bretton Woods institutions.

Many plans to attack global problems must now be implemented on a regional level. Several new regional institutions have appeared, such as EBRD, the European Bank for Reconstruction and Development. When the Soviet Union, in 1989 and early 1990, participated in negotiations with other leading countries to create this institution, the Soviet leaders tried to create just one more source of loans. But, then some Party bureaucrats understood that in order to play an important role in this bank, and not just act as a country with its hand out, it was necessary to invest amounts comparable to that which other leading countries were investing. And, they finally did it. As a result, EBRD became one of the first institutions where the former Soviet Union, and now Russia, plays a role not only as a recipient, but also as a decisionmaker. Unfortunately, this institution did not properly focus its activity. As a result, EBRD is not terribly visible in post-Communist countries. In addition, the fact that they are also active in Asia, which is not part of Europe, is a mistake not only of a geographic nature. Multilateral institutions, global and regional, do not give any special attention to the Central Asian republics, and so a very dangerous situation has evolved—

because countries like Iran and Iraq *do* give these republics special attention. As a result, through business activities, the political influence of Iran and Iraq has increased in this part of the world. It seems it is necessary to create a Central Asian institution to work with these republics, and perhaps to work with the southern part of Siberia and the Russian Far East. Now, for the first time in history, Central Asia is comprised of established, independent countries. They don't yet play a geo-political role, nor are they yet a major target of the world business community, but both will happen within the next ten years. In addition, large multinational corporations are not wasting time. They are already investing in this part of the world.

Another very important point for business people is to understand that multilateral institutions are not world institutions. Many countries, even with formal participation in the World Bank, are not recipients of funding. For example, of the Eastern European countries, Poland has the best connections with the multilateral institutions, and then perhaps Hungary and Romania. But Bulgaria definitely lies outside the vista of these agencies. To them, Bulgaria is like a forgotten land in Central Europe. As a result, international business is only very slowly focusing on this country. And business people have not yet benefited from this country—one that offers a relatively stable political environment and significant opportunities for business. There are of course, several possibilities as to why this happened—they did not have lobbyists (which are very important), and they had to pay more attention to settling debt with the Paris and London Clubs. But these are not the reasons. The main reason Bulgaria has been all but forgotten is that the Bretton Woods Institution does not have a sound strategy. If we are to speak about the immediate future, an ironic picture could take shape: One or two of the biggest beggars and recipients, Russia and China, will also be key players among country donors. The G7 could soon be G8 or even G9, with Russia and China as participants. In the Paris Club, Russia will be a full member, in spite of Russian debt. This new reality has to be in the forefront of the minds of business leaders. It is very important to understand that any political decision made by the G7 is not like news of a football game, but can provide an opportunity to earn money.

CONCLUSION

Foreigners have gained experience. More and more information is available to the world regarding this market—from newspapers, newsletters, and magazines that sprout like mushrooms after the spring rains. Regulations in the former USSR are developing more and more quickly. The limits put on foreigners are diminishing. Foreign business people have become the darlings of the Russian, Kazakhstan, and Kyrgyzstan business communities.

The form of joint ventures has changed from simple incorporated firms to firms that are privately and publicly held by shareholders. In 1993-1994, the process of transforming joint ventures to wholly owned subsidiaries of foreign firms began. Also, 1993-1994 saw the flight of mining companies to Siberia and the Russian Far East to mine nonferrous and precious metals, oil, and gas. Russia, Ukraine, Kazakhstan, Turkmenistan, and Kyrgyzstan have many small foreign businesses investing in the food processing and services industry, as it becomes easier to convert rubles to hard currency.

The failure of the the coup and the formal disbanding of the Communist Party also played a catalytic role in the future of foreign investment and especially regarding American joint ventures. Americans believed that the political risk in Russia had lowered. Between 1992 and 1994, there was a marked increase in the creation of American joint ventures, with America having invested more than any other country. In terms of capital invested, Germany tied with the United States. By March 1995, the number of American joint ventures or wholly-owned American companies in the former Soviet Union will exceed 4,000.

There are many misconceptions about foreign investment in Russia. One of them is that while all joint ventures are registered entities on paper, none of them is actually in operation. This is a fallacy. While both exports and imports were fairly low and consistent (below $1,000,000) through 1992, both skyrocketed thereafter. By June 1993, imports had jumped to nearly six billion, while exports increased nearly three times to three billion.

One may wonder how it is possible that imports of joint ventures are three times higher than exports. Where are they getting the hard currency to make this possible? The answer is the following: executives of joint ventures are afraid to take money from their exports and put it in Russian banks due to prior negative experiences, e.g., when Vnesheconombank froze accounts in 1991-1992.

As a result, the real exports of joint ventures are approximately four times higher than the official figures on this table, while import figures are correct. Money for imports is generally held by the joint venture in foreign banks abroad. As a result, officially, imports are higher than exports. According to my estimate, Russian joint ventures have approximately $8 billion in foreign banks abroad.

The period of 1994-1995 will also be a time for transportation firms and telecom giants like U.S. West, AT&T, Cable and Wireless, MCI, Sprint, Alcatel, and Italtel to create a new infrastructure and business environment, enabling the next phase of internationalization of business in the former Soviet Union.

The Soviet Union is dead and in its place are newly emerging markets that have just started to be really open for foreign investment. Competition in these markets is a new occurrence. One form of a successful firm is a joint venture that is properly prepared and whose operations management is appropriate to the conditions in this new business world.

10

Foreign Investment and Joint Ventures in the Former Yugoslavia, 1967–1990: A Success Story in Southeastern Europe

Mile B. Jovic

The practice of joint business investment in the world is rather diversified. However, the modalities and characteristics of individual national or regional solutions remain within the framework determined by the specific economic, political, and legal environments as well as the marketing practices. Therefore, there are procedural and status-related differences in individual solutions in connection with the capitalization of investment, ownership, operational activity, foreign exchange and financial operations, accounting records and control, fiscal obligations, management, etc. In fact, it all depends on the relation the host country has toward foreign investment as a model of performing international business activities of specific enterprises on the market and, accordingly, on the relation that affects or shapes the decision to embark on such a venture. This is true despite the fact that the key role in the company's decision on applying such a modality of business operation is determined by the market factors.

These few factors have considerably influenced the defining of national joint venture models, particularly in countries that have opted for such a practice in the rather recent past. Therefore, among the basic goals to which individual countries are striving are:

—acquisition of new technology and/or technical know-how,
—expansion of the export sector of the economy and, consequently, an increase in foreign exchange earnings,
—import substitution and on this basis economizing where the outflow of foreign exchange is concerned,
—provision of foreign capital,
—provision of managerial know-how for enterprises,
—modernization of the domestic industrial basis,
—creating new jobs, increased labor productivity, and training of personnel in the economic sector,

—better economy in employment, material spending, energy, financial, and other sources with an increase in profitability.

It is within this framework that the basic determinants of individual national models should be sought. Many national JV models are based on favoring the minority concept as a form of foreign partner's participation. In many cases this may produce a destimulating effect as many international companies are not ready to accept a weaker position in decisionmaking and control. But this does not automatically mean that the minority share is simultaneously an inferior position for the second partner; today international companies do not always need a majority share in order to control the joint venture (Roman and Puett 1983).

While the experience of market economies in joint venture arrangements is relatively uniform, in the East, there are higher rates of cooperation between two partners who have known each other for several years. In other words, in the developed market economies, the application of the joint venture concept on a specific market is the integral part of the marketing strategy in the companies' international business operation. In their relations with partners from the less developed or the former socialist countries, this makes a part of the marketing policy of every enterprise the consideration of the considerable market limitations and limits of the character of business in these countries. Therefore, where joint venture arrangements with developing or socialist countries are concerned, only specific firms from market economy countries got involved in such arrangements. Besides entrance into a specific market, cooperation exists for a number of other reasons (obsolete technology, fleeing from competition in their own market, expansion into certain areas, etc.). This practice was also very much supported by the orientation in developing individual national JV models—also the case with the former socialist bloc, better known as CMEA countries, and with the former Yugoslavia. Prior to 1989 the number of joint ventures in CMEA countries and Yugoslavia was fairly low relative to other types of contracts. In 1989 joint ventures exceeded other types of contracts for the first time.

Considering the JV practice in the Yugoslav economy in the years 1967-1990, several basic characteristics may be clearly distinguished:

—experience in legal regulation and directing of international business operations of domestic enterprises through joint business investment for a period of over 20 years was evident,
—until recently the economic policy and legislation had been committed to the practice of nonproprietary investment, i.e., contractual or non-equity joint ventures, a concept abandoned with legislation in 1988,
—the legal possibilities created for such a type of business activity were, in fact, the first experiences of this kind in the group of former socialist countries (for instance, Romania and Hungary in the 1970s; Bulgaria, Poland, Czechoslovakia and the USSR in the 1980s).

The importance of joint ventures in Yugoslavia became particularly evident from 1965 on, with the implementation of the economic reform measures. Legal provisions directly regulating the foreign engagement in the Yugoslav economy were adopted in 1967, and amended and adjusted several times (in 1973, 1976, 1978, 1984, 1986, and 1988). In fact, the legislation regulating the investment of foreign partners resources in Yugoslav enterprises evolved through four stages, namely:

Stage 1:   from 1967 to 1976 and/or 1978;
Stage 2:   from 1978 to 1984;
Stage 3:   from 1984 to 1986 and/or 1988;
Stage 4:   from 1989, with the adoption/passage of the new JV Law
                  (parallel with the company law).

All these stages have distinct characteristics and a specific profile.

In the first stage there was a fairly liberal approach to the conclusion of contracts on investment in domestic organizations, giving a rather wide autonomy where relations between partners were concerned. The second stage had an expressly restrictive orientation; it contributed, in fact, to the slowdown of the pace and the dynamics of the national economy in this sphere due to considerable restrictions in the autonomy of the parties. The third stage may be defined as a repeat effort of the official economic policy to liberalize those regulations between Yugoslav and foreign companies in the country, but such legislation had a rather limited scope with no particular results. The fourth stage is connected with the change of the complete legal regime and regulations in the sphere of foreign economic relations and, within this context, the issue of joint ventures as well. It is a comprehensive set of activities aimed at introducing changes in the national economy, initiated in 1988, continuing through 1989, until the outbreak of political problems that were the beginning of the process of disintegration of the then Yugoslav federation. The fourth stage ended in 1990/1991, when new states, still not fully shaped, emerged in the former Yugoslavia.

In former Yugoslavia, the business practice and legal regulations governing this sphere were based on some fundamental principles:

—joint risk sharing of the partners, meaning that the risk was proportionate to the share of the individual partner's investment,
—the long-term quality of the investment (it was not an ad hoc or individual foreign trade transaction),
—provision of legal security to the foreign partner based on the Yugoslav constitution, and
—the need for the adjustment of the joint venture to the social development plan and the responsibilities accepted by the domestic enterprise.

The specific features of foreign investment and joint ventures resulted from the characteristics of the economic and political system of the country. The

Yugoslav joint venture model required the fulfillment of the following conditions:

—the foreign partner invested his resources in domestic organizations with the aim of achieving joint business objectives,
—the resources were invested at joint risk,
—decisions concerning joint business operations were taken by the foreign partner's and domestic organization's mutual consent,
—the resources invested were restituted depending on the results of joint business operation, which means there was no guarantee for the restitution of all the invested resources except through successful operation on the market,
—the foreign partner received its share of the profits obtained through joint business operation.

The fundamental principles of this Yugoslav joint venture model were de facto based on the following elements:

—the defined (minimum) share of the domestic partner and the limits for the foreign investor,
—the respect for the workers' rights stemming from the constitution,
—full protection of the foreign investor's rights stemming from the investment arrangement,
—the proportionate share in the distribution of profits or in the losses incurred, and guarantee when repatriation of capital was concerned,
—equal treatment for both partners without discrimination when their legal and business status was concerned.

The characteristics of the Yugoslav legal system also resulted in the essential differences between the investment of foreign persons' resources into domestic enterprises and similar investments in other countries. These differences based on the characteristics of such investments in Yugoslavia in the 1967-1988 period manifested themselves in the following:

—the investment of a foreign person's resources under such a model did not affect the regime of social ownership in Yugoslavia,
—the foreign investor had no proprietary rights over the invested resources,
—the activities in the joint business-managing body, regulated and defined by the contract, did not provide any opportunity for the disruption of self-management in the newly created joint organization,
—by the investment of the foreign person's resources, the organizational form of business operations was not changed as no mixed enterprise or corporation was established,
—the mutual relations between investors were based on a contract (in writing, approved), so that for the definition and determination of the rights and obligations, the rules of the contractual right were in force (regardless of the fact

that regulation of some issues from the sphere of the status right was also involved).

Through such a structure, a community of interests and business objectives was de facto created; the overall rations between the partners were regulated by the joint venture contract expressing the meeting of minds based on the legal regulations in force. All the regulations envisaged a joint venture contract, which was given a central position in the regulation of investment of foreign resources.

The Yugoslav joint venture model experienced substantial amendments with the adoption of the Joint Venture Law at the end of 1988. This Law introduced two legal joint venture models already known in legal and economic systems in other countries as contractual and equity joint ventures. The former of the two models was known in the Yugoslav practice while the latter presented a novelty, in line with the orientation toward change.

Until the new Law had been adopted, the investment of foreign persons' resources in Yugoslavia was not treated as direct or portfolio foreign investments, because the investment by the foreign person did not give them the right of ownership, control, or management. The only similarity to direct investment was that the foreign person, on the basis of his investment into the Yugoslav enterprise, secured an active relationship in the operation and business activities of the organization into which his resources were invested, with the aim being the realization of both partners' long-term economic interests.

According to the Law mentioned above, foreign persons may invest assets with a view to performing economic and social activities in the form of foreign exchange, things, rights and dinars (Yugoslavia funds) that are accorded to foreign exchange regulations transferable abroad. A foreign investor may also invest dinars acquired through the buy-out and conversion of obligations arising from specific foreign credits (direct conversion of external debt into share capital in an existing enterprise or bank) and through other forms, in conformity with the regulations governing foreign credit relations.

A foreign investor has rights as specified by contract and, in particular, the right:

—to manage or take part in the management of the business of the enterprise concerned, proportionally to the assets invested,
—to transfer the contractual rights and obligations to other domestic or foreign investors,
—to share in profits proportionally to the resources invested and to free transfer and reinvestment of such profits,
—to the return of individual things invested, provided he has explicitly retained this right in the investment contract,
—to the return of the share capital invested, i.e., what has remained from the resources invested in a socially-owned enterprise (SOE),
—to a share in net assets and the repatriation of this share if he has invested resources in a mixed enterprise after the dissolution of such enterprise.

The rights of foreign investors arising from resources invested (the rights established by the investment contract and enterprise bylaw) are protected and may not be curtailed by any other law or regulation. An enterprise with foreign investment has the same status, rights, and responsibilities as any other domestic entity.

The foreign investor may invest resources in:

—an SOE,
—mixed enterprise (joint-stock company, limited liability company, limited partnership, and company with unlimited joint and several liability),
—private enterprise and private shop,
—bank or other financial organization,
—cooperative,
—insurance organization,
—other forms of cooperation and joint business as specified by the Company Law.

A foreign person may also establish a wholly-owned enterprise.

Investments by foreign persons are regulated by investment contract or memorandum of association. Investment contract regulates mutual relations of the investors and it has to be made in writing. An investment contract or a memorandum of association may be made for a specified or indefinite period of time.

An investment contract shall particularly contain:

—contracting parties,
—the object of enterprises' business,
—the amount of resources invested by each investor and mode of determining the share of each investor in total investment,
—the form of investing and/or what the share capital consists of,
—the designation of the enterprise in which investments are made if it already exists, or of the kind of the enterprise to be established,
—the mode of distribution of profits and mode of covering the enterprise's losses,
—the mode of decisionmaking by the investors,
—the duration of the investment contract,
—the mode of the return of the share capital, and
—settlement of disputes.

A memorandum of association in a mixed enterprise shall in particular contain:

—contracting parties,
—the object of the company's business,
—the nominal capital of the company and the parties' share in it,
—investments that are made in a joint-stock company,
—the type of shares and the bank through which they are issues,
—the bodies of the company and representation of the investors in them,

—the duration of the company,
—a possible obligation of the domestic investor to buyout share capital or shares, and
—settlement of disputes.

Investors shall have the right to inspect the books of the enterprise in which they have invested resources, in the way specified in the investment contract and its bylaws, and/or to audit annual statements of accounts themselves, or to have them audited by authorized representatives.

Foreign banks, other foreign financial organizations, and investors may invest in insurance organizations, banks, and other financial organizations, or they may establish joint banks, insurance organizations, or some other financial organizations and jointly invest in them. Investing in insurance companies, banks, and other financial organizations is regulated by a specific statute.

A foreign investor may also establish a wholly-owned enterprise, in the way and under conditions upon which domestic persons may establish private enterprises. A foreign investor may *not* establish a wholly-owned enterprise 1) for the manufacture and distribution of armaments and military equipment; 2) in rail and air transport, communications and telecommunications, insurance, publishing and mass media; or 3) in areas that are designated as significant to the total national defense for the security of the country. An investment contract shall be reported to the Ministry for Foreign Economic Relations; to establish a wholly-owned enterprise, the foreign investor shall obtain an approval from the same Ministry (the investment contract shall be submitted together with an outline of the expected effects of the investment), which assesses the conformity of the memorandum of association with the Constitution and the Law on Foreign Investments and renders a ruling within 30 days from the date of receipt of the contract.

Any reinvestment of the profit of, or any additional investment by, a foreign investor, or any transfer of foreign share capital from one to another person (the expiration of the validity of the investment contract or the memorandum of association, and/or other important changes in status) shall be reported to the Ministry for Foreign Economic Relations, and the original and translation of the relevant document shall be delivered to it within 30 days from the date the document was signed.

According to the Law on Corporation Profits Tax, each newly founded enterprise (which when founded employs at least 50% of the unemployed workers registered with the Employment Bureau) shall be exempt from the corporation profit tax (the regular profit tax rate is 40%): in the first year of operation—100%, into the second year—70%, and in the third year—30%. The corporation profits tax in an enterprise in which a foreign person's capital investment accounts for at least 20% of the total invested capital of the enterprise shall enjoy a tax reduction for a period of five years from the date such investment was made, proportionately to the share of the foreign capital in the total capital invested. Agreements on Avoiding Double Taxation have been concluded with some 20 countries. Custom duties are not paid on imports of equipment that comprise the foreign investor's share or that are imported on the basis of foreign investor's assets (under the condition the investment is larger than 20% of the total capital invested and the investment has been made for a period of at least 5 years).

Where joint ventures as a form of business cooperation with foreign partners practiced by enterprises in former Yugoslavia are concerned, it should be noted that several were just continuations of some existing forms of cooperation (usually a license arrangement, purchase of equipment, raw materials, business and technical cooperation, etc.). It is one of the factors that positively influenced the cooperation of domestic organizations with foreign partners in the period under observation (1967-1990).

The orientation toward the practice of joint business ventures in Yugoslavia resulted from the need for wider and long-term integration into the international division of labor, the acquisition of modern technology, increased exports, supplying the domestic market, reduced imports, and improvement of business performance of the domestic organizations engaged in production and trade. The practice has shown that through this form of cooperation, besides securing resources for financing specific ventures, the domestic organizations could also provide for:

—the acquisition of modern technology for the production process and for the equally important market development and product marketing,
—modern organization of production and labor productivity on a worldwide level,
—better marketing of their products, particularly in foreign markets,
—better supply of the domestic market and import reduction,
—greater security where completion of projects is concerned, during the period of capital construction as well as in the process of production and marketing of finished products and/or services,
—provision of raw materials and products in short supply, and
—broader and long-term integration into the international division of labor, etc.

The decision of foreign partners to invest in a Yugoslav organization was usually based on the estimate of their business interests and the assessment of the benefits such a venture offered or might offer on the whole, although the expected profit from the earnings realized through a joint business operation was not their primary motive at all.

Based on the joint venture practice so far, we may say that the foreign firms' motives and policy depended on the specific strategic objectives of the big companies. Consequently, the dominant motives for investing in former Yugoslavia could be listed as follows:

—penetration into the Yugoslav market as a basic motive in most cases,
—profit making,
—penetration via Yugoslavia into CMEA markets (because of the former's specific relations and connections with this group of countries),

—securing raw materials and semi-manufactures (in certain cases),

—cheap labor and skilled manpower,

—rather difficult penetration through usual marketing channels due to the world economic crisis (this form being used as a model for overcoming such problems),

—the long-term policy of stability pursued in Yugoslavia during the period under observation,

—application of the strategy of relocation of the so-called "dirty" industries (ferrous metallurgy, production of chemicals, rubber processing, nonferrous metals processing, etc.),

—possibility for the application of transfer prices through contractual cooperation within the system of the corporation, and

—a most favorable geographic location.

The assessments of some foreign authors who studied the practice of foreign investment in Yugoslavia are quite similar. Chitle (1977) points out that one of the most important motives for joint ventures in Yugoslavia is the foreign partners' desire to penetrate the CMEA markets, while Coughlin (1983) places emphasis on the attractiveness of the Yugoslav market for many foreign partners. Lamers (1976) also points out the approach to the domestic market (26.5%) as the basic motive, although favorable marketing of licenses, patents, and know-how (24%) are also of major importance, while low costs, and provision of raw materials are ranked much lower. In any case, these experiences from various sources and connected with different cases clearly bring to the foreground a number of business motives the enterprises reckoned with when developing their own marketing strategies. The possible motives of Yugoslav enterprises were similar, as they were mostly oriented toward the advancement of the technological level of production and success in the world market place (BI 1988). The contribution of many contractual relations on the basis of joint venture projects with well-known foreign partners was certainly noted in the practice so far. In fact, each of the partners chose the contents that would enable the achievement of the desired objectives, so that the subjects of cooperation in joint venture contracts concluded in Yugoslavia greatly vary—ranging from investment of resources for joint business operation and acquisition of material rights to technology, to the training of personnel, mutual deliveries, joint appearance on the market, granting and raising credits, design, construction work, erection work, and many other activities.

In the period when the former legislation was in effect (until 1988), the total number of joint venture contracts concluded with domestic organizations was 342, which means the number of contracts concluded annually in the period between 1968 and 1988 amounted to 17 (Table 10.1). Observed by development stages, there is evidently a high degree of correlation between the more liberal vis-a-vis the restrictive approach of the legislator and the interest of foreign partners in investment in Yugoslavia. In stage 1, which encompasses the first 10 years of the joint venture practice in the country, there were twice as many contracts concluded (164) compared to each of the next two stages—in each, 89 contracts were registered between domestic and foreign partners. A slow rise in the number of contracts may be noted up to 1978, followed by stagnation. This is correlated with the restrictions of the regulations after 1978. It is also very clearly manifested by the number of contracts concluded after 1984, when the Law was amended and certain restrictions abandoned. After all, the average annual number of contracts concluded in stages 1 and 2 are below the average for the whole period, while in stage 3, they are considerably above it—29 compared to 17, which is the average for the 1968-1988 period.

Table 10.1. Trends in the Number of Concluded Joint Venture Contracts by Specific Periods (1968-1990)

Time Period	Total Number of Joint Ventures	Annual Average
Stage 1 (1968-1977)	164	16
1968-1972	72	14
1973-1977	92	18
Stage 2 (1978-1984)	89	13
1978-1982	63	13
1983-1984	26	13
Stage 3 (1985-1988)	89	29
1985-1986	53	27
1987	36	36
Stage 4 (1989-1990)		
Estimate	700	NA
TOTAL (1968-1988)	342	17

Source: Jovic (1990)

Certainly, the number of concluded contracts does not mean that all the JVs became operational, and because the period concerned is more than 20 years long, the fact should not be forgotten that many contractual relations—the successful as well as the unsuccessful ones—became obsolete by the very nature of things.   According to some estimates, about 1/4 of the contracts were terminated either because the term of the contract had expired or because of cancellation, which left some 150 contracts in effect by 1988.

At the beginning of stage 4, when the new Joint Venture Law was adopted, a sudden increase in the number of these arrangements could be noted. Moreover, during 1989, the first year the new Law was in effect, over 300 J contracts were concluded—more than in the entire preceding 22-year period. Most (over 2/3), of these joint venture contracts concern mixed enterprises, the setting up of foreign persons' own enterprises, as well as investment in the already existing ones. The main characteristic of these new investments is an increased number of smaller investments, although the sum total of foreign residents' investments in the first year amounted to more than $120-150 million. In 1990, the number of new joint venture units, as well as the invested amounts, were several times that amount.

On the basis of the contracts registered earlier, it may be noted that most of the investment monies went into industries that developed faster with the help of the domestic market. This means that the biggest investments were made in the production of basic chemicals, metal processing, production of means of transportation, and electrical machinery and apparatuses (Table 10.2). It is also typical that foreign persons invested in the existing facilities (expansion, reconstruction, modernization) and less in the construction of new projects. In this way, by investing relatively modest resources, foreign persons tried to secure faster activation of investments and participation in joint business operations.

According to UN experts (UNECE 1988), the resources invested in the J by companies from developed countries and their Yugoslav partners in the period 1968-1980 totalled $2.5 billion. The foreign partners' share was about 20%, which means investment of some $500 million of foreign resources in Yugoslavia. Five years later, in 1985, foreign partners' investments were estimated at some $200 million.

Domestic organizations concluded J contracts with partners from over 21 countries, i.e. about 1/6 of the countries that Yugoslavia traded with, while the share of trade on this basis amounted to only 0.5% of the total trade of Yugoslavia with the world. This indicated the exceptionally low level of foreign trade coming from these operations.

As for the regional distribution, most of the J contracts were concluded with EEC partners, followed by partners from the USA and EFTA. There is considerable similarity in this between Yugoslavia and the CMEA countries (see Table 10.3).

It also should be noted that concentration on individual countries becomes even more important if, instead of contracts, we take their sources invested. This may be explained by the fact that, as a rule, the most important J partners of Yugoslavia are also her major partners in foreign economic relations.

Making a general assessment of joint ventures between domestic organizations and foreign persons in Yugoslavia in the 1967-1990 period, we could state:

—the utilization of such a form of business cooperation developed rather unevenly, which is confirmed by the fact that there were stages of legal and business regulation,
—in many cases, through joint venturing, problems of investment nature resulting from the shortage of local sources, as well as the need for other contents accompanying the investment were successfully solved,
—most of the contracts produced positive balances in general, (e.g., employment, productivity, balance of payments, etc.), which was highly important for both the enterprises and the country,

—the contracts concluded mostly involved higher stages of processing, in
enterprises in the developed regions,

Table 10.2. Distribution of Joint Venture Contracts in Yugoslavia by Sector

Rank	Sector	% of J Share by Sector
1	Metaprocessing	17.0
2	Chemical industry	16.5
3	Production of means of transportation	10.4
4*	Electric machinery industry	8.5
	Non-electric machinery industry	8.5
	Food, beverages and tobacco	8.5
7	Other processing industry (car tires, etc.)	6.7
8*	Building industry	4.9
	Paper, printing, and publishing	4.9
10*	Textile	2.4
	Wood and furniture	2.4
	Bricks, cement, and ceramics	2.4
13	Production of instruments	1.8
14*	Agriculture, forestry, and fisheries	1.2
	Service sector	1.2
16*	Mining and quarrying	0.6
	Clothing and footwear	0.6
	Professional and scientific services	0.6
	Other activities (games of chance, etc.)	0.6

*indicates a tie

Source: Artisien and Buckley (1985)

—through this form of cooperation domestic organizations solved problems in
connection with the transfer of technology and know-how (technical, organizational, marketing),
—joint ventures helped develop new production lines, while some activities in the
country developed on the basis of such arrangements.

However, the results could probably have been better, especially because the
actual potentials of the Yugoslav economy could be better utilized. Specific
weaknesses could be noted in the J practice in Yugoslavia, as follows:

—a relatively large number of contracts failed to be realized (because both sides
did not fulfill the necessary preconditions),

Table 10.3. Industrial Cooperation Contracts by Western Partner Countries, August 1989-July 1990

Partner	CMEA	Yugoslavia	Total
Germany	100	7	107
Austria	32	3	35
United States	20	4	24
Italy	10	4	14
France	10	4	14
United Kingdom	8	2	10
Japan	1	5	6
Switzerland	—	5	5
Belgium	—	5	5
Finland	—	4	4

—there are a large number of joint ventures where the foreign partner's investment is small and insignificant,

—complex legislation was passed which the foreign partner had difficulty understanding,

—joint ventures were concentrated in developed regions (although one of the intentions was development of economically underdeveloped regions),

—very often there was an unrealistic valorization of foreign technology (overvaluation, as a rule),

—insufficient selectivity of foreign partners (very often the reputation and standing of foreign partners were inadequate),

—the personnel and organization of domestic partners and entities were frequently insufficiently prepared,

—there was an orientation toward processing industries, and to a much smaller extent toward basic sectors,

—very often the foreign partner's superiority in the business arrangement as a whole could be noted,

—there was a low rate of capital formation,

—there was bigger investment in existing organizations, and much less investment in newly established ones,

—limited export resulted, very often due to the restrictive practices,

—there was an uncritical acquisition of foreign technologies, causing dependence on foreign countries,

—a major diffusion of foreign investment (in 25 activities) existed, which enabled the foreign partners to exert stronger influence on the entire productive structure of the country, and

—there was an absence of the most sophisticated and appropriate technologies in arrangements based on joint investment.

However, the positive effects predominate, because of the creation of positive experiences in the spheres of know-how—primarily technological, marketing, and organizational and a better supply of products coming from the joint venture into the domestic market. In addition, domestic enterprises achieved an enviable level of international recognition on global markets.

REFERENCES

Artisien, P., and P. J. Buckley (1985), *J in Yugoslavia: Opportunities and Constraints*, Columbia, SC: JIBS.

BI (1988), *Investing in Yugoslavia,* Business International, Dubrovnik, London: International Business Conference.

Chisnall, M. P. (1977), "Challenging Opportunities of International Marketing," *European Research,* 5 (June), pp. 13-18.

Chitle, C. R. (1977), *Industrialization and Manufactured Export Expansion in a Worker Managed Economy—The Yugoslavia Experience*, Kiel: Kiel papers series.

Coughlin, C. C. (1983), "An Economic Analysis of Yugoslav J," *Journal of World Trade Law* 27, (Jan-Feb), 54-63.

Jovic, M. (1992), "Experience in Foreign Investment and J in Yugoslavia," in *International Business and Marketing*, Kip Becker, ed., Boston: Allyn & Bacon.

Jovic, M. D. (1990), *Medjunarodni Marketing/International Marketing: Co-operative Concept, Approach and Modalities,* Publ. House "Savremena administracija" Yugoslavia: Belgrade.

—— (1990a), *Foreign Investment and J in Yugoslavia-Strategic Turnaround or Needs for Changing International Marketing Strategies in the 90s,* 6th IMP Conference, SDA Bocconi, Milan, Conference papers, Part II.

—— (1990b), *Deregulation in Economy and Economic Reform in Yugoslavia,* Key Note Paper on Business Section, Meeting-place Europe 90, International Conference, CIB NHH, Bergen.

—— (1988), *A Tripartite Approach to International Marketing—Does It Works Today,* Second World Conference on Marketing and Development, Budapest.

Jovic, M., and Z. Zlatkovic (1988), *Economic Reform in the East—Great Chance for Improving Economic Cooperation with West,* East-West Special Session, the 41st ESOMAR Congress and Exhibition, Lisbon, Portugal.

Lamers, A. (1976), *J Between Yugoslav and Foreign Enterprises*, Amsterdam: North-Holland.

Roman, D. D., and J. F. Puett, Jr. (1983), *International Business and Technological Innovation*, Amsterdam: Elsevier Science Publ.

UNECE (1992), "Economic Survey of Europe in 1991-1992," Geneva: United Nations.

—— (1988), "East-West Joint Ventures: Economic, Business, Financial and Legal Aspects," Geneva: United Nations.

11

The Strategic Behavior of Dutch Multinational Enterprises Toward International Joint Ventures: A Multidimensional Analysis

John Bell
Pieter K. Jagersma

International expansion is a very important strategic decision for most companies. The reasons for this are well documented elsewhere (Jagersma 1991). The international dimension of competition became an increasingly important academic discipline in the 1970s and 1980s. Theory followed practice, and in these years some remarkable and interesting publications were introduced (e.g., Contractor and Lorange 1988a; Porter 1986). This created the conceptual context in which many scientists are operating today. In this chapter, the object of study is the international joint venture (IJV). We are interested in a number of questions about this phenomenon. This chapter tries to conceptualize the IJV from different angles. This conceptualization is empirically investigated, by analyzing 80 IJVs during the period 1985 through 1989.

As usual, this chapter is the result of some important shortcomings. These shortcomings are intrinsic to the Dutch context. In the Netherlands we have the unique situation that only a few authors are really involved in the field of International or Comparative Management. This made us aware of the importance of initiating an empirical study to fill the gap with other investigations from other countries.

Our study is explorative in the sense that it tries to give some answers to questions that have never been asked before in the Dutch "state of the art." We also have been disappointed by the marginal attention paid to the IJV as a way of expansion and competition in the theory of the multinational firm. The literature about multinational firms focus on competition and concentration issues. This chapter shows that inter-organizational alliances in general, and IJVs in particular, are an important—instead of a marginally—competitive mechanism. We also believe that most of the multinational companies (MNEs) are still not aware of the utmost importance of international collaboration. Even large MNEs do not have the resources to win the global and local competitive battles completely on their own (Ohmae 1985). In our view a partner firm can be an important source of skills. These skills may be complementary to the skills of the other partner. This combination may transform an on first sight unimportant productive factor into a sustainable competitive advantage.

In advance of the introduction of our multi-dimensional approach, we have to outline what in our opinion makes an IJV distinctive from other mechanisms of coordination. Our definition of an IJV is followed by a review of our dimensions and the research methodology. The main part of this chapter contains the results of our empirical study concerning a number of interesting dimensions of IJVs. The chapter ends with an evaluation.

TOWARD A DEFINITION

International expansion by international contractual agreements can be implemented by different mechanisms. The literature introduces a diverse array of concepts. Strategic alliances (Hamel, Doz and Prahalad 1989), contractual alliances (James 1985), joint ventures (Reich and Mankin 1986), cooperative agreements (Mariti and Smiley 1983), cooperative arrangements (Contractor and Lorange 1988b), coalitions (Porter and Fuller 1986), and strategic partnerships (Teece 1988) are but a few. It is remarkable that there is little if any discussion about the inherent meaning of these concepts (Jagersma 1992).

We defined an IJV as "an international agreement on collaboration between two or more independent companies who exploit an (in)tangible asset in an autonomous entity" (Bell and Jagersma 1992). The partners are not necessarily of the same size or of the same quality. Partners share in the financial assets of the new company. This financial participation is embedded in a formal contract. An IJV is a formal arrangement, not an informal one. The IJV is intentional not temporary. The IJV, in our view, is a coordination mechanism, which has to be reserved for an autonomous entity in which two or more partners are participating financially with the intention of improving or sustaining their competitive position in the international or local environment. This interpretation has been known as the "strategic behavior" approach.

LITERATURE

An IJV can be interpreted from a whole set of perspectives. We isolated ten important dimensions. These dimensions are important because they all have far-reaching implications for the competitive position of the multinational partner participating in the IJV. We called this interpretation the "multidimensional approach" of the IJV. The dimensions are as follows:

Product and/or Process Objectives

An IJV has two core objectives: generating a product or a service (the so-called product dimension) or learning how to produce a product or service (the process dimension). Figure 11.1 is a visual representation of these dimensions. The formation of an IJV can be motivated by the product dimension, the process dimension, or both.

Offensive or Defensive

Offensive IJVs are distinctive mainly in terms of their consequences for the competitive position of the multinational participating partner. MNEs are in this regard motivated by the realization of a potentially stronger competitive position. The input of the multinational partner in the IJV is of a distinctive nature. Only that partner has a specific skill, which may be based upon technical and marketing know-how.

A defensive IJV, on the other hand, is not the result of the activities of the participating MNEs, but the result of actions of other firms (mainly competitors) and institutions (governments, for example). A discriminating policy of a host government can be the sole reason to initiate an IJV in that country. In other words, an MNE can be forced to form an IJV. Other motivations for a defensive IJV are influenced by the "pre-emptive strategy" argument. This argument implies that a joint venture can be motivated by the actions of a third party. The defensive IJV sometimes operates as an entry-barrier (Rugman and Verbeke 1991).

In summary, the offensive IJV is pro-active and funded in, and the direct implication of a strength of the participating companies. The defensive IJV, on the other hand, is reactive and the indirect consequence of the activities of firms other than those participating in the IJV.

Direction

An IJV can be executed in three directions: horizontal, vertical, and diagonal. These directions are determined by the number and the peculiarities of the businesses. They are formed at the same level of the value-chain in the same line-of-business. Horizontal IJVs are also formed between companies from the same level of the value-chain in different businesses. In this sense, horizontal IJVs are aimed at the common development, production, and/or marketing of products or services. Vertical IJVs institutionalize activities in the same value-chain. The transfer of know-how about the generation of products or services can be exchanged against the know-how about the distribution of those products or services. In diagonal IJVs, the input of the partners is originally located in different businesses at different levels of the value-chain.

Motives

IJVs are initiated by specific motivations. These motivations are the direct consequence of the central tendency to strengthen or consolidate the competitive position of the participating MNEs and to attain some degree of flexibility. These motives have been called "generic motives" (Bell and Jagersma 1992). An IJV can be the key to a competitive advantage. Companies share their distinctive skills that, on their own, could never fulfill the promise of a sustainable competitive advantage. In this way, latent advantages (distinctive skills) can be transformed into manifest advantages (sustainable competitive advantages).

An IJV is an important mode of international expansion. Other modes are start-ups and acquisitions, which have important disadvantages: both international start-ups and international acquisitions are expensive and time-consuming. Those modes are to some extent what we call inflexible. IJVs, on the other hand, are a more flexible approach toward international expansion. International start-ups and acquisitions require commitments that an IJV does not necessarily require. This makes the IJV a flexible international expansion mode.

We distinguish three specific motives: risk reduction, market entry, and efficiency advantages, which are embedded in the two "generic" motives: "competitive advantages" and "flexibility." They are well documented in the literature (Contractor and Lorange 1988b). In this study, we take the "generic" motives for granted and instead focus on the specific motives in activating IJVs.

Financial Participation

The partners in the IJV share in the financial base of the autonomous organization. The financial participation often reflects the position of the partners in the venture. There is the possibility of a 50/50 partnership, a minority participation, or a dominant participation. The reasons for a 50/50, a minority, or a dominant participation are diverse (Harrigan 1985).

Other Research Dimensions

How many partners are involved in the IJV? This dimension is important because of the relationship between the number of parties within the IJV and the complexity of managing and controlling the IJV.

The IJV can be located in the home country (in our study, the Netherlands) or in some foreign country. This is also an important question, because one's influence on all kinds of decisions (mainly operational) may lose force when the venture is located in a foreign country. This is an important actuality in IJVs that are located within unknown cultures. These situations can be platforms for conflicts and counterproductive actions.

Closely related with the earlier discussed "direction" of the joint venture relationship is the "nature" of the activities. This nature can easily be defined in terms of the value-chain of a business. We assume that the value-chain contains three components, namely: development, production, and marketing (see Hergert

Figure 11.1. Product and Process Dimension of an International Joint Venture

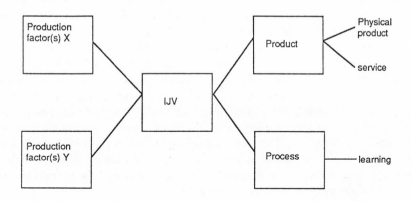

and Morris 1988). An IJV is, theoretically, not bound to one activity (for example, developing new products or services). An IJV is able to activate all kinds of activities. In other words: MNEs are able to strive for narrow or broad value-chain strategies. Market circumstances as well as characteristics of the MNE determine the narrowness (or broadness) of this value-chain strategy.

Some MNEs are experienced in using IJVs; others are not at all interested in initiating IJVs. In order to determine whether some statements can be made about the level of interest of Dutch MNEs, we will look at the number of IJVs formed by Dutch MNEs.

METHODOLOGY

In the empirical investigation we looked at IJVs in the period 1985-1989. Only IJVs with at least one Dutch MNE as a partner, of which enough information could be gathered, and which were actually set up were selected as objects of study. Eighty IJVs met these requirements.

The scoring of a dimension was consistently interpreted from the Dutch partner's point of view. In cases where two Dutch firms were involved in an IJV, only the largest one was considered for classification. In the classification process, the choice of a particular score on the different dimensions was determined by the dichotomy latent-manifest. For example: if the process dimension was latently present in a certain IJV, and the product dimension manifestly, that IJV was classified as being set up to generate a product (or a service see Figure 11.1). For two dimensions, all subdimensions can be in force at the same time—they, unlike the others, are not mutually exclusive. These two dimensions are: 1) objective: product and/or process; and 2) value-chain: development, production and/or marketing.

The data about these IJVs were gathered by studying all international partnerships, as documented in "Het Financieele Dagblad" (the Dutch financial newspaper) in the period January 1985 until January 1990 (5 years). This source was examined thoroughly page by page to trace all IJVs with at least one Dutch MNE as a partner. In order to be more certain about the completeness of the dataset, three additional actions were undertaken. At first, we inquired at "Het Financieele Dagblad" if there happened to be a change of editorial policy concerning the publication of information about IJVs and other strategic partnerships in the period 1985-1989. They declared that there had not been such a change of policy, and that such (rather radical) changes always would be announced in their newspaper. We did not find any announcement of that tenor. Secondly, we scanned year reports of the 25 largest Dutch MNEs, and did not detect any large, deviating differences. Thirdly, we compared a printed list of all the articles published in "Het Financieele Dagblad" saying anything about joint ventures with our own traced articles. This list, taken from the database of "Het Financieele Dagblad," contained only a few IJVs that we missed initially. We included these missing IJVs in our analysis.

The data were arranged in conformity with the intended multidimensional interpretation of IJVs. All eighty IJVs were studied conscientiously and successively scored on the following dimensions:

- the objectives the IJV strived for (product and/or process);
- the offensive or defensive character of the IJV;
- the direction of the IJV (horizontal, vertical, or diagonal);
- the motive to set up the IJV (risk-reduction, market-entrance, or efficiency gains);
- the financial participation of the Dutch partner in the IJV (< 50%, 50/50, or > 50%);
- the number of participants in the IJV;
- the location of the IJV's headquarters (the Netherlands, or abroad [by region])
- the level of the value-chain on which the IJV is active (development, production, and/or marketing);
- the number of IJVs Dutch MNEs have formed in the period 1985-1989;
- is the partner a local or a multinational firm?

RESULTS

The study yielded 80 IJVs that met our definition and the aforementioned criteria. The results by dimensions, are as follows.

Frequency

There was a remarkable change in the number of IJVs from 1985 to 1989. Although in 1985 and 1986 about 25 IJVs were set up, the number of IJVs decreased significantly in 1987 and in 1988 to thirteen and seven, respectively. In 1989 the number of IJVs appeared to recover increasing to eleven. As compared with 1988, there was an enormous increase in 1989. The asymmetric division of the frequency seems clear, because in 1985 and 1986 together, more than 60% of the total number of IJVs were already set up.

Objective

IJVs are seldom directed only at the process dimension (5%). Nearly every time the product dimension, whether or not in combination with the process dimension, was the most essential objective for Dutch MNEs strived for. This is summarized in Table 11.1.

Offensive or Defensive

Not all IJVs are aimed at influencing directly the Dutch partner's competitive position (offensive character); a small number of the IJVs (20%) are of a more defensive nature. This is summarized in Table 11.2.

Direction

More than 75% of the total number of IJVs were formed with a (potential) competitor, while only 8% of the IJVs were set up with the intention to attain a quasi-integration. New, possibly unknown, activities hardly ever developed by (diagonal) IJVs. This is summarized in Table 11.3.

Table 11.1. Objectives of Dutch Multinational Enterprises Product Versus Process by Year

Year	Product	Process	Product + Process
1985	12	3	7
1986	14	1	12
1987	8	0	5
1988	4	0	2
1989	6	0	6
TOTAL	44	4	32

Motives

The most important specific motive for setting up an IJV was gaining access to a market (over 60%). Other motives balanced each other more or less. It is very striking that in the most recent years of the study, almost no motive other than market-entrance could be distinguished. This is summarized in Table 11.4.

Table 11.2. Objectives of Dutch Multinational Enterprises Offensive Versus Defensive by Year

Year	Offensive	Defensive
1985	21	2
1986	19	7
1987	8	3
1988	7	1
1989	9	4
TOTAL	64	17

Financial Participation

The financial stake was equally distributed over the partners in more than half of the IJVs. The Dutch partner had a financial minority stake in about 25% of the cases. It can be concluded from our study it can be concluded that the Dutch partners' influence in IJVs are increasing, since fewer minority stakes are taken, while more and more majority stakes are established. Dutch MNEs apparently experience financial participation information as an important strategic advantage, as this participation often could not be detected from "Het Financieele Dagblad." By using additional sources (like year reports and inquiries by telephone), this problem was largely eliminated. Only one financial participation account appeared untraceable. This is summarized in Table 11.5.

Table 11.3. Directions of Dutch Multinational Enterprises by Year

Year	Horizontal	Vertical	Diagonal
1985	20	3	1
1986	17	2	5
1987	12	1	2
1988	5	0	1
1989	8	0	5
TOTAL	62	6	14

Number of Partners

In almost 85% of the observations, only two partners are involved in the relationship (that is the IJV); cooperation by IJVs appears mainly to be executed with only one other firm. Multi-partner relationships are probably particularly difficult to realize in an international context. This is summarized in Table 11.6.

Table 11.4. Motivations of Dutch Multinational Enterprises by Year

Year	Risk Reduction	Market Entry	Efficiency Advantage
1985	3	16	6
1986	10	10	5
1987	1	8	3
1988	0	7	1
1989	0	8	2
TOTAL	14	49	17

Location of Headquarters

IJVs with at least one Dutch MNE as partner are usually situated in the Netherlands or in the Far East region (both add to 60%). Less important regions of establishment are the non-Dutch countries of the European Community and North America (principally the United States). Very striking is the strong decrease of the total number of IJVs set up in the Far East and to a lesser extent in the European Community. Only a few IJVs with firms of an Eastern European origin were initiated in the most recent years. The effects of the political revolutions in these countries will probably cause an increase in future IJVs.

Table 11.5. Financial Participation of Dutch Multinational Enterprises by Year

Year	< 50%	50%	> 50%
1985	8	13	2
1986	6	13	7
1987	4	6	2
1988	1	4	2
1989	3	5	3
TOTAL	22	41	16

Value-Chain

Dutch multinationals appear to prefer IJVs aimed at a shared production of a product or a service (over 35%). Interesting is the trend from aspect-based cooperation toward more integral cooperation. Instead of cooperation in developing, producing, or marketing a product or a service, the combination of these three successive activities, as well as the combination of production and marketing are becoming more and more important.

Table 11.6. Number of Partners Used in Dutch Multinational Enterprises by Year

Year	Two	Three	Four or more
1985	19	4	1
1986	11	4	1
1987	11	1	1
1988	7	0	0
1989	10	0	2
TOTAL	58	9	5

Number of IJVs

From our research it is obvious that not all Dutch MNEs set up an equal number of IJVs. In the period 1985-1989, there were only four Dutch MNEs that formed more than four IJVs (Philips, AK30, DSM, and Shell). These firms, active in industries with a high technological intensity, were involved in more than 53% of the total number of IJVs in our research period. One firm (Philips) was really active in forming IJVs, as it was involved in 25 of them (more than 30%).

Type of Partner

In almost 75% of the cases Dutch MNEs choose an MNE as their partner in the IJV. As a whole, MNEs seem to be preferred to local firms. This is summarized in Table 11.7.

Table 11.7. Type of Partner by Year

Year	MNE	Local Firm	Both
1985	16	7	3
1986	19	6	0
1987	10	3	0
1988	5	1	0
1989	9	2	0
TOTAL	59	19	3

EVALUATION

In the present research the IJV as an international expansion alternative is analyzed. This exploration has lead to a number of remarkable conclusions that deserve more attention and investigation.

From our study it appears that there is no explosive growth in the number IJVs, as many researchers assert (e.g., Anderson 1990; Harrigan 1985, 1988) but rather an adversary pattern. If and to what extent this trend will continue in the 1990s can not be traced with the current dataset. A possible explanation for the rather striking decrease in 1987 might be that Dutch MNEs were less willing to make their strategic partnerships public (by "Het Financieele Dagblad"). Nevertheless, as already mentioned, no evidence for this speculation was found. Also a global exploration of a number of year reports did not lead us to form deviating conclusions. The only conclusion that emerges is that there was a significant decline in the number of IJVs in 1987 as compared with 1985 and 1986.

Dutch MNEs seldom form IJVs that are solely directed toward learning skills or obtaining know-how (the process dimension). Generating a product or a service (the product dimension) is, whether or not in combination with learning in and from the relationship, the dominate objective behind IJVs.

More than three out of four IJVs were of a horizontal nature, which means that they were set up with a (potential) competitor. This observation fits other researchers' findings (e.g., Hergert and Morris 1988), but differs from other findings. For instance, Hoekman (1984) found a difference in the direction of Dutch joint ventures set up in 1980. In his study it turned out that less than 30% of the total number of joint ventures were horizontal, while almost two out of four joint ventures were of a vertical nature. These differences may be explained by another research period or by the fact that Hoekman considered national joint ventures and participations in his study.

Another conclusion that can be drawn is that IJVs above all form an excellent medium to gain entrance to a foreign market, to a competitor, and to (specific) know-how. Many Dutch MNEs expand their range of activities by means of IJVs just because of the market entrance. IJVs are often the best way to conform to local content requirements of national and regional governments of the respective host countries. The IJVs in the Far East especially confirm this.

It should be stressed that the specific motives are of a rather idealistic nature. Besides risk reduction, market entry, and efficiency advantages, other—sometimes very specific—motivations can be observed (Contractor and Lorange 1988).

As could be expected, most IJVs (almost 85%) were formed by two firms, a result also confirmed by earlier studies (Hergert and Morris 1988; Hoekman 1984). The division of control, as reflected by the financial participation in the IJV, is generally spread equally between the partners. This financial participation is, however, not the same as the real influence that can be exerted (Killing 1983). More specific data about this division of control could not be detected from the available sources of information. A possible explanation for the often chosen 50/50 relation could be that such an equal division indicates some trust in the partner (see Bleeke and Ernst 1991).

The strong decline of the number of IJVs set up by Dutch MNEs in the Far East is interesting, although it was expected that firms want to be present in growth markets. This sharp decrease may indicate that the current presence of

Dutch MNEs in this region is satisfactory or that other entry modes (such as takeovers, or greenfield new plant investments) are preferred. Bad experiences with earlier IJVs might play an important role in this regard. Unfortunately, no information is available to support this statement.

The cooperation in an IJV seems to embrace more and more activities; this may deepen the relationship. Because of this, partners' dependency on the relationship and on each other is growing. This intensifying mutual dependency will discourage or even prevent opportunistic behavior of one of the partners, and so improve the stability of the IJV (Buckley and Casson 1988).

The year 1987 was one in which much interesting data was gathered. Besides the already mentioned strong decline of the number of IJVs, an increasing care concerning the forming of IJVs can be observed too. In 1987—as compared to 1985 and 1986—relatively more IJVs were defensive, horizontal, motivated by attaining efficiency advantages, were production based, and had Dutch minority financial participations. These characteristics indicate a more reserved attitude of Dutch MNEs in forming IJVs. A clear explanation of such an attitude of Dutch MNEs is lacking. The economic recession, with the "crash" on "black Monday" (October 1987) as the anticlimax, may have been an important factor. Firms probably anticipated the growing uncertainty. As a real tough recession failed to occur, and there turned out to be a great flexibility in absorbing the consequences of the "crash", multinational corporations may have revised their reserved attitude toward forming international joint ventures.

Very interesting is the observation that regardless of the fact that fewer IJVs were formed in 1988 than in 1987, little or no indication of such reserved attitude can be detected in that year. In 1988 (and in 1989), the IJVs appeared to be of a relatively more offensive nature, more often motivated by acquiring market entrance, more production- and marketing-oriented, and contained more frequent majority participations than in previous years.

Not all IJVs will be a success story. This chapter does not evaluate the success or failure of IJVs, mainly because of methodological restrictions. It is not possible to make valid statements about success and failure considering only a period of five years. Further research is required.

REFERENCES

Anderson, E. (1990), "Two Firms, One Frontier: On Assessing Joint Venture Performance," *Sloan Management Review* (Winter), 19-29.

Bell, J., and P. K. Jagersma (1992), *Internationale Joint Ventures [International Joint Ventures]*, Research Memorandum FEW 541, Faculty of Economics, Tilburg University, The Netherlands.

Bleeke, J., and D. Ernst (1991), "The Way to Win Cross-Border Alliances," *Harvard Business Review* (November/December), 127-135.

Buckley, P.J., and M. A. Casson (1988), "A Theory of Cooperation in International Business," in *Cooperative Strategies in International Business*, F. J. Contractor and P. Lorange, eds., Lexington, MA: Lexington Books, pp. 31-54.

Contractor, F. J., and P. Lorange, (1988a), *Cooperative Strategies in International Business*, Lexington, MA: Lexington Books.

—— (1988b), "Why Should Firms Cooperate?," in *Cooperative Strategies in International Business*, F. J. Contractor and P. Lorange, eds., Lexington, Lexington Books, pp. 3-28.

Hamel, G., Y. L. Doz, and C.K. Prahalad (1989), "Collaborate With Your Competitor—And Win," *Harvard Business Review* 89 (January/February), 133-139.

Harrigan, K. R. (1985), *Strategies for Joint Ventures*, Lexington, MA: Lexington Books.

—— (1987), "Strategic Alliances: Their New Role in Global Competition," *Columbia Journal of World Business* (Summer), 67-69.

—— (1988), "Joint Ventures and Competitive Strategy," *Strategic Management Journal 9*, 141-158.

Hergert, M., and D. Morris (1988), "Trends in International Collaborative Agreements," in *Cooperative Strategies in International Business*, F. J. Contractor and P. Lorange, eds., Lexington, MA: Lexington Books, 99-109.

Hoekman, J. M. (1984), *The Role of the Joint Venture in the Strategy of Corporations*, Ph.D. Dissertation, University of Amsterdam, 1984.

Jagersma, P. K. (1991), "Horizontale Internationale Expansie van de Onderne mingsscope: Het Waarom [Horizontal International Expansion of the Scope of the Firm: The Why]," *Maandblad voor Accountancy en Bedrijfseconomie* [Journal of Accountancy and Business Administration] *65* (September), 399-407.

—— (1992), *De Strategie en Structuur van Nederlandse Multinationale Ondernemingen* [The Strategy and Structure of Dutch Multinational Enterprises], Groningen: Charlotte Heijmanns Publishers.

James, B. G. (1985), "Alliance: The New Strategic Focus," *Long Range Planning 18* (3), 76-81.

Killing, J. P. (1983), *Strategies for Joint Venture Success*, New York: Praeger.

Mariti, P., and R. H. Smiley (1983), "Co-operative Agreements and the Organization of Industry," *The Journal of Industrial Economics 31* (4), 437-451.

Ohmae, K. (1985), *The Triad Power: The Coming Shape of Global Competition*, New York: The Free Press.

Porter, M. E., ed. (1986), *Competition in Global Industries*, Cambridge, MA: Harvard Business School Press.

Porter, M. E., and M. B. Fuller (1986), "Coalitions and Global Strategy," in *Competition in Global Industries*, M. E. Porter, ed., Cambridge, MA: Harvard Business School Press, pp. 315-343.

Reich, R. B., and E. D. Mankin (1986), "Joint Ventures with Japan Give Away Our Future," *Harvard Business Review* (March/April), 78-86.

Rugman, A. M. and A. Verbeke (1991), "Trade Barriers and Corporate Strategy in International Companies—The Canadian Experience," *Long Range Planning* *24* (3), 66-72.

Teece, D. J. (1988), "Capturing Value From Technological Innovation: Integration, Strategic Partnering, and Licensing," *Interfaces 18* (3), 46-61.

12

The Evolution of Polish Joint Ventures

Stanley J. Paliwoda
Zbigniew Dobosiewicz

By the year 1992, Poland had a market economy and a fully convertible currency. Its traditional export market, the Soviet Union, no longer existed and even the separate republics that made up this former Soviet Union, while still able to consume Polish goods, were not able to pay for them in convertible currency. These markets were lost (Ohmae 1989). At the same time, the domestic Polish market has been opened up to worldwide competition with the introduction of convertibility. The seller's market that existed before has turned into a buyer's market for those fortunate to have enough dollars to spend (Merritt (1991). Western competition and the inevitable comparison of goods for sale has, therefore, hit Polish enterprises hard. Lacking the latest sophisticated technology and having demanding customers, there has been no investment in product research and design (Ohmae 1988). One example of this is the television set. Until recently, the Polish market for color TV sets was dominated by Polish production (Neptun, Jowisz, etc.) from big state-owned enterprises; Soviet sets constituted the majority of imported color TV sets. During the last several years, TV sets imported from Japan, Korea, Taiwan, etc., captured an important part of the market, and at the same time imports from the Soviet Union decreased. The French company Thomson became the owner of the Piaseczno enterprise (one of the biggest in Europe) and modernized it. Today, the Soviet television has increased in price to the point where it is competing unfavorably alongside Japanese competitors, such as Panasonic, who have since captured the market. The reasons are simple. Soviet televisions sold when they were available for soft currency and no other serious competitors existed on a market; Japanese sets could be bought only for dollars only. Today, the change that was introduced with currency convertibility has created choices for consumers; they can now buy from any one of many suppliers offering goods from a wide variety of sources. For the state enterprises, the urgent mission is now the quest for survival.

It is worth considering the concept of "value subtraction" put forward by McKinnon (McKinnon 1991). An enterprise might be so inefficient that its revenues fail to cover even the cost of materials. The enterprise uses scarce capital and labor to subtract value from its other inputs. As McKinnon puts it: valuable metal, plastic, cardboard, rubber, energy go in at one end: Trabant cars worth less than the sum of these parts emerge at the other. While devaluation can cut labor costs and make a loss-making enterprise profitable, a value-subtracting enterprise loses money even if labor and capital are free. It is a failure irrespective of the exchange rate.

There are many Polish state-owned manufacturing enterprises today who have consistently failed to match the design, quality, and sophistication of Western competitors. For all of them the choice is a joint venture or death. As Ohmae (Ohmae 1987) has pointed out, the world economy is now ruled by manufacturing and trading corporations, not nations. The need is urgent, and so the enabling legislation is now in place. To retrace the steps by which we arrived at this point, it is worth examining the historical development of Polish joint ventures.

PHASE 1

This was the period during the 1970s, which was characterized by the word "detente." It characterized a relaxation of controls on East-West trade while the West still continued to eye the East warily as the potential enemy. Certain industrial sectors were subject to control, e.g., telecommunications, and the Eastern side was always the one to decide the scope and duration of projects to be fulfilled by means of contractual joint ventures termed "industrial cooperation." Western companies also found themselves publicly embracing the political regime in question, often as a result of the political progaganda machinery, which was more effective than the political machinery itself. Western control and influence was variable in projects identified as national priorities within the terms of a national or CMEA Five Year Plan. Equity stakes were limited for, ideological reasons: the ownership of the means of production (such as they were) had to remain with the people. Industrial cooperation held certain advantages over joint-equity ventures in such situations because, in the face of high risk, Western companies preferred a fixed term duration and for responsibilities to be clearly defined. What has not changed is the basic underlying motivation prompting joint ventures, but the negotiating atmosphere, the legislation, taxation, and expectations have all since changed.

PHASE 2

After the implosion of the Soviet Union, the rather cautious Poles, and their would-be investors, waited to assess the political climate for change in their own country. Poland's elections, held in 1989, were not very democratic, but they transformed the political panorama of Central Eastern Europe. The first free elections in Central Eastern Europe were held in Hungary and Czechoslovakia. The period from 1989-1991 was characterized by a series of faltering steps not only toward marketization of a command economy but toward freeing the controls over foreign direct investment within Poland. As the urgency for outside help with the restructuring increased, successive measures were taken to try to liberalize the workings of the domestic economy and create a more favorable climate and treatment of foreign investment. Initially, as the old rules were abolished, old statutes dating back to 1933, and never repealed, were reintroduced. The period was marked by confusion and ambiguity, which made Western investors nervous as they sensed fear amongst Poles of a possible political backlash. Once the failed August 1991 Kremlin coup was over, the end of an era was clearly marked. The way ahead was through opening the domestic market to global trade and in sealing political and trading ties with the widest possible number of trading partners. There would be no going back from this point.   The Communists had lost decisively; the people had succeeded in overthrowing over forty years' of Communist rule in a skillful revolution without any bloodshed. Stronger relations with the West would be guaranteed, because that was where their future and their continued independence lay (UNECE 1991). Yet a subsequent worldwide recession and the aftermath of a war in the Persian Gulf were to create the worst possible background against which to launch an investment drive.

In the new mood of goodwill toward a newly independent state, the "Group of 24" took a number of steps to try to reduce the level of outstanding Polish foreign indebtedness. Years of industrial neglect and economic mismanagement had created a debt mountain of $48.5 billion (which included $11 billion to commercial banks). This was a level that ran to approximately two and a half times Polish export earnings. First the group of countries belonging to the Paris Club rescheduled the moneys owed to it— 2/3rds of the total debt—and about 60% of that total was due to the capitalization of unpaid interest. Twenty percent of the debt was owed to commercial banks. In the main, this was medium and long-term debt; it was rescheduled with an eight-year interest grace period. Further, in March 1991, Western governments agreed to cut the $33 billion owed to them and cut interest repayments on government-to-government debt from $3.3 billion to $660 million and agreed to a voluntary debt swap facility representing 10% of the claims (UNECE 1991). The largest creditors were Germany, Austria, France, Canada and the United States. It is the United States that created the greatest media attention in announcing their 70% write-down of Polish debt. However, this amounted to only $2.9 billion and made little impact on the $33 billion still outstanding.

Since then, however, Poland has received assistance from the European Community, its PHARE program and the European Investment Bank; the OECD and its "Partners in Transition" program for Poland, Hungary, and the CSFR; the IMF; the World Bank; the European Bank for Reconstruction and Development (EBRD); and a number of countries (Dobosiewicz 1992). Nevertheless, Poland still requires a massive amount of private capital to restructure its economy. Export increases have created a surplus in the Polish balance of trade and have increased the creditworthiness of the country. Today, it is much easier to obtain credit from foreign banks.

PHASE 3

A free political will, a market economy in place, and an urgent need to modernize created new pressures for attracting foreign investment. This period started in 1992 and marks another shift. It is a period of maturity as regards attitudes and general expectations of what a market economy can bring. It is also tinged with a sense of frustration at both the low levels of inward foreign investment and the prices at which Western firms are able to negotiate their entry. There is no turning back to communism. The greatest existing danger is that the people may see in socialism a less painful road toward capitalism. Yet there can be no such half-way house. The Polish government is weak but has to deliver on IMF promises. The inexperience extends to President Lech Walesa. The people, unable to understand what is happening and inexperienced in the way of free elections, have voted into power more than twenty-nine political parties. This makes coalitions necessary, but political coalitions do not create the ideal atmosphere of confidence that investors look for in an economy. A government able to command a parliamentary majority and able to govern with a clear mandate from the people would be more reassuring to foreign investors. Tinkering with the investment regulations continues to produce minimal effect. Statistics on joint ventures fail to report any qualitative assessment as to their investment quality relative to the domestic economy.

The management of private companies will not bother about low productivity if costs overall are low and large-scale asset acquisition is possible at opportunity prices. But workers are still demanding, and there is an increasing social fear of privatization by foreigners being directed against Jews, Germans, and other prominent investors.

Of a total world-wide foreign direct investment of U.S. $1.5 trillion, the UN Economic Commission for Europe estimated the value of total foreign investment in Eastern Europe at U.S. $23 billion as of March 1994. This is equivalent to less than one-half of one percent of the value of the world stock of FDI abroad. As regards Poland, the UNECE (UNECE 1991) reported the total number of joint ventures and wholly owned foreign subsidiaries to have been 5,000 on October 1, 1991, as against 2,799 on January 1, 1991, and 918 in January 1990. This growth is significant, for in 1989, 867 foreign investments were authorized, 40 authorized in 1988, and 13 in 1987. In the first half of 1991, 282 authorizations were approved per month. However this does not mean that all of these in fact materialized.

Business International S.A. made this point clearly in Table 12.1. As the number of joint ventures increase, though, the size and quality of the investments decreases. There are few examples unfortunately of the size of the $75 million GM joint venture with the Polish car producer, FSO, announced on February 28, 1992. GM Europe intends to prepare a comprehensive program of cooperation between FSO, its branches, and the Polish suppliers of parts, and between specific GM branches and departments, as well as GM suppliers. As talks continue along these lines, GM Europe has announced a link between one of its subsidiaries—Automotive Components Group Europe—and the shock absorber factory in Krosno, Poland. More standardization will be required for the assembly of the GM Astra/Kadett car from its European range and the future production of new jointly researched and developed models from the FSO plant (*Warsaw Voice* 1991). Elsewhere, American International Group, Inc., has formed a majority-held joint venture with the Polish PKO Bank S.A. to participate in the Polish insurance market (*National Underwriter* 1990). The creation of East European Investment Funds for private investors in the West has been affected by the very limited stock markets of Poland and Hungary and by the world recession (Dodsworth and Webb 1990).

THE JOINT VENTURE CONCEPT HAS CHANGED OVER TIME

"Joint ventures" as a concept has always been poorly defined (Lynch 1990). In the particular context of Poland, there has been a significant difference as to what is meant and understood by the term "Joint Ventures" at any point over the last twenty years. In the 1970s, joint ventures were also known as "industrial cooperation" and so industrial cooperation agreements or ICAs became a term that passed into the language of East-West trade. Joint venture possibilities in the 1990s have moved sharply away from the industrial cooperation of the 1970s in a number of very important respects. The year 1980 was a watershed with the appearance of Solidarity and the politicization of social unrest; and although the joint-equity venture was floated in the 1980s, there continued to be the uncertainties of the political situation and the debt burden to discourage Westerners. Joint-equity ventures were promoted in the 1980s as a means of obtaining technology in the absence of finance for industrial cooperation. With joint-equity ventures, financing was supposed to be found through the Western partner, but this did not happen. Given the ideological straight-jacket that Poland was in prior to Solidarity becoming the government, this meant not that joint equity venture legislation would be amended but that joint equity ventures simply did not happen.

HOW POLISH JOINT VENTURES IN THE 1990s DIFFER

Firstly, there has been significant political change. Pragmatism has replaced an ideology that demanded that the ownership of the means of production must remain with the people and therefore with the government. Although a joint-equity venture may have been theoretically possible before, it was hitherto limited to a Western participation of 49%, a minority holding. The Communist regimes wanted to control that which they did not understand including finance, management, marketing, and product development. In fact most things related to management.

In the 1970s industrial cooperation was a preferred alternative to the joint venture because with an ICA, the Polish side determined the size and timescale for projects with a Western company and arranged payments guaranteed by government-backed lines of credit over a medium- to long-term period; often this was accompanied by a form of countertrade such as "buy-back". This might take repaying 25% of the total contract price in the form of final goods manufactured under the supplier's own license; to take the example of Fiat in Poland, partpayment took the form of delivery of Fiat 126P cars to Fiat.

Table 12.1. Joint Ventures in Poland (1990)

At the end of 1990, some 2,400 joint ventures were registered in Poland (1989: 860 registered). However, only 954 were operational and around 70% involved Polish individuals rather than companies.	In 1990, joint ventures contributed 2.5% of total sales of goods and services in Poland, and 3.4% of the country's hard-currency exports.
Total investment capital at the end of 1990 amounted to $320 million. On average, the share of foreign equity was 52% with investments of $163,000. The majority of joint ventures are operating in the clothing industry (19%) followed by the cosmetics and plastics section (11%). The remaining ones are primarily in household products, construction, food processing, electronics and medical equipment production.	The bulk of joint ventures in Poland were situated in the Warsaw area, with over 182 JVs registered there, employing close to 22,000 people. Another 93 ventures are located in Poznan (employing 7,310), 58 in Katowice (5,989 employed) and 49 in Lodz (5,684 employed). The remainder are spread out evenly across the country.

Source: Industrial & Commercial Chamber of Foreign Investors.

During the 1990s, the remaining constraints have been swept away with the reintroduction of pre-war legislation where applicable, and so a joint venture can now be as far-reaching in Poland as any other part of the globe. The Polish enabling legislation, in many instances, dates back to 1933 (pre-dating the communist regime). At the same time, the markets of Eastern Europe have been changing. The sudden and very dramatic moves toward establishing free-market economies in Poland and Hungary, which require convertibility of the domestic currency, affected not just the domestic economy but also the existence of the CMEA or Comecon region (now defunct as an organization), which are now increasingly moving toward trade settlement in convertible currencies. In 1989, Poland, for example, received payment for 20% of its exports to the USSR in U.S. dollars (UNECE 1991). As this pattern is being replicated elsewhere, the continued existence of the EECT (East European Cooperation and Trade), established October 1991 as the second successor to the defunct CMEA (after the speedy demise of the OIEC as the organization for International Economic Cooperation), is now very much in doubt (UNECE 1991). The so-called transferable ruble payments were never transferable and were simply bilateral trading arrangements that failed to deal with the difficult question of accumulated surpluses and deficits. Most of the previously Communist countries have now turned toward currency convertibility and shun soft currency transactions. Only Albania and Cuba remain as stalwarts of the old Communist system.

The CMEA (Council for Mutual Economic Assistance) had been created as an internal market with payment for goods traded between members in soft non-convertible domestic currencies. The market was undemanding of quality, and as quantities delivered were always below market needs, there was little incentive to invest in improved and increased production technology, marketing, or distribution skills. The CMEA simply identified priorities for the region over a five year period and aranged for suppliers to the region for those priority goods over those five years. As isolationism from world markets continued, and there were the added problems of CoCom controls prohibiting the sale or export of strategic goods and services in addition to the difficulty of access to funding, there were no incentives to actively pursue meaningful joint ventures.

What has changed is that in the wake of political change, central planning has now been completely dismantled throughout Eastern Europe. Poland moved suddenly and very dramatically on January 1, 1990, from a centrally planned economy to a free-market economy with an IMF-backed $1 billion plan that allowed for only a limited transition period. The cost has been great, introducing an initial 40% interest rate and the risk of social unrest developing into a backlash as inflation rates for a monthly year-on-year comparison exceeded 1,000%. Since then, with the structural change required in a "once and for all" realignment of prices, this has fallen to single digit levels.

Poland needs to reduce its state deficit, reduce government spending, tighten monetary policy, and suppress domestic demand. Everyone realizes that without inflation control, there can be no possible economic revival. Until 1989, more than 80% of items available on the Poland market were produced within the country; since then the share of imported goods has increased substantially. The more time that passes without social unrest, the greater Poland's chances of pulling through its economic crisis. The need to create a realistic pricing structure has never been in doubt; only the speed with which these changes can take place is the subject of discussion.

STRATEGIC INTENT OF JOINT VENTURES

Within a joint venture, what actually brings two sets of people together can often be the confluence of what are in effect disparate interests (Geringer and Hebert 1987). Where these interests are conflicting, the future of the joint venture itself is in danger. Opportunities to dominate the joint venture are not limited to the possession of capital, the ownership of equity, or the control over the flow of technology. It is impossible to have the equal interests of the partners represented in a strictly equal share of actual control over the joint venture, as, for one consideration, there will be three sets of management involved. The possible relationship between the two partners (parents) and the joint venture (child) give rise to a number of possible outcomes both anticipated and unanticipated. Table 12.2 shows joint ventures that parents will settle on initially as they negotiate if their respective needs for cooperation are high. If firms value potential partners' resources highly enough to negotiate, they would prefer to acquire them. They are often not for sale. Joint ventures are a compromise point.

Table 12.2. Strategic-Importance Relationship and Joint-Venture Formation (Assuming Firms Will Cooperate)

	Firm A	
	High strategic importance	Low strategic importance
High strategic importance	Stalemate—no cooperation	B acquires A
Firm B	Joint venture	B makes minority investment in A
Low strategic importance	A acquires B / A makes minority investment in B	Cooperative agreements (no separate entity is created)

Source: K. R. Harrigan (1985), *Strategic for Joint Ventures*, Lexington, MA: Lexington Books, p. 63.

The opportunity for Poland to make a quantum leap can only be achieved if there is an equal willingness by the West to accept these joint ventures and the risks they bring with them. There is no parallel with what Poland is currently trying to achieve, which has been compared to converting scrambled eggs back into fresh eggs. Political resistance can be expected of the economic adjustments being made, bringing with them recession, falls in industrial output and individual consumption, unemployment, and a worsening of the balance of trade and payments situation. However, projections are for 4 million people to be unemployed by 1996 concentrated in a few areas such as manufacturing, mining, construction, and agriculture.

PRIVATIZATION AND ECONOMIC REGENERATION THROUGH JOINT VENTURES

With regard to joint ventures, approximately one-third are being concluded with Germany. ICL Ltd. of Britain formed one of the first and largest joint ventures under the new legislation, now employing 5,500 people in six furniture factories and one computer assembly factory—making the joint venture—Furnell International—one of Poland's top exporters. In the last two years, ICL has been acquired by Fujitsu, putting the Japanese in control. The largest joint ventures in Eastern Europe are with G.M. in Warsaw, Volkswagen at the Skoda enterprise in Czechoslovakia, and with Fiat at the FSM enterprise in Poland. FSM has been at the center of prolonged strikes, including a hunger strike, ostensibly over wages. Industrial unrest and wage demands killed off the joint venture proposed between Lucchini (Italy) with the Huta Warszawa steel mill. As for FSM, it is effectively bankrupt. Meanwhile, this rather idiosyncratic method of selling cars in Poland through an installment plan and drawing lots among customers to get to the head of the waiting list to actually obtain a car is not an experience to be found elsewhere.

The FSM agreement was signed in October 1992 and involves investment of U.S. $2 billion of which only some U.S. $800 million is to be directly invested by Fiat. Similarly, Chrysler has held talks with the Ministry of Industry on modernizing Fabryka Samochodow Rolniczych, a producer of trucks and vans in Pznan. The U.S. firm offered a U.S. $20 million investment. Iveco (Italy) and Volkswagen (Germany) are also interested in cooperating with the factory. Also in the automotive sector, Volvo (Sweden) is expected to finalize a joint venture with the Jelcz enterprise to produce trucks and buses in a project that would involve Volvo investing U.S. $80 million. Saab-Scania of Sweden has signed a letter of intent with the Kapena bus repair enterprise of Slupsk to assemble Scania buses using Swedish components. Volkswagen (Germany) has been involved in joint venture talks with the Tarpan factory in Poznan to produce VW-T4 minivans from semi-knocked down kits. Elsewhere, Conoco, a subsidiary of Du Pont de Nemours (United States) is negotiating with the Plock and Gdansk refineries on setting up a joint venture to refine oil. Conoco is to invest U.S. $1 billion over a ten-year period in the Gdansk refinery. Also in petrochemicals, Bechtel (United States) is carrying out a feasibility study for the construction of a petrochemical plant near Kedzierzyn, and Amoco (United States) has concluded an agreement with the Ministry of Environmental Protection & Natural Resources & Forestry to carry out petroleum exploration work in Poland. In Krakow, Otis Elevator of the United States has acquired a 70% stake in a joint venture with PRDIE to install, service, and modernize elevators in Krakow. Bata (Canada), which used to have two factories and 300 shoe shops in Poland, is setting up a joint venture with Intercan to establish 30 shops, but is not applying for restitution of property lost to them during the communist period of control.

A 1990 telephone survey by London-based Merton Associates (Merton Associates and Transearch International (1990) of 200 British executives with Russian and Eastern bloc language fluency skills revealed that all respondents viewed with less than optimism the chances of more British companies successfully setting up joint ventures unless there is a change of attitude:

- at the Corporate Board level about the importance of taking a long term strategic view,
- amongst senior managers who are prepared to commit themselves wholeheartedly to making joint ventures work at local levels.

Respondents did not believe that British companies were doing enough or showing enough enterprise to compete with foreign countries for joint ventures with the USSR and Eastern Bloc.

West Germany was by far the favorite to succeed in this respect and was cited for:

- superior management
- greater entrepreneurial foresight
- long-term economic planning
- geographical proximity

In order of perceived success thereafter, the following countries were thought most likely to succeed over the United Kingdom in the long term:

1. France
2. Italy
3. USA
4. Japan
5. Finland
6. South Korea

The various scenarios described for the Soviet Union and for Eastern Europe agree in one important aspect: that the change that is taking place must be seen as permanent rather than ephemeral. Elections that took place throughout

Eastern Europe in 1990 reinforced this, and the newly enlarged community of interest created thereby has led to international coalitions to cement further political ties and economic union between the newly liberated democracies of Eastern Europe. However, without a change of attitude on the part of business-men outside of Germany, we can only look forward to the German economic invasion of the East. In terms of current debt holding, Germany holds more than 20% of Poland's $33 billion debt. With regard to credit, Chancellor Kohl has also offered Poland much more than others.

The Merton survey has proved true in fact, for although Germany has a very large number of JVs and the largest single amount, the value and quality of these JV investments could be greatly improved. Nevertheless, as Table 12.2 shows, over the last three years change has taken place. While some long standing problems are no longer so, some new problems have emerged in the transition to a market economy. Clearly, companies investing now are investing for the longer term.

BACK DOOR FOREIGN DIRECT INVESTMENT: ACQUISITION THROUGH JOINT VENTURE

It is almost impossible now to gauge exactly the number of joint ventures in Poland now because of the lack of reporting requirements. With only certain exceptions relating to the security, defense, and economic interests of the state, the regulations introduced in November 1991 state that authorization is no longer needed even for 100% foreign ownership, and there are also no stipulations requiring any fixed sum of start-up capital. Most involve small- to medium size enterprises (5 million small businesses were registered in 1994 through 1995 consisting mainly of 1 to 2 individuals, but only 60% of these are thought to be active), and there is an increasing gradual incremental foreign ownership in preparation for January 1995 when the rules change once again. Some Polish enterprises will have a minority foreign partner until then. Yet, in these circumstances, joint venture is a misnomer because we are really dealing with foreign direct investment (FDI). As the new system comes into being, the old system is simply being discarded without any formal acknowledgement. The need for investment and for technology drives this move to attract foreign investors. Western Europe as a consolidated investor accounts for over 80% of the total value of foreign capital in Poland (UNECE 1991). The EEC share of projects in Poland is approximately 53% and EFTA, 26%. Foreign companies now compete on equal terms with Polish enterprises. Tax holidays have been abolished but exemption from income tax may be granted where an investment exceeds 2M ECU (approximately U.S. $2M) and the investment is planned for an area of high unemployment, introduces new high technology, and where export sales are in excess of 20% of the value of total sales. Changes introduced in June 1991 had already introduced important changes regarding profit repatriation, approval of investment, and investment guarantees (Cole, Corette, and Abrutyn, Solicitors 1991).

MANAGERIAL RESISTANCE AND THE CONTINUED
EXISTENCE OF THE "NOMENCLATURA"

Like managers the world over, but even more so, Polish managers have resisted change for as long as it was possible to do so. It is said that 56% of the Polish labor force in September 1992 was in the private sector, but this ignores their contribution to GDP. Thirty-nine percent of Polish industry is unprofitable and certain industrial sectors, e.g., steel, have no private ownership. Provided the Polish government does not embark on any ill-conceived plan to curb this

Table 12.3. Problems Solved and Remaining Related to IJVs in Poland

Problem Areas	No Longer Problem Areas
1. Statistics on investment are virtually hopeless as the delegation of authority to municipal bodies has done away with much of the reporting of actual cases.	1. Investment possible now in virtually all economic sectors.
2. Privatization of state-owned bureaucracies swathed in regulation.	2. Links with Polish government bureaucracy have been streamlined and new agencies created to offer a "one-stop" service for Western investors. Governmental approval not required.
3. Warsaw Stock Market still in its infancy; ability to raise capital is very limited.	3. Majority or total foreign ownership of assets in Poland.
4. Pricing of goods and services on a full-cost basis.	4. Convertibility of the Polish currency has likewise removed many previous difficulties.
5. Intellectual Property. No protection from piracy in areas such as compter systems. Copying software in Poland and selling it is not illegal.	5. Shortages are no longer a problem. Everything is available at a price.
6. Accounting concepts of the Eastern Bloc traditionally differ from the West.	

growth, change should be long-lasting. However, change in ownership by itself is no solution to Poland's economic crisis, and even this change is being deliberately stalled by the old Communist party faithful. The FSO car works in Warsaw is a good example. After visiting Britain, France, and Germany, the directors of the enterprise said that the workers could not accept the proposals of foreign companies.   The directors have in fact really been fearing for themselves, looking at examples of what has taken place elsewhere. With Polkolor, even changing the director did not create any organizational change in attitude because of the entrenched management positions below. Yet change has taken place despite these obstacles, often introduced by the communist old-guard, the so-called "nomenclatura," less committed now to an outdated ideology and more fearful for their own futures. Through joint ventures, working practices have changed.

A further example is the French company Thomson, which made guarantees to retain the workforce when it came into the Polkolor enterprise in Warsaw. However, no wage increases were given to those working in the unprofitable parts of the Polkolor enterprise. In the first year of marketization, inflation in Poland hit 1,000% and this in turn took care of the excess workforce problem; those workers were now forced to look elsewhere for work. One year later Polkolor is manufacturing globally competitive products and exporting three quarters of its output. Polkolor is now a fully vertically integrated producer of picture tubes, and Thomson's investment has been steadily increasing from the $35 million originally to a reported figure of $100 million. The large companies that Poland needs to develop her economy are looking now at the longer term. David Hunter of the Swedish firm Asea Brown Boveri spoke of his firm's two large joint ventures, and minority involvement in four others, and put this down to "ABB's particular style—we're not afraid to invest in firms with an uncertain future."   ABB's investments in Poland include steam and gas turbines; generators; electrical motors and drivces; railroad signalling equipment; electron tubes and broadcast transmitters; and environmental protection project support and transformer manufacture. Poland has a higher degree of foreign investment than Hungary, but Hungary has a better publicity machine. The question of private enterprises is also difficult to define because in the early stages, there were stock market share flotations, but this proved to be slow. The Stock Market has not developed beyond 16 companies whereas privatization of state enterprises has shot ahead through liquidation sales of unprofitable enterprises. Retailing as a sector is now largely privatized, while the manufacturing sector is still in need of privatization measures (Sowinska 1991). The Ministry of Ownership Changes, which is responsible for privatization, produced a September 1992 legal draft for the Mass Privatization Program (known by the intitials PPP) which would privatize somewhere between 400 and 600 enterprises. This would make ownership theoretically available to all Polish citizens over eighteen years of age, 27 million potential shareholders. This will happen in practice because while details are scant, shareholders would have to pay a registration fee fixed to the monthly wage, which is currently around $200. This, though, is no more than a legal conveyancing mechanism designed to transfer the ownership of assets from the state to the private sector without the injection of new working capital.

However, while there has been substantial progress made over the last two years toward lifting barriers to FDI, the UNECE (UNECE 1991) points out how the privatization of state-owned enterprises, which generally offers the prospect of greater inflows of capital than through joint ventures or greenfield investments, has been accompanied not by less regulation but by more. The Ministry of Ownership Changes would have to create 20 National Investment Funds as joint-stock companies to act as a conduit for this investment money. It has to be said, though, that Poland is very short of domestic investment capital and has not been very successful in pulling in foreign investors. The net effect, therefore, will be a change in ownership but no addition to working capital for these newly privatized enterprises.

COMPARING POLISH JOINT VENTURES WITH "FOCUSED" CHINESE JOINT VENTURES

Looking at what has been successful in China, Newman (1992) found that highly flexible, participative, democratic management is not the key. Instead, these Chinese joint ventures have been successful in transforming the economy because they are focused. It is argued that they could play an important role in developing countries seeking a quick rise in GNP and which have low-skilled ambivalent workers. These focused joint ventures have the following characteristics:

1. Highly prescribed operations
2. Narrow product lines
3. Sustained commitment of partners
4. Top-down motivation of employees
5. Strict performance standards for local suppliers

These enterprises, which are tightly managed, are then capable of producing goods to world class standards while also keeping control over costs.

There is a role model for Eastern European countries, such as Poland, as they assess the quantum leap that their economies have to make to become internationally competitive. The transition required can be enormous and, in any event, joint ventures are inherently unstable. Newman argues that the successful joint venture is one that does not deviate from its narrowly defined business mission. A successful simple focused joint venture establishes relationships. Success becomes conspicuous and will allow the joint venture to be extended perhaps into helping suppliers improve their product, offering to move them closer to world standards. Polish joint ventures have been less successful in attracting foreign capital than, for example, Hungary or Czechoslovakia. In number, they are very small relative to China, which has over 30,000 joint ventures. In part, Polish decentralization has caused a situation where no one really knows the full extent of foreign investment in Poland, but it is estimated to be about U.S. $800 million. Again, the numbers of joint ventures in Poland are often taken together with the number of wholly owned foreign subsidiaries, but data is incomplete. The Polish Foreign Investment Agency (PAIZ) themselves are lacking this information, and a *Warsaw Voice* estimate of July 26, 1992, of 2,749 conflicts with earlier figures cited by UNECE.

Assets	Liabilities
- Elimination of previous CoCom barriers to technology transfer	- No economic model to follow
- Hungry market for Western goods	- Western aspirations but Eastern wage levels
- Social cohesion, a bloodless revolution away from Communism	- lack of management skills so reliance on expatriate managers
- Relatively homogeneous nation with proven democratic traditions	- Weak infrastructure
- Skilled, educated workforce	- Political uncertainty of a split parliament
- Professional cadre educted to Ph.D. level	- Large number of weak state enterprises
- Proportionately more young people in the population than other Western nations still suffering from the "baby-boomer" effect	- Two generations lost to Communism
- Industrialized nation	- Lack of a significant work ethic while aspiring to Western materialism
- Associate membership of the EEC has introduced conformity with other Western countries	- Role of unions unclear
- Frequent attempts to joint NATO reassures potential investors	- Economic uncertainty if social cohesion breaks down
- Low wage country relative to Western European neighbors	- Strong neighbors in Russia and Germany who have traditionally posed both an economic and defense threat
- Located in Central Europe	- Low value-added to be found in Poland
- Rich in raw materials	

- Pragmatic approach to foreign
  investment

- Large Polish communities abroad,
  e.g., United States defense threat

- International goodwill

- Many Polish entrepreneurs with
  vision

- Assets for sale at low prices

- Western management training,
  development to be found
  everywhere

- Western management practices
  being integrated into business

- Nomenclature (old communist
  faithful) still entrenched
  in some sections of the
  economy

- Personal tax and value-added
  tax are new
- Tax authorities undermanned and
  underfunded so statistics based
  on taxation collected will be
  unreliable of total potential

- Official statistics generally poor

- Communications poor

- Language skills weak (German
  more popular than English)

- Low quality reputation, low
  work ethic will force low
  asset sale price

- Lack of general funding
  possibilities

- Bureaucratic traditions
  remain

- Procrastination is endemic

- Few Polish brands known
  in the West

- No established distribution
  networks in the West

The potential for joint ventures in Poland is enormous. In actual practice, these are not taking place with the speed or size desirable to ensure a smooth transition to a market economy. It is to be hoped that Poland will make it through very difficult times ahead without continued violent demonstrations of the social unrest now evident. The politicians are divided and have nothing to offer, and without them Western businessmen are reluctant to enter. No new alternative scenarios have been offered by any political party. More than just a massive injection of foreign capital is required. An infusion of new technologies is required, and a whole series of marketing networks and strategic business alliances needs to be instituted. Management training and development programs are now in place in Poland and it is to be hoped that these will help not only create more owner-managers, but assist them in the transition that their companies will go through as they increase in size and total owner control becomes unfeasible. To address this, there will be heavy demands on joint ventures, but given the list of Poland's assets and liabilities (see Table 12.4), these joint ventures are likely to be more jointly shared than any of their predecessors.

REFERENCES

Business International Limited (1991), *Doing Business with Eastern European, The Economist*, London.

Cole, Corette, and Abrutyn, Solicitors (1990), "Critical Legal Issues Affecting Investment and Trade in Poland," Warsaw, London, Washington, Moscow, December 1.

Dobosiewicz, Zbigniew (1992), "Foreign Investment in Eastern Europe," London: Routledge.

Dodsworth, Terry and Sara Webb (1992), "So You Fancy Making a Fast Buck Behind the Curtain?" *Financial Times*, January 27, pp. B1-B3.

Geringer, J. Michael (1988), "Selection of Partners for International Joint Ventures," University of Western Ontario School of Business Administration, Working Paper No. 88-30, September.

Geringer, J. Michael and Louis Hebert (1988), "Control and Performance of International Joint Ventures: An Analysis of Theory and Research," University of Western Ontario School of Business Administration, Working Paper No. 88-20, June.

Gillespie, Ian (1990), *Joint Ventures*, A Eurostudy Special Report, London: Eurostudy Publishing Co. Ltd.

Knight, Russell M. (1987), "Entrepreneurial Joint Ventures Strategies," University of Western Ontario School of Business Administration, Working Paper No. NC 87-05, March.

Lukowicz, Maciej (1990), "Guidelines for Foreign Investors Interested in Joint Ventures," *Warsaw Voice*, October 13, 12.

Lynch, Robert Porter (1990), *The Practical Guide to Joint Ventures and Corporate Alliances*, New York: John Wiley and Sons.

McKinnon, Ronald (1991), "The Order of Economic Liberalisation: Financial Control in the Transition of a Market Economy," Stanford University Press, as reported in the *Economist* (January), 51.

Merritt, Giles (1991), *Eastern Europe and the USSR: The Challenge of Freedom*, London: Kogan Page.

Merton Associates and Transearch International, "Survey into the Management Attitudes into Working with the Eastern Bloc and the USSR," London, February 16.

National Underwriter (1990), "AIG Licensed for Poland and Hungary," Vol. 94 (47), November 19, pp. 57-88.

Newman, William H. (1992), "'Focused Joint Ventures' in Transforming Economies," *Academy of Management Executive*, 6 (1), 67-75.

Ohmae, Kenichi (1989), "Managing in a Borderless World," *Harvard Business Review* (May-June), 152.

—— (1988), *The Borderless World*, New York: Harper Business, 181.

—— (1987), "Companies without Countries," *The McKinsey Quarterly*, (Autumn), 51.

Piotrowski, Zbigniew (1991), " New Conditions for Investing Capital in Poland" *Warsaw Voice*, (September 7), L1-L4.

Sowinska, Magda (1991), "The Transformation—One Year Later," *Warsaw Voice*, October 20, pp. B5.

UNECE (1992), *Legal Aspects of Privatisation in Industry*, ECE/TRADE/180, Geneva and New York.

—— (1992), "Statistical Survey of Recent Trends in Foreign Investment in East European Countries." TRADE/R575, November 25.

—— (1991), "Promoting Foreign Direct Investments in the ECE Region," TRADE/R572 November 25, pp. 1-2.

—— (1991), "Review of Recent and Prospective Trends, Policies and Problems in Intra-Regional Trade," TRADE/R 571 November 15, pp. 6, 4, 2.

—— (1990), "The Promotion of Foreign Direct Investment in the ECE Region," TRADE/R572, November 29.

Warsaw Voice (1991), October 13, p. 12.

—— (1991), March 8.

Index

Abkhaz Republic, 165
Accountancy, 33
Agency: relationships as a contract, utilization of rules, 22
Agreements on Avoiding Double Taxation, 181
Aguilar, Francis J., 145
AIG Insurance, 167
AK30, 198
AKZO subsidiary: Ketjen, 127, 136
Alcatel, 174
Alchian, Arman A., 22
Alliances: relating to market access, 128; types of, 4
American Chamber of Commerce, the Netherlands, 130
American International Group, Inc., 207
Amoco, 212
APV, 97—100
Armenia, 165
Arrow, Kenneth J., 23, 26, 29
Asea Brown Boveri (ABB), 215
AT&T, 174
Austin, Anne L., 21
Automotive Components Group Europe, 207
Avishai, Bernard, 142

Azerbaijan, 165
Babolna Agricultural Cooperative, 8, 11, 13
Baker and McKenzie, 163
Baltic states, 164
Bank of Credit and Commerce International (BCCI), 33
Banks, John C., 21, 23, 26, 79, 85
Bargaining agreement, control mechanisms (decision-making power), 84
Barnard, Bruce, 21
Beamish, Paul W., 21, 23, 26, 67, 79, 80, 85, 107, 108, 142, 144, 147
Bechtel, 212
Belarus, 165
Bell, J., 190, 192
Bell Labs, 167
Berg, Sanford V., 109, 130
Bergen, Mark, 21
BI 1988, 183
Biemans, Wim G., 5
Bivens, K.K., 108
Bjorkman, Ingmar, 7, 17
Black Box Corp. Inc, 134
Black Box Datacom BV, 134
Bleeke, J., 199

Blodgett, Linda Longfellow, 21, 24
Bounded Rationality Model: of decisionmaking, 6—7, 17
Buckley, Peter J., 23, 24, 26, 28, 200
Bulgaria, 173
Burnette, J.J., 109
Bush, President George, 170
Business International S.A., 206
Business plan, 87
Butarker, IKEA joint venture, 13—16
Buzzell, Robert D., 34, 142
Cable and Wireless, 174
Campbell, Donald C., 6, 56
Case study research, 6—18; evaluation, 7—8; goal of, 6; IKEA-Butarker joint venture, 13—16; McDonald's-Babolna joint venture, 8—13; methods, 6—7
Casson, Mark, 23, 24, 26, 28, 200
Cavanaugh, Richard E., 34, 55
Central Committee of Communist Party, 161; perestroika, 160
Chase Manhattan, 167
Cheung, Steven N.S., 22
China: coordination of investment objectives, 70; critical economic and political changes, 141; development of market and reform of prices, 64; economic reform process, 63; feasability study, 68; foreign exchange balance, 72—73; foreign investment, attracted to, 141; foreign investors prefer joint ventures, 66; government in 3 levels, 144; incentives in Special Economic Zones, 66; International Monetary Fund, World Development Bank and United Nations, 142—43; low technical and managerial

skills, 66; market main objective of foreign companies, 71; organizational structure, 74; privatization of state-owned companies, 64; socialism developing, 63; transfer of production factors, 71
China, joint ventures compared with Poland, 216
China Business Review, 146
China's Governmental Planning Department, 69
China's motive for promoting joint ventures: access to technology, 71
China Statistical Yearbook, 143, 145
Chinese business cooperation: improvement of products and new products, 71
Chitle, C.R., 183
Christensen, John, 22
Chrysler, 211
Cindu Chemical Industries, 129, 133
Citicorp, 167
Clifford, Donald K., 34, 55
CMEA countries, 176
Coalitions, 190
Coase, Ronald H., 22
Coastal/open cities: 45 opened, 145
Cohen, M., 6
Cole, Corette, and Abrutyn, Solicitors, 213
Collins, Timothy M., 25
Communism, in Poland, 205, 207—8
Comparative Management, 189
Competition: dimension of, 189
Competitive advantages, 192
Computerization of Russian industry, 160
Conant, Jeffrey S., 33, 36
Connolly, S.G., 78, 85

Conoco, 211—12

Contractor, Farok J., 4, 23, 27, 79, 84, 85, 189, 190, 192, 199

Contracts: alliances, 190; governed by Law of the PROC on Chinese-Foreign Cooperative joint ventures, 67; nonrepeated asymmetric information, 22; separate legal entity with limited liability, 67; writing, 87, 89

Control: degree achieved by partners, 24; issue of furniture venture, 15; of venture members coordination of actions, 21

Cooperation: coordination through mutual forbearance, 24

Cooperative agreements, 190

Cooperative arrangements, 190

Cost/benefit analysis, 85—86

Coughlin, C.C., 183

Council for Mutual Economic Assistance (CMEA), 209

Country Report on China, 142, 143

Creation-implementation process, 3

Credit Lyonnais, 167

Currency convertibility, in Poland, 204, 209

Cyanamid, 127, 129

Cyanamid International Development Corp., 133

Cyanamid-Ketjen, 133

Cyert, Richard, 6, 17

Czechoslovakia, 13

Datta, D.K., 108, 109

Davies, Howard, 129

Davies, J.R., 78, 80

Dean, Richard, 37

Debevoise and Plimpton, 163

Decisionmaking: Bounded Rationality Model, 6—7, 17; characteristics, 4—5; in creating an IJV, 4; flow phases of, 8; foreign direct investment (FDI), 17; Garbage Can Model, 6 — 7; implementation phase, 8, 13; joint venture design phase, 8, 13; joint venture proposal evaluation, 8, 13, 15—16; solution-opportunity identification phase, 8—12, 14

Decision process, phases in, 8

Decision systems analysis (DSA), flow-diagrams, 7

De Jong-Coen BV, 133

Demsetz, Harold, 22

Denzin, Norman K., 34, 37

Design and implementation: of the fast-food joint venture, 13; process, 3, 8, 13

Dess, Greg S., 33

Dodsworth, Terry, 207

Dominant-parent ventures, 81

Doorley, Thomas L., III, 25

Dougherty, Deborah, 33

Doyle, Peter, 33, 34, 36, 37, 38, 43, 55

Doz, Y.L., 82, 190

DSM, 198

Dual organizational model, 74

Duncan, Jerome, 130

Dunning, J.H., 144

DuPont de Nemours, 211

Dutch: defensive or offensive character of ventures, 191; financial participation of Dutch partner, 192; level of value-chain, 192; motive to set up ventures, 192; number of participants in ventures, 193; objectives strived for, 191

Dutch American Plant Breeders BV, 138

Dutch Innovation Board, 136

Dutta, Shantanu, 21

Dyson, Esther, 37

Easley, David, 22

East European Cooperation and

Trade (EECT), 209
East European Investment Funds, 207
EBRD (European Bank for Reconstruction and Development), 172
Economic reform process: in China, 63
Economist, 10
Emmott, Bill, 4
Equity joint venture, governed by Law on Joint Ventures Using Chinese and Foreign Investment, 66
Ernst, E., 199
Esso Europe, 130
Esso U.S.A., 130
Evaluation: alternatives follow conjunctive decision rules, 7; implementation of Hungarian-Swedish furniture venture, 15; of proposed Hungarian-U.S. fast-food joint venture, 13
Exxon Europe, 136
Fama, Eugene F., 22, 25
Farley, John U., 7
Feasability study, 68; of joint venture defined, 69—70
Fiat, 159, 211
Fleck, Robert A., 3
Flexibility, 192
Flexifloat Systems BV, 130
Flow-diagrams, in decision systems analysis (DSA), 7
Focus of control, scope of activities, 24
Foreign direct investment (FDI): decisionmaking, 17; in Poland, 213, 216
Foreign-owned enterprises: governed by Law of the PROC on Enterprises Operating Exclusively with Foreign Capital, 67
Former Yugoslavia: foreign investor

had no proprietary rights, 178; foreign investor has rights as specified by contract, 179; foreign investor may establish a wholly-owned enterprise, 180; foreign investor may not establish enterprise in communications, insurance, publishing and mass media, 181; foreign investor may not invest in areas deemed in the national defense, 181; foreign investor seeks penetration via Yugoslavia into CMEA markets, 182
Former Yugoslavia Joint Venture Law, 179
Franko, Lawrence G., 34
Friedman, Phillip, 109, 130
FSM, 211
FSO, 215
Fuller, M.B., 190
Furnell International, 211
Gale, Bradley T., 34
Garbage Can Model, 6—7
Georgia, 165
Geringer, J. Michael, 21, 24, 34, 37, 107, 109, 127, 128, 210
Gerlach, Michael L., 146
Germany, 212, 213
Glaser, Barney G., 3, 8
GM Europe, 206—7
Goldberg, Victor P., 22
Government policy, fade-out agreements, 80
Government suasion, in developing countries, 80
Great Britain, 212
Guanxi, friendly network, 71, 145
Gullander, S.O., 108
Gyori Keksz, 91—94
Habib, G.M., 109
Hamel, G., 82, 190
Hamill, J., 77, 78, 80
Harrigan, Kathryn R., 37, 79, 83,

84, 85, 86, 87, 101, 109, 192
Hart, Oliver, 23
Hebert, Louis, 21, 24, 34, 37, 128, 210
Heckathorn, Douglas D., 22
Heenan, D.A., 37, 107
Hendryx, Steven R., 144
Hennart, Jean-Francois, 129, 134
Hergert, M., 192, 194
Het Financiëel Dagblad, 130
Hidden Action Model, 23
Hidden Information Model: of moral hazard, 23; resolution based in reputation, 28
Hisrich, Robert D., 5
Hladik, K., 108
Hoekman, J.M., 199
Holmstrom, Bengt, 23
Holton, R.H., 80, 82, 85, 87, 109
Howard, John A., 7, 38
Hulbert, James, 7
Hume, Scott, 9
Hungarian-Swedish furniture joint venture: as strategic opportunity, 13
Hungaroton, 94—97
Hungary: criteria for success of joint ventures, 77;
IBM, 166
ICL Ltd. of Britain, 211
IKEA-Butarker joint venture, 13—16; McDonald's-Babolna fast-food joint venture, 8—13, 17—18; toward a market economy, 89, 90
IKEA-Butarker retail furniture joint venture, 13—16
Implementation, design and time, 3
Implementation phase, in decisionmaking process, 8, 13
Industrial cooperation agreements (ICAs), in Poland, 207
International cooperative alliances. See Alliances
International cooperative venture

(ICV), 4
International Finance Corporation, 170
International joint ventures (IJVs): contributions of each party, 4—5; decision-making process, 4—5; defined, 3; design-implementation process, 3, 8, 13; distribution of rewards and their composition, 108; effectiveness, 109; financial managemen, 190; a formal arrangement, 190; form of, 3—5; globalization of the economy and, 21; government and trade relations; a legal entity, 107; management style, 82; marketing policies and practices, 82; personnel and industrial relations policies, 82; production policies and technology transfer, 82; R & D 82; time scale of the venture, 82; unification of Europe and, 21
International Management, 189
Italtel, 174
Itoh, Hideshi, 25
Jagersma, P.K., 189, 190, 192
Jain, S.C., 82
James, B.G., 190
Janger, A.R., 80, 81, 107, 108, 109
Jensen, Michael C., 22
Jick, Todd, 35, 37
Johnson-Hamstra BV, 138
Johnson Inc., 138
Joint equity ventures, in Poland, 207
Joint venture: failure, 80; as a foreign market entry, 78; global competition, 79; minimum cutoff criteria, 17; objectives, 85; strategic opportunities, 17
Joint Venture Implementing

Regulations (1983): policies on patents, profit repatriation and foreign exchange clarified, 143

Joint Venture Law (1979): established principles and procedures for foreign investments, 142

Joint ventures: acquisition through, 213; case study research, 6—18; changing concept of, 207; in China, 144; design phase, 213; in Poland, 203—19; Polish vs. Chinese, 216—19; proposal evaluation phase, 8, 13, 15—16; strategic intent of, in Poland, 210—11

Joint ventures in former Yugoslavia, 177

Joint ventures in Hungary: criteria for success, 77

Joint ventures in Russia: dominated by Germany and United States, 168; growth in Research and Development, 167; heavy industrial production, 166—67; industrial waste and raw materials, 166

Jowisz, 203

Kandiko, Jozsef, 4, 8, 17, 34, 36

Kazakhstan, 165, 173, 174

Keck, E., 143

Ketjen, AKZO subsidiary, 127, 136

Key success factors (KSFs), 3

Killing, J. Peter, 23, 80, 81, 85, 107, 108, 109, 199

Klein, Benjamin, 23, 28

Knowledge of structure of Russian government, 162

Kogut, Bruce, 34, 37, 81, 107, 135

Kohl, President Helmut, 170

Kohler/Wascher, 67

Koot, William T.M., 23, 24

KPMG, 161

Kuiper, W.G., 128

Kyrgyzstan, 165, 173, 174

Lafayette Publications, 21

Lamers, A., 183

Lane, H.W., 107, 108

Law on Corporation Profits Tax, 181

Lee, Allen S., 33, 38

Lee, Ming-Kwan, 142

Leffler, Keith B., 23, 28

Levinthal, Daniel, 22

Lithuanian Parliament's Declaration of Independence, 164

Local partner, supplies infrastructure, 79

Lorange, Peter, 4, 23, 27, 82, 109, 189, 190, 192, 199

Lotus, 166

Lovell, E.B., 108

Lyles, M.A., 108

Lynch, Robert Porter, 207

Lyons, Michael P., 127

MacDonald, Glenn M., 22

Managerial dimension, 78

Managers, resistance to change, in Poland, 214—16

Managers carry perceptions, observing sequence of steps, 4

Mankin, E.D., 190

March, John, 6, 17

Mariti, P., 190

Martinez, C.L., 109

Maser, Stephen M., 22

McDonald's-Babolna fast-food joint venture, 8—13, 17—18

McDonald's USA, 8

MCI, 174

McKinnon, Ronald, 204

Meckling, William H., 22

Merritt, Giles, 203

Merton Associates, 212

Microsoft, 166

Miles, R.E., 36

Milgrom, Paul, 23, 28

Miller, Danny, 33

Ministry for Foreign Economic

Relations, 181

Ministry of Communication and Post, 160

Ministry of Education and Culture, 94

Ministry of Foreign Trade, 159

Ministry of Machinery Building, 160

Ministry of Non-Ferrous Metals, 160

Mintzberg, Henry, 7, 33

MNE provides knowledge of: management, 79; technology, 79

Mokwa, Michael P., 33, 36

Moldova, 165

Moral hazard problem, 23

Morganroth, William A., 38

Morris, D., 193, 194

Morrison, Alan J., 33

Moscow, McDonald's in, 9—10

Moscow location for 85% of joint ventures, 164

Mudge, Rose, 163

Multidimensional approach, 190

Multilateral Investment Guarantee Agency, 170

Multinational corporations (MNCs), 109

Multinational enterprise (MNE), 6; knowledge of capital markets, 79; managers, decision-making process, 4—5

Multiple goals: used in valuing investments, 5

Multiple performance criteria, 5

Mutual forbearance, 24

National Underwriter, 207

Negotiation: of the agreement, 87; planning paradigm-calculation of rates of return, 84

Neptun, 203

Neville Chemical Corporation, 129

New Economic Mechanism (NEM), 90

Newman, William H., 23, 216

Nichols, Henry W., 25

Nike, 144—45

Non-profit organization: distinctive competencies, 33; strategic focus, 33

Nooderhaven, Niels, G., 23

Nowak, Phillip, 25

Nueno, P., 128

Occidental Petroleum, 168

O'Hara, Maureen, 22

Ohmae, Kenichi, 153, 190, 203, 204

Olsen, J., 6

Oosterveld, J., 128

Otis Elevator, 212

Parkhe, Arvind, 4

Pattern matching, 6

Patton, Michael Quinn, 33, 37

Pearson, M.M., 142, 143

People's Republic of China (PROC), 63—74

Performance evaluation, 89

Performance standard, a signal as a parameter, 22

Perlmutter, H.V., 37, 107

Peter, J.Paul, 3

Peterson, R.B., 23

Pettibone, Peter J., 142

Pettigrew, Andrew M., 38

Pfeffer, Jeffrey, 25

Phase theorem, from Rational Model, 7

Phillips, 198

Piaseczno enterprise, 203

Poland, 203—19; acquisition through joint ventures in, 213; changing concept of joint ventures in, 207—9; Communism in, 205, 207—8; currency convertibility, 203, 209; detente period, 204; foreign direct investment (FDI) in, 205—7, 213, 216; free-market economy, 209; industial cooperation agreements (ICAs), 207; joint venture assets and liabilities, 217—19; joint ventures compared with China, 216; loss of traditional markets, 203; managerial resistance in, 214—16; Ministry of Ownership Changes(PPP), 215, 216; privatization, 211—13, 215—16; strategic intent of joint ventures in, 210—11; western competition, 203

Polish Foreign Investment Agency (PAIZ), 217

Polkolor, 215

Pooling of resources, 80

Porter, M.E., 82, 189, 190

Post-incorporation requirements, 120—22

Prahalad, C.K., 82, 190

Pratt, John W., 22

Pre-emptive strategy, 191

Pre-incorporation requirements, 119—20

Principal-agent relationship, 25

Privatization, in Poland, 211—13, 215—16

PROC People's Republic of China

Product and/or process objectives: of IJV, 191

Product-market opportunity, 5

Profits: division of, 80

Provisions for the Encouragement of Foreign Investment, 143

Puett, J.F., Jr., 176

Pye, L., 143, 144

Quelch, John A., 142

Raisinghani, Duru, 7

Raveed, S.R., 108

Reciprocal agency: in the context of joint ventures, 25; provides framework to anticipate problems, 21

Reciprocal interdependence, 24

Reagan, President Ronald, 160

Reich, R.B., 190

Renforth, W., 108

Reputation, contract enforcement device, 23

Research models, case study research method, 6—18

Retail site location, 13

Reward and control systems, 80

Richardson, John D., 142

Ricks, D.A., 109

Roberts, John, 23, 28

Robinson, Richard B., Jr., 33

Robishaw Engineering Inc., 130

Rock, Stuart, 142

Roebers, Th. J., 128

Roman, D.D., 176

Roos, J., 109

Roth, Kendall, 33

Rugman, A. M., 191

Russia, 174; enrichment of industrial waste, 166; GNP declined every year, 160; IMF and World Bank, 170; industrial production conversion of military plants, 167

Russian Central Bank, inconvertibility of ruble, 162

Russian economy since 1993, inflation and devaluation of the ruble, 163

Russian joint ventures: dominated by Germany and United States, 168; growth in research and development, 167; industrial waste and raw materials, 166

Russian joint ventures failed: financial problems, 162; inappropriate partners, 161; unfavorable negotiation results-difference in mentality, 163

Saab-Scania, 211

Salama, Eric R., 142

Sanders, John, 33, 34, 36, 37, 38,
    43, 55
Schaan, J.L., 108, 109
Schuchardt, Christian, 67
Selecting partners, 86
Shanghai Jiaotong University, 67
Share of initial capital investment:
    division of profits, 162
Shaw, Vivienne, 38, 55
Shell, 198
Shenkar, Oded, 4, 107, 109, 144,
    147
Short-term profits vs. future market
    share, 43
Simon, Herbert, 6
Smiley, R.H., 190
Snow, C.C., 36
Socialist market system, 63
Solution-opportunity identification
    phase, in decisionmaking
    process, 8—12, 14
Somogyi, Piroska, 36, 39
Sowinska, Magda, 215
Special Economic Zones (SEZ),
    143, 145
Sprint, 174
Starks, Laura T., 22
State Committee for Foreign
    Economic Ties, 159
State Investment Company (Russia),
    168
State Property Agency (SPA), 90
Stertil BV, 132, 136
Stopford, M., 129
Strategic alliances, 190; many
    forms, 146
Strategic auditing, 33
Strategic behavior approach, 190
Strategic dimension, 78
Strategic orientation of IKEA's
    product, 15
Strategic partnership, 190;
    Hungarian-Japanese enterprise,
    34
Strauss, Anselm L., 38
Studer, Margaret, 142

Sullivan, Daniel P., 36
Sullivan, J., 23
Sung, Yun-Wing, 142
Swap-center, exchange Chinese
    currency, 73
Sweden, IKEA-Butarker joint
    venture, 13—16
Tallman, Stephen B., 4
TDF Tiofine BV, 133
Tebodin Engineering Consultants,
    128
Technische Universität Berlin, 67
Technology transferring
    co-venturer, 130
Teece, D.J., 190
Theoret, Andre, 7
Third-party stakeholder, 4, 5
Thompson, James D., 24
Thomson, 215
Thorn-EMI, 94—97
Tomlinson, J.W.C., 81
Transfer of power, HRM policy,
    122
Trappey, Randolph J., III, 36
Triangulation: application of to
    strategic auditing, 34; research,
    37
Trommsdorff, Volker, 67
Tsui, Anne S., 23
Turkmenistan, 165, 174
Ukraine, 165, 174
Ultra Carbon Inc., 136
UNCTC (United Nations Centre on
    Transnational Corporations),
    80, 85
United Biscuits (UB), 91—94
U.S.-Dutch joint ventures, 127
USSR Council of Ministers, 161
U.S.West, 174
Value subtraction, 204
Varadarajan, Rajan P., 33, 36
Vnesheconombank, 174
Volkswagen, 142, 211
Volvo, 142, 211
Walker, Orville C., Jr., 21

Walmsley, J., 85
Wang, H.Y., 142, 144
Warsaw Voice, 207
Webb, Sara, 207
Wells, L., 129
Westchester Country Syndrome,
    143
Wheeler, C., 78, 80
White and Case, 163
Wholly owned subsidiaries (WOS),
    5
Williamson, O.E., 79
Wilpert, Bernard, 67
Wilson, David T., 17
Wilson, Elizabeth I., 17
Winfrey, Frank L., 21
Witte, Erhard, 7
Wong, Veronica, 33, 34, 36, 37, 38,
    43, 55
Woodside, Arch G., 4, 8, 16, 34,
    36, 39, 40
World Bank, 68–69
Xiaoping, Deng, 63
Xycarb BV, 136
Xytel Corporation, 128
Yeltsin, President Boris, 168
Yin, Robert K., 6, 7, 56
Young, S., 78, 80
Zeckhauser, Richard J., 22
Zeira, Y., 107, 109

About the Contributors

KEVIN Y. AU was born in Hong Kong and is studying Organizational Behaviour/International Business at UBC. His research interests include foreign direct investment, cross-cultural management, and social justice. His dissertation is on grievance processing for an ethnically diverse workforce. E-mail: yfau@unixg.ubc.ca

ANNE L. AUSTIN is currently a third-year law student and contributing editor to the *Case Western Reserve University Law Review.* She is also employed as a law clerk for the Office of the General Counsel of Ernst & Young in Cleveland, Ohio. Her scholarly research interests focus on export trading companies, international franchising, countertrade, and issues of promissory estoppel. Papers by Dr. Austin have been presented at meetings of the Academy of International Business, the American Marketing Association, the Academy of Management, the Association for Consumer Research, the International Association for Business and Society, and the Society of Franchising.

JOHN BELL is Assistant Professor at the Department of Business Administration of Tilburg University in The Netherlands. His research interests include entry mode choices, interfirm relationships (e.g., joint ventures, strategic alliances, networks), international management, and strategic decision making. He has published several articles on these topics in different Dutch journals, and in a book edited by Rugman and Verbeke (1993). E-mail: J.H.J.Bell@KUB.NL

ZBIGNIEW DOBOSIEWICZ is an established author with books published in Eastern and Western Europe, including *Foreign Investment in Eastern Europe* with Routledge Ltd., London. He is Senior Advisor to the UN Development Programme in Warsaw and served at the Polish Institute of International Affairs before becoming Professor at the Higher School of Commerce and at the High School of Insurance & Banking, both based in Warsaw, Poland. He is an experienced economic analyst and has published widely throughout Africa and Europe, East and West.

GUNNAR GRÄF is working as a consultant to Arthur D. Little International Inc. and the Chief Technology Advisor of the Berlin Senate specialized in innovation co-operation projects in reforming countries. He has worked as research assistant at the Shanghai Jiao Tong University in the P.R. China.

JIM HAMILL is Reader in International Business and Academic Director of the MSc in International Marketing (Open Learning) at the Strathclyde International Business Unit, Department of Marketing, University of Strathclyde, Glasgow, Scotland. He has researched and published widely in international business and marketing. His works have appeared in *European Management Journal; Journal of General Management; Employee Relations; Industrial Relations Journal; Textile Outlook International; Journal of East West Business;* and elsewhere. He has held visiting professorships in the United States, France, and Italy. He has undertaken consultancy on behalf of the Economist Intelligence Unit; International Labour Office, and the United National Conference on Trade and Development.

MATTHEW D. HEAPS is a Research Associate at the Freeman School of Business, Tulane University. He completed the M.B.A. at the Freeman School in 1992. He served as the Principal Investigator on the Freeman School Strategic Management and Marketing Audit Study at several Hungarian firms during 1991-1994. His current research projects include the investigation of the resulting changes in international strategies and the impacts of these changes on performances of firms following final reporting of research findings by outside consulting firms.

GRAHAM HUNT is a graduate of the University of Strathclyde and currently Marketing Manager with Hyward-Tyler, East Kilbride, Scotland.

PIETER K. JAGERSMA is a consultant in his own consultancy firm. His research interests include international management and strategic management. He has published a large number of articles on these topics in different Dutch journals.

MILE B. JOVIC has about twenty years of experience in research, consulting, and teaching in marketing and international business. He is senior Research Fellow at Institute of Economic Sciences as well as Associate Professor of Marketing and International Marketing in the Faculty of Economics, University of Novi Sad. He is the author of five books in marketing.

VLADIMIR L. KVINT is a Professor of Management Systems and International Business at Fordham University's Graduate School of Business Administration and Senior Consultant with Arthur Andersen LLP. He is a specialist on the economy and natural resources of Russia and other former Soviet Republics on foreign trade and political economy. He participated in drafting joint ventures and free economic zones regulations and has helped start a number of successful joint ventures in Russia and other Soviet Republics using experience gained as Deputy Chairman of a large Siberian company. A contributing writer to *Forbes* magazine and the *Harvard Business Review*, Dr. Kvint is the author of seven award-winning books and more than 200 articles. His most recent book is the *Barefoot Shoemaker: Capitalizing on the New Russia* (1993). He is a life-time member of the Russian Academy of Natural Sciences and a member of the Bretton Woods Committee. Other achievements include the development of a theory of regionalization of scientific technical progress and a system of optimizational models of strategies of companies in emerging markets.

STANLEY J. PALIWODA is Professor and Chair of Marketing at the University of Calgary, and Visiting Professor in Marketing at the Warsaw School of Economics, Poland. His interests are primarily in international marketing, focusing on business-to-business marketing strategy and marketing relationship management. He is the editor of *The Journal of East-West Business* and the author of ten books including *International Marketing*; *Business Opportunities in Eastern Europe*; *Essence of International Marketing*; and *The International Marketing Reader* (with Dr. John K. Ryans, Jr.). Dr. Paliwoda is on the editorial board of six journals including; *Journal of Global Marketing; Journal of Euromarketing; Asia Pacific International Journal of Marketing; International Business Review; Journal of Transnational Management Development;* and *Journal of Teaching in International Business.* He is listed in a number of international directories including *Who's Who in the World.*

BARBARA PARKER is Associate Professor of Management in the Albers School of Business and Economics, Seattle University. Her research reflects a variety of interests, but major research emphasis is on international strategy, managing decline, gender, and diversity. Publications appear in *Sex Roles; Human Relations; Management International Review; Review of Higher Education; Journal of Business Research; and International Journal of Intercultural Relations.* E-mail: parker@seattleu.edu

ROBERT E. PITTS is Professor and Chair, Department of Marketing, and the Director of the Kellstadt Center for Marketing Analysis and Planning, DePaul University. He has served as a member of the faculty at Jacksonville State University, the University of Notre Dame and the University of Mississippi. Internet: rpitts@wppost.depaul.edu

THEO ROEBERS joined Delft University in 1990 on a part-time basis after a more than thirty-year business career. He is teaching (industrial) marketing; his research interest is in business alliances. He also teaches International Management at The Hague Polytechnic. Until 1992 he was marketing director worldwide for food ingredients with a Dutch company, while concurrently serving as executive vice president with its U.S. office. Apart from his academic work, he is a management consultant.

DAVID K. TSE is Professor of International Business in the Department of Business and Management at the City University of Hong Kong. He taught at University of British Columbia for ten years and visited universities in China and Europe. He has published more than thirty journal papers and book chapters in international marketing and consumer satisfaction. His work has appeared in such international journals as *Journal of Marketing; Journal of Marketing Research; Journal of Consumer Research; Journal of International Business; Journal of Advertising; and Journal of International Marketing.* He serves on the editorial board for two academic journals and actively reviews for eleven other journals.

ILAN VERTINSKY is Vinod Sood Professor of International Business Studies at the University of British Columbia. He is also a senior fellow and director of the Centre for International Business Studies. He previously taught at Northwestern University and he held an appointment as a senior fellow at the Science Centre in Berlin for several years. His current research interests focus on foreign direct investment and trade policy.

FRANK L. WINFREY teaches courses on strategy/policy and organizational theory. His research specialties center on agency theory, corporate governance and control, corporate acquisitions, and pricing issues. Papers by Dr. Winfrey have been presented at conferences of the Academy of Management; the Strategic Management Society; the American Marketing Association; the Association for Consumer Research; the International Association for Business and Society; and the Southern Management Association.

ARCH G. WOODSIDE is the Malcolm S. Woldenberg Professor of Marketing at the Freeman School of Business at Tulane University, New Orleans. He has completed several research projects on international management and marketing strategy topics involving Austrian, Hungarian, Finnish, U.S. and Yugoslav firms. He has served as a Senior Fulbright Lecturer in Finland (1976), Yugoslavia (1980), and Hungary (1989). His research reports on international management and marketing strategy have appeared in European Society of Opinion and Marketing Research proceedings, the *Journal of International Consumer Marketing*; the *European Journal of Marketing*; and the *Journal of Euromarketing*.

GUO-LIANG XUAN is Associate Professor, Vice Director of the Department of Management Engineering in the Management School of Shanghai Jiao Tong University, and Economic Advisory of Shanghai Nan Shi District Government. His major research interests include the economic analysis and feasibility study for investment projects and Sino-foreign joint ventures.

YORAM ZEIRA is on the Faculty of Management, Tel-Aviv University, as well as the Stern School of Business. His major research and teaching activities focus on multinational business management, especially the management of international joint ventures, strategic alliances and comparative human resource management in wholly owned subsidiaries and strategic alliances. He has published extensively on these topics in major American and European academic journals. He also has had visiting teaching appointments at UCLA, University of Maryland, Rutgers University and Baruch College, CUNY.

ISBN 0-89930-970-4

HARDCOVER BAR CODE